A Legitimate

A Forbidden Journey of Self-Discovery

Memoir of an Adoptee

MELINDA A. WARSHAW

Edited by ELLEN C. MAZE

A Legitimate Life
A Forbidden Journey of Self-Discovery
By Melinda A. Warshaw

Edited by Ellen C. Maze

NOTE: This is a partially fictionalized memoir of a journey into the mind of an adoptee in a closed adoption searching for her lost DNA identity. The names of some of the family members have been changed to protect their privacy. Text of Public Record documents included has not been altered, but facial identities have been preserved. Any resemblance to real people with these fictitious names is purely accidental and no harm was intended in the execution of this memoir.

Interior Design: Ellen C Maze, The Author's Mentor,
www.theauthorsmentor.com
Cover Graphic Design: Elizabeth E. Little, Hyliian.deviantart.com
Author Website: www.melindaawarshaw.yolasite.com

ISBN-13: 978-1475252538
Also available in eBook

PRINTED IN THE UNITED STATES OF AMERICA

"Adoptees have been emotionally marginalized."

~ Anonymous

"I cannot even begin to imagine what it's like to be adopted, let alone never ever knowing your true, *true* roots, or ever being allowed to ask or know."

~ Karin Pelletier

"Nothing is 'normal' for an adoptee. Accept it and don't miss it. Life can still be good."

~ Morten Johanssen

"Denial is the lifeblood of adoption. The entire industry relies upon it, and the legislation enshrines it in law."

~Robert Wilson Harrington McCullough Haight

"Although she was adopted into a wealthy WASP family, it becomes apparent that no amount of money nor privilege can replace the lack of 'mirrors' and 'genetic markers' that closed adoptions demand."

~ Dr. Gina Bailey

The Author, Melinda A. Warshaw.

Dedication

To my husband and my sons, for their understanding, their patience, their love, their forgiveness, and their undying support as I searched for my true identity. I can never repay you, and I thank you that you have never asked me to try.

Dear Reader,

In this memoir, you will find that I use the term "birth mother" to refer to the woman who gave birth to me, as was common in the era in which I was raised. I am aware that some people today find this term offensive and prefer the use of terms such as "natural mother," "biological mother," or even, "first mother." Please know that I mean no disrespect to those who no longer use the 1960's terminology and it my deepest hope that this causes you no distraction as you read. Thank you for understanding,

~Melinda A. Warshaw

Secret (se'krit) adj. kept from the knowledge of others, beyond general understanding; mysterious, concealed from sight, hidden. n. a secret fact, cause, process etc. – in secret

1

Unknown

Orphaned at birth.

2

Grafted In

"Dad & Linda 9/2/47. Linda wearing her first orchid from Gaga as she leaves for home in Aurora, Illinois," is written on the back of the picture in Mother's beautiful script.

In the photo I am five months old nestled in my maternal grandfather Gaga's lap, looking anxious as he sits holding down my tiny arms, in a huge wooden chair in the back yard of his house in South Pasadena, California. We're surrounded by lush, lavender lilac bushes in full bloom. Gaga, a 6'7" American of British and Irish descent has straight, white, hair, slicked down and parted in the middle. He's refined and erudite in his wire-rim glasses, cuffed, pinstriped trousers, and starched, white dress shirt as he smiles down at me. I'm elegantly dressed in a beautiful white lace bonnet and a pristine long, white, organdy dress with one of Gaga's rare home-raised orchids pinned to the front. The Victorian pearl hat pin that attaches the flower to my chest is from Nannie's vast collection.

While my grandfather's pride and the orchid pinned to

my tiny chest suggested heritage and a link to Gaga, for years my true origins remained a secret; as if I didn't exist before I landed in his lap.

Was it intimacy problems between my parents that caused them to adopt? Sex was a whispered word, a shameful and dirty part of life that wholesome people did not discuss nor ponder at length. Plus, without a doubt, Mother wanted a girl. As a result, she and Father took the easy route: adopt a child, seal the original Birth Certificate containing the names of the birth parents, issue an amended document naming the adoptive parents as the birth parents, make it illegal for the adult adoptee to obtain a copy of their OBC for 99 years, all the while, pretending the baby was born to the adopters. Ultimately, this practice often forces the adoptee into a life of confusion, grief, and the split-personality of general identity crisis.

But I digress…

To put it simply, Mother, forcibly and without an ounce of wisdom or foresight, grafted me into her family tree. The social workers matched my looks to theirs so that really only my eyes gave me away. Big, blue-turning-to-hazel, and almond-shaped, mine were not small, round, and baby blue like those of my adoptive parents. Still, despite the photo capturing my grandfather's obvious pride, I never had a chance to know him well. Because of this and her driving desire to teach me my (adopted) heritage, over and over, Mother made a point of filling in those memory gaps.

"Linda, your Grandfather, Ira, was born in 1878 in Decatur, Illinois. He went to the University of Illinois, Phillips Exeter, and Harvard where he graduated in 1903, cum laude."

"What is koom loud?" I asked.

"It means 'with honors' in Latin," she said instructing me as she was a graduate of Pomona College with a double major in English.

"He met Nannie in Auburndale, Massachusetts in 1901. Ira's sister, Dot, introduced them."

"What kind of name is Dot?" I asked, bored to death as

she continued on about her genteel, elegant, and refined parents, not understanding that she was trying to give me a connection to her family roots. Looking back, even as a child, I sensed a false note about it all. When she reached the details of Nannie's and Gaga's wedding, she caught my attention again with one sharp, shiny red fingernail.

"Being married before you have children is very important," she said, pointing in my face. "One day you will be married and have the most beautiful wedding in the whole world."

My eyes might have glazed over for she repeated herself directly afterwards.

"Do you hear me?" she asked again in a louder, albeit kind voice.

"Yes, Mother, I hear you," I answered as I perked up, smiled, and rolled my eyes.

Gaga died when I was three years old. All I remember about him is running at top speed and leaping high into his loving arms. We visited Nannie every few years after Gaga was gone, but it wasn't the same. Mother's older sister, Carolyn, lived there, too, with her husband, my Uncle Bob, and their three children. Aunt Carolyn had a beautiful face and small blue eyes like Mother. Both Aunt Carolyn and Mother were brunette, but while my aunt wore her hair in a long braid down her back, mother wore hers short, curly, and in the latest style. Mother once told me her sister was not only Gaga's favorite, but also a wild flapper in the roaring 20's. I discerned early on that she was jealous of her sister and had been her entire life.

As for my grandmother, Nannie was an artist, quiet, soft-spoken, and a sensitive soul. We were very much alike, and our eyes spoke volumes to each other. Even though I felt close with Nannie, I never successfully bonded with my aunt and cousins when I visited Nannie. No matter how much time passed, they always seemed like strangers to me with no legitimate physical or spiritual connection.

Another vivid memory of Nannie's house was the trains that passed through her town twice daily. My brothers loved to make the long walk down the palm tree-lined street to put pennies and buffalo head nickels on the train tracks. When they returned later, they found the coins had miraculously flattened. Without fail, as the train conductors passed by, I'd become overexcited, waving and yelling "hello," as if they might slow the train and let me hop on for a ride. Mysteriously drawn to them, I sensed an odd emptiness when they were gone. Even odder, once we returned home to Illinois I forgot all about them.

3

Mommy's Little Girl

Mother was high society all the way and extremely proud of her aristocratic English roots. She loved the beach, and Father who was German, loved the mountains. They slept in twin beds in those days and their lives revolved around golf. Power, privilege, the proper name, family background and, above all else good breeding, was of the ultimate importance, and I learned early on that if you didn't have an important name, image, and position in society you were no one.

I had two older brothers; Jack and Rob. Jack, the oldest, was born in Chicago, and—like me—joined the family from a closed adoption orchestrated by The Cradle Adoption Agency in Evanston, Illinois. Rob was my adoptive parents' natural son. Jack was seven and Rob was three when I arrived in 1947. Their last biological child, Darin, was unplanned and was born a year and a half later, making the total of Meyers children four: three boys and myself.

Living with the Meyers resembled someone right out of a novel. I found myself the daughter of a highly educated, sophisticated, and impeccably dressed English American who deported herself as a true British blue-blood. Mother observed the rigid rules of the English aristocracy and her children were required to do so as well. She and Father came from old money and we were taught the ways of royalty and how to obey her orders without question. Talking about money, sex, or emotions was taboo and considered in poor taste. Reading movie magazines was forbidden. Elegance, manners, the Queen's English, and impeccable manners were Mother's cardinal rules.

When I was five we moved from Aurora, Illinois, to Kettering, Ohio, a wealthy suburb near Dayton, into a gorgeous, white four story colonial mansion on the top of a hill on a dead end street. Our house overlooked the even bigger mansion of famed inventor Charles Kettering, who amassed considerable wealth for his time. Mother and Father had arrived in this famous town and joined St. Paul's Episcopal Church in Dayton where we were baptized and confirmed.

There, Mother groomed me to be her clone. I was to be a bride and homemaker and to marry a wealthy WASP from the power elite so I would have social standing and be financially secure. In Mother's mind, women from the educated upper classes didn't work; they volunteered, organized fundraisers for charity, entertained, and never married down. What she didn't know, but I discovered in my youth that many adoptees have a preverbal catastrophe visited upon them; they are not simply blank flesh canvases on which identities can be painted without negative consequence. These precursors manifested early in my life, and trying to be made into Mother's image only exacerbated the issue.

Mother's high energy and enthusiasm for life made mornings in our household like preparing for a race. Once our eyes opened, it went like clockwork: wake up, get properly dressed for the occasion, and eat a formal breakfast around the circular antique oak table in the breakfast room. Breakfast was served by Joy Ella, our Black, live-in maid. Joy Ella, donning a freshly starched white uniform and black apron, greeted us with a big smile every morning.

"Make sure you take your vitamin pill," Joy Ella instructed me.

"I did already," I told her as I hid it deep inside a left over raisin in the bottom of my cereal bowl when no one was looking. Swallowing pills without gagging was difficult and I knew Mother did not tolerate my inability to comply.

"Now drink all your milk, Linda," Mother ordered.

"I don't like milk, it gives me a tummy ache," I replied.

"You will sit here at the table until you finish your milk," she said and left me alone until I did as she said. Once she was gone, I called Father's hunting dogs, our two German short-haired pointers, and they drank it for me.

Getting dressed in the morning remained a joint effort between my Mother and me. She never let me choose what I wanted to wear. Any time I tried, she marched me right back up the long, spiral staircase to my room and directed me to wear what she'd put out for me. She loved formality and parties. I was shy, easy going, and a bit of a Tomboy. Being like her did not come naturally or easily.

I loved to wear riding jeans and spend my free time drawing pictures with my crayons. By the age of six, I was in love with a retired American saddle bred three-gaited show horse at Miss Belle's riding stable where I rode on Saturdays. My short life was off to a great start. It wasn't until a few months after my seventh birthday that Mother told me something that gave me insight into our many differences and changed my life forever.

"Linda, I have something to tell you," she said as she lit her Kent cigarette. "Come sit next to me." Once I was settled, she sighed. "When you were five months old we adopted you."

"Adopted? What does that mean?"

"It means that your mother couldn't keep you and you are ours now."

Mother's words caused my chest to hurt and she must have seen the distress in my face. "Where is my real mother?" I asked. "Is she coming back to get me?"

"Darling, I'm your mother now and you are a Meyer. We wanted you so much and so we adopted you." I must have appeared unconvinced, for Mother touched my hair and softened her gaze. "Your brothers loved you so much that they held your tiny hands the entire way home from The Cradle Adoption Agency. You are my child and special in my eyes." When she stopped speaking, tears rimmed her crystalline blue eyes.

Mother's sadness and her forlorn tone made it very clear that I was not to ask any more questions regarding my adopted status, even though as each year went by, my natural origins became more confusing and upsetting. As time passed, I found a nest of hidden thoughts and unhappy emotions deep inside of me. My new parents required me to ignore my grief, so I smiled and became the greatest actress of all time, pretending to be what they wanted. I had been abandoned. Why didn't matter. I was living with strangers. How wealthy or caring they were paled when compared with the plain truth: this isn't my real mother.

I never spoke to Mother again about it, but I could fill a small lake with the tears I shed over the years wishing I had someone to talk to about it all.

Little Orphan Barbie

Mother's seemingly arbitrary rules about our high class upbringing meant I wasn't allowed to have a Barbie. "If you want a doll, it will be Tiny Tears," she stated emphatically.

"Can't I have a Barbie doll? All my friends have them," I pleaded.

"No daughter of mine will have a Barbie; she is too common," she assured, dismissing my complaint.

I sulked and lowered my voice. "My real mama would let me have one."

"Your who?" she asked, obviously pretending not to hear.

"Nothing," I replied, once again disappointed that I had to keep my secret self quiet as not to hurt Mother.

It didn't occur to me to ask Mother Barbie's last name, or if there was an adoptee Barbie she might allow me to have. How ironic that Mother thought she was protecting me from sexuality and immorality by the type of doll she allowed me to have. I never played with my Tiny Tears doll because changing wet baby diapers and wiping away tears wasn't fun. I played with my plastic horses instead, and when I did it right, they were ever as much fun as Barbie and Ken.

Mother constantly instructed me on what good girls do and don't do. Once, when I was ten years old, Mother began to speak of her relatives between sips of her highball.

"Your Nannie came from a well-respected Kentucky family in the South," she slurred, not entirely drunk, but definitely looser of tongue. "The communities where they lived were small and everyone knew everyone else's business. They wouldn't have anything to do with people who weren't from the right family." With the last word, Mother's gaze turned hard and it seemed she was looking right through me. Did she think I was from the wrong family? More than ever, I was reminded that I did not belong there. The "orphan me" began to wonder who are these strangers I'm living with? From that point on, I became two different people: outwardly, a true Meyer, and inwardly, someone who didn't fit in with the Meyers at all.

Joy Ella's Little Sugar Bear

Meals were invariably formal in the Meyer household, and our servants played a big role in every meal. Joy Ella announced each meal with a hearty, "Breakfast (or lunch, or dinner) is served!" Quietly elegant, the butler Raymond (also Joy Ella's husband), never spoke. He performed his duties with pride and with no waste of time or effort. Joy Ella and her husband resided in the attic and I learned to listen for her on the creaky stairs each bed time. Her nightly ritual of reading to me until I fell asleep gave me something to look forward to each day.

"Joy, please read about Dorothy and Oz," I asked. "I love the drawings and Dorothy's adventures."

I especially loved Dorothy's struggle to return to her real home. One night, I asked Joy Ella a particularly important question.

"Dorothy lived with her aunt and uncle. What happened to her parents?"

Joy Ella smiled on me like the sun. "I don't know, child. Maybe they're in Heaven. She's an orphan like you and Jack."

Not satisfied, I pressed on. "Did the wicked witch turn her into an orphan?"

"No," she assured.

"Was Goldilocks an orphan? Why did she end up in the woods with the Three Bears?"

"Never you mind, child. I think you are The Little Engine That Could!"

"Joy Ella, where did I come from?" I asked, still undeterred. She gave me a friendly grin that accompanied a low chuckle.

"I don't really know, but probably the stork because that is where all babies come from. Now go to sleep," she said quietly as I gazed with confusion into her dark velvety brown eyes. Then she would head to the basement laundry, putting in more hours after the sun set.

One of her responsibilities was to starch and press our monogrammed sheets, linen napkins, some of our clothes and even our underwear. I always felt sorry for her, when I would see her as she slaved away in front of the huge steamroller press, feelings of guilt would consume me. She developed bad arthritis in her knees from the frequent and constant scrubbing of floors and eventually, she could hardly walk.

Joy Ella called me her Little Sugar Bear and her large but gentle brown hands relaxed me when she rubbed the soap-filled washcloth across my back in the bathtub. When I was clean she would gently comb the tangles out of my long hair and dry it with a towel. Then I would sit on her lap in the rocking chair next to my bed, lay my head on her big bosom, and listen while she read to me. When I was sad, she rocked me and sang beautiful spiritual songs about Jesus until I stopped crying. One night, in her generous lap, I touched on the subject I was forbidden to approach with Mother.

"Joy Ella, where do you think my mama is?"

"She's out for dinner with your father."

"No, I mean my real mother."

"Well, child, I don't know, but I'm sure she loves and misses you."

"Why doesn't she want to see me?"

"Sugar Bear, I don't rightly know, but she must have a good reason."

The subject seemed closed and I sniffled. "Don't tell Mother I asked about her, okay?"

"Okay, sweet, I won't. This will be our little secret," she promised.

My mind scampered to Raymond's frequent assertion that I was going to be a famous actress someday. I looked into Joy Ella's eyes and felt peace.

"Why does Raymond tell me I'm going to be a famous lesbian some day?"

"Child, what did you say?" Joy Ella asked, surprised. "He never said that."

"Well, Mother told me that a lesbian is an actress, and he said I'm going to be a famous actress one day." Joy Ella laughed.

"No, he thinks you're going to be an actress on the big movie screen someday. Never you mind about lesbians, ya' hear? Raymond just wants you to know that he thinks you're beautiful."

"How come he's so skinny?" I asked her thinking her rotund body would crush him when they were in bed together. I giggled at the thought. Joy Ella would never answer that one.

"God, She's Funny."

We used the dining room table for assembling the Nixon buttons in 1952. Mom and Dad were conservative, right-wing Republicans and feverishly worked on the campaign to get Eisenhower and Nixon elected. The posters and the red, white, and blue Nixon-Ike and I Like Ike buttons were strewn all over the dining room table so Mother dropped her usual formalities and let us eat on trays in front of the television. I loved this; it was one of the few times I could relax. My favorite show was The Lone Ranger because, like me, he had a "secret identity." However, I was much too young to know why I identified with him. It was something about having a secret identity, being adopted, and wearing a mask. One of these nights, Mother turned to me to make the blessing before we ate.

"Linda, you are old enough now to say grace. Rob, you say it and she'll say it after you."

"Thank you for the birds so sweet, thank you for the food we eat, thank you for the birds that sing, thank you, God, for everything," Rob, Mother's favorite son, recited it perfectly. I took a deep breath, and gave it my best shot.

"Thank you for the food so sweet, thank you for the birds we eat… Oh, no that's not right," I whispered and sunk into my chair. Father busted out laughing, followed by my brothers.

"God, she's funny!" Father said as Mother took over and finished it for me. She didn't see the humor.

I never said Grace again and kept my distance from Mother, although to me almost everything seemed funny after that.

4

To the Manor Born

As a child, Mother dreamed of becoming a professional ballet dancer, but her father wouldn't let her dance. He thought wearing a tutu was too risqué. In an effort to fulfill her dreams, at age eight, I was enrolled in ballet classes. Even though I had a dancer's body, and I did my best to please her, I did not share Mother's passion for ballet.

I was more relaxed like Father who was less uptight. He played the organ and accordion on holidays and I loved to sit on the organ bench next to him and sing along while he played chords. Father preferred jazz, and before he was married, he spent many nights in jazz clubs on Chicago's West Side enjoying the musicians there. It wasn't until after he died that I found out he was a womanizer. This and his budding alcoholism were never discussed.

"Children, go to your rooms right after dinner tonight because we're having some friends over," Mother told us before a night of entertaining.

Their friends appeared for after-dinner drinks, billiards, and bridge when they weren't playing golf at the country club. Mother was the social butterfly who hated that father preferred to smoke and drink alone. Mother once told me he was a reverse snob.

Much of my parents' social life revolved around drinking

and playing games. Alcoholism ran through the family and their friends like a tsunami and the socializing was simply an excuse to drink. I loved to sneak down the spiral staircase and spy on them. Once, I saw one of their friends passed-out on the front foyer floor. Another time I snuck under the tablecloth of the dining room table at a dinner party and listened to them speak about me.

"…that daughter of yours would have made a perfect Ziegfeld girl with those long legs," a man said as I watched a hand that wasn't Father's disappear up Mother's skirt. I held my breath hoping no one would realize I was there.

"That Linda will drive the boys crazy. Why did you chop off all of that gorgeous blonde hair?" I heard one of the drunken men say.

"She's going to be a knockout," Father agreed, "but she's a bit too quiet for me."

"Did you hear that Funkhauser shot his brains out on the 7th hole?" someone said. I gasped and put my hand over my mouth and waited until they were gone to sneak back to my room on the second floor.

Suicides were another common occurrence among my parents' social set in those days. To anyone on the outside our family seemed idyllic. It seemed people were coming and going all the time. Mother created beauty everywhere in our mansion in Kettering. The rooms were professionally decorated, the house was filled with fresh flowers all the time, and we were ready to receive guests at a moment's notice. When their important friends came over for cocktails, dinner, and after-dinner drinks, Mother always sent us to our rooms.

"Children are to be seen and not heard," she told us over and over until I was afraid to even say I love you to her aloud.

Mother did volunteer work in a psychiatric hospital, which was ironic since depression and dysfunction ran rampant in our family. Father worked at the Y.M.C.A. like his father and mother and did volunteer work for the church guild at St. Paul's Episcopal Church. Above all, Mother made sure our family looked perfect to anyone looking in.

A Natural Talent

I don't remember Father's parents at all. His younger sister, my aunt Mildred, was big and fat and never said a word to me when she visited every year. She simply sat in the big yellow and green chintz-covered armchair smiling as she knit or darned my father's socks. I did hear Mildred tell Mother I had musical talent after she heard me play my rented flute. She emphatically encouraged Mother to buy me a flute of my own. I began classical flute lessons in second grade and Mother bought me my very own 1939 United States Navy Selmer Manhattan Band flute. Playing in the band and orchestra was fun; as always, Mother was grooming me for great things.

"Just think, if you keep practicing, you will play lovely classical music in lovely places when you get older," Mother said as she gazed out the window after a deep drag on her cigarette one night.

"What kind of lovely places?" I asked.

"Perhaps in Austria, Sweden, Italy, or France," she replied in a faraway voice.

"Where are they?"

"In Europe."

"Europe?" I asked. It sounded wonderful, but I couldn't be sure.

"Remind me to show you. I don't have time now. Go get ready for bed," she said as I reluctantly left her side wondering why she cut me off and rarely answered my many questions.

While my free time was spent practicing and honing my musical talents, being adopted began to eat away at me and consume my thoughts. I had everything a girl could want, and yet I didn't have my real mother, the mother I longed for. If I asked Mother about Jack's adoption, she'd make light of it and simply reiterate how much they wanted us. But deep down the rejection of my biological parents nagged at my peace. I was especially lonely for my natural mother, whom I christened Mama. In my secret thoughts, Mama would spend lots of time with me because she belonged to me and would want to do the same things I liked to do. I felt afraid and lost without her. No one in my adoptive family enjoyed the same activities I did. Some mornings upon waking the tears flowed as thoughts of being away from Mama surfaced from a bad dream. The pain was so deep there was no way to stop it. I was able to love Mother Meyer, but it was a bit awkward and I kept her at arm's length, always waiting and hoping that Mama would return and rescue me. No one could ever take her place and I missed her. The loss of my natural father was also an issue, but not nearly as severe. This separation and disconnection ate away at me like acid and I was only ten years old.

A good day was one when I didn't think of being adopted at all; a bad day was I couldn't get my Mama out of my mind for a second. Nonetheless, I slowly and painstakingly adjusted to my adoptive family without realizing I was losing much of my genetic self in the process.

Horses, My Refuge

Mother had the good sense to put me on a horse when I was six. It was at Miss Belle's riding stable that I fell in love with riding Star, a beautiful 16-hand retired American Saddlebred three-gaited show horse from Kentucky. Miss Belle told me I had great hands and was a gifted rider. She mentioned more than once that I was headed for the Olympics one day. Unfortunately, her stable burned down just as I was getting good. I made certain Mother found another place for me to ride soon after. Kings Riding Stable was close to the Dayton Country Club and there I picked up riding again with Saturday lessons.

Riding at Kings was a bit boring because the instructor continually sat me on a small horse with no spirit. I preferred Star's size and vigor, and none of the current mounts could match her attributes. Mother refused to demand a larger horse for me so, to spite her I went against her advice and told my new riding buddies that I was adopted.

"You don't look adopted," said a fat boy.

"You don't act adopted," said his friend.

"You're stupid," I said to them and never mentioned it again.

I stopped talking about it after that and sadly retreated into myself. Their reaction made me feel bad and confused me. I thought that being adopted made me special; yet talking about it to others made it clear that it was actually something to be ashamed of. These kids felt that I was a mistake, that I didn't belong. For years after that, instead of share my emotions on the topic, I fell into a low-grade depression. My outward smile never faltered, although keeping such a secret identity exhausted me daily.

The Engineer, the Sadist, and the Little Lost Boy

While I was living in turmoil, my brothers adjusted easily to the hands that they had been dealt. Jack never mentioned his adoption. He kept tropical fish. He collected rare coins and stamps that he inherited from Gaga and would sit for hours sorting and cataloging his stamps on the dining room table.

Jack also loved toy trains and Father filled the Summer Room with a Lionel track, complete with switches and sidings. Jack built little houses and created bushes and roads. He made mountains out of plaster of paris and painted them to create a realistic and scenic model railroad. Father bought two Santa Fe streamliner engines, some Pullman passenger cars, plus a number of freight train cars, and the electric trains ran 'round and 'round whistling and smoking through the beautiful miniature manmade countryside.

"I'm a locomotive engineer on the CB&Q! All aboard," Jack announced as I sat on the velvet upholstered couch to watch him play with the trains.

"What's an engineer?" I asked.

"The one who runs the engines on the trains and solves

problems," he offered.

"Could I do it, too? I have some furniture in my doll house that we could put into one of the freight cars," I suggested.

"Girls don't do that sort of thing, but you can watch me," he replied.

"Come over and push the red button, and the whistle will blow and smoke will come out of the smoke stack."

There was something about a train whistle and that puff of smoke that really gave me a thrill.

"Are the men on the trains that go by Nannie's house driving the CB&Q?" I asked, wishing I could be on one of those trains at that moment. Jack shrugged.

"All I know is that the CB&Q stands for the Chicago, Burlington and Quincy railroad line and transports all the furniture that Kroehler makes. 'Boss' Kettering lives in Ridgeleigh Terrace pretty near us. He's famous for designing the Zephyr on the CB&Q, but I think Dad is famous for selling furniture for Mr. Kroehler and grandfather handles all the money for the entire company!" he replied.

"Wow," I said in wonder thinking the "Boss" might be my real father.

Mother's natural son, Rob, kept his room like a museum of natural history. He would catch butterflies, moths, and bugs and watch them slowly die in jars filled with cyanide before he pinned down their wings to mount in frames. On his shelves, dead snakes and lizards floated in jars of formaldehyde. It was Uncle Bob, Mother's sister's husband, who collected butterflies and taught Rob how to catch, kill and prepare them for framing. One might say Rob was an amateur herpetologist, entomologist, zoologist and lepidopterist although his sadistic streak made him more like the Marquis de Sade. He loved to watch his female praying mantis bite the head off the male in the huge aquarium he kept in his room. His also collected cicada shells, snake skins, animal pelts, bugs, and many other creepy crawlers.

One summer night he filled an entire jar with lightening bugs. The light from the jar lit up the entire living room with a beautiful other worldly glow.

"You have to let them go or they'll die," I told Rob.

"I don't care if they die," he replied and shook the jar as hard as he could to prove his cruelty.

Darin got lost in the shuffle. He always ended up with the baby rabbits every spring after the mowing of the fifty acres. We fed them with eyedroppers full of warm milk but we could never keep them alive long enough to grow up. He was a Cub Scout and an all-around good boy. When he took up playing the trumpet I helped him figure it out. I mothered him because Mother treated him like he never should have been born. Later I found out that she blamed my father for getting her pregnant on a vacation down south. Darin and I built things with wooden blocks and I taught him to play jacks. He followed me around like a little puppy, but I didn't mind. Somebody needed to love him.

5

Good Rob, Bad Rob

In our seemingly lovely home roamed a monster named Rob. He put on a phony, sweet persona in front of our parents, but when they were away, he turned into a sadistic fiend and hurt us at every opportunity. Darin and I were afraid for our lives; neither knowing that the other was living with the same resident evil and in complete terror of Rob.

Rob was the one who put cherry bombs in our neighbors' mailboxes and shot off a homemade rocket that blew a hole through a neighbor's roof. And although he was never caught, I knew he was the one who pulled down our neighbor's panties when she came over to play with us. Rob watched the little girl run home in tears with her underwear around her ankles, all the while pretending he wasn't involved.

The good Rob was very talented. He and Father could build and make anything in Father's basement woodshop. The two of them even made go-carts and would race them around our front circle.

The bad Rob surfaced when Mom and Dad were away playing golf or bridge. Rob was really bad to Darin and me when Father went away to hunt for quail and pheasant. I was so afraid of his Dr. Jekyll and Mr. Hyde personality, I dared not tell anyone about the abusive evil side that made us cry.

When Mother was around Rob acted normal. Darin and I happily went outside after dinner to play Red/Light Green/Light, Kick the Can, Mailbox, Freeze Tag, and Croquet with my brothers and the kids in the neighborhood . Sometimes we went swimming at the country club while our parents played golf. I was on the swim team and loved to eat lunch at the club.

Mother was forever dropping me off at ballet class, tap class, riding class, flute lessons, the Brownie group, or one of my friend's houses for a play date which thankfully kept me away from Rob and the anxiety he caused me.

Human Chameleon

Darin and I kept the chameleons we brought home from the Ringling Brothers Circus in shoe boxes with holes punched in the tops. The pet lizards wore strings around their necks and could be pinned to our shirts. We loved to watch them change colors and tried keeping them alive with little cups of sugar water and dead flies.

"What a miracle of nature!" I exclaimed once as Darin and I examined the lizards. "They escape predators by blending into the color of their surroundings. It's like they're two different lizards living in one body."

"Where'd they come from?" Darin asked.

"They came all the way from Madagascar!" I answered.

"Where is that?" Darin asked.

"I think from another planet," I assured him.

"Did they come from another planet like you came from another mother?" asked Darin.

"Yes, and I wonder where she is?"

Darin didn't say anything more, and I made him promise to never speak of my adopted status in front of Mother. It occurred to me that by slowly adapting to my adoptive family I was forming a false self. I was losing my authentic self and becoming a human chameleon. The DNA-person living inside of me was far removed from the one I pretended to be. I was happy that I didn't change color when I thought about my biological mother; what a giveaway that would have been!

Polio Strikes Jack

When I was eight years old, Jack was diagnosed with Polio. On a very snowy Christmas Eve, Jack collapsed while carolers sang Joy to the World at our front door. Petrified, I watched the ambulance from my bedroom window as Mother readied herself for the trip to the hospital. How could God let this happen? Jack's legs became paralyzed, and he had to undergo numerous bone operations. Mother was so consumed with his physical therapy, and her regular duties at the garden club, the country club, and the ladies church guild that we only saw her briefly in the morning and now and then before we went to sleep.

On Jack's fifteenth birthday, Mother organized a huge polio benefit at our house. Game booths, ice sculptures, and various rides peppered our expansive lawn while numerous contests of all types and a dinner dance under the stars were scheduled throughout the day and into the early evening. The hired dance band employed a gorgeous blonde trumpet player and I couldn't take my eyes off him. Eventually Mother pulled me from the floor for fear that I was dancing just for him. The fundraiser was a tremendous success and raised quite a bit of money for Polio research. Afterward the write-up in the newspaper told the whole city what Mother had accomplished.

Jack wore a stiff back brace and both legs were supported as well with the latest medical treatments. Pins stuck out of his legs, and he eventually ended up with scoliosis. Sometimes, a family friend with Cerebral Palsy came over to play with Jack. I was not permitted to join them, but I managed to see him and note his peculiar appearance. A deep sense of compassion for the disabled filled my soul from that day on, and remains with me to this day.

Wicked Rob Takes Advantage

With Father passing out at the dinner table from too much liquor more and more often, Mother stepped up her drinking and was rarely sober. With both parents literally incapacitated most of their time at home, Darin and I were left to Rob's devices much too often. We both enjoyed playing with him when the adults were about, but when left alone with him, he became a devil.

"You know, don't you, that your boney shoulder blades stick out so far on your back that they look like wings. You'll have to have them surgically removed." Rob laughed an evil chuckle. "And you'll never be able to pronounce spaghetti right," he added as I brushed my teeth one morning.

"Scabetty, puschetti," was all that came out of my mouth until I burst into tears.

"Too bad for you," he said and walked out of the room snickering.

My third grade teacher was the first to notice my burgeoning anxiety disorder. She called Mother to report my frequent tears and fits of crying that followed any kind of correction or request to speak aloud in class. Hoping to help, she also placed me in the back of the room so I could run from the room if I felt an anxiety attack coming on. Still, I loved school and did everything I could to not miss class. Who wanted to be at home? Rob might be there, and I could live without that as often as possible.

At home, in private, Rob delighted in my tears and I believed everything he said. It didn't occur to me that my own brother would purposely lie to and stalk his little sister. He was supposed to protect me. Just being around him made me afraid and filled me with apprehension.

Rob's lies often landed me in trouble with Mother.

"Linda, why did you throw the cat off the porch? She fell twenty feet onto the asphalt. Midnight could have died," Mother asked.

"I wanted to see if she would land on her feet like Rob

told me," I confessed to her even though I was taking my rage out on the cat instead of my abuser.

"Go to your room this instant," she commanded, her face red.

"No," I replied with my lip out.

"Go to your room right this minute," she said as she marched me up the spiral staircase to my room and locked me in.

"I hate you! I hate you," I screamed. Seeing red, I tore the head, legs and arms off of my Tiny Tears doll and hurled the pieces against the walls of my room. When my room looked like a tornado had come through, I collapsed on the floor sobbing until I couldn't breathe.

My pent up anger at Rob eventually manifested itself as violence against the only one I loved: Darin. One night, I shoved a marble up Darin's nose, knowing it was a crazy way of getting back at Rob for his abuse of us both.

Rob's growing obsession with catching snakes was bordering on insanity. He made frequent trips deep into the woods around our house to hunt and trap the slimy serpents. One time, a dozen snakes escaped from the bucket he had in his room to slither all over the house. I came home one day to find Joy Ella on a chair in the dining room screaming at a black racer water snake that had fallen from the second floor on her head while she was vacuuming. What a sight she was with her hands in the air and the tops of her knee-highs disappearing into the rolls of fat above her knees.

Another of Rob's favorite "games" was to tie Darin and I to chairs and gag us with our cowboy scarves until we could barely breathe, much less yell out. Then he would tip us over and "leave us for dead." His presence alone was enough to make me nervous, afraid and scared speechless.

Rob used various tools of torture to hurt us. The wooden paddle with the holes in it stung when he hit us with it and the wet towel rolled up in such a way as when he snapped it on our bodies it stung like crazy. He loved to scare and hurt Darin and me. It made him laugh.

Rob also enjoyed playing strip poker, and Darin and I

were his unwilling playmates. Cheating and rigging the cards meant that invariably, at the end of the game, Rob was fully dressed and Darin and I were naked. Rob became so excited as I took off my blouse and then my skirt followed by my slip and underpants. I shivered with cold as I sat on the chair in my room trying to cover my crotch with the cards.

"I call you. I have a full house," said Rob.

"What do I have?" I asked him.

"Two Kings and you lose. Now you have to take something off," he ordered in Mother's authoritative tone.

"What do I have?" asked Darin.

"You have a pair of Aces and you have to take something off too," said Rob.

Darin lost his shirt, his pants, and his underpants, too. We were totally in his power. Rob had the door locked and stuffed a tissue in the key hole so no one could look in and see what we were doing. When I cried and begged him to let me redress, he laughed and nodded his head. When an adult neared the door, Rob would urge us to dress more quickly, threatening us that if we ever told anyone about our strip poker games, he'd make us sorry. He also convinced us that we were bad and dirty and if we told Mother, she would take his side because he was her favorite. He also used a miniature guillotine that he'd built to behead mice as a scare tactic to keep me compliant and silent.

"I'll chop off one of your fingers if you tell Mother," he threatened. And we believed him.

Rob also wrote the word "fuck" on the frosted window of our car. We were living with an evil so chilling that neither one of us could speak about it. Thus, I learned how to lie, deceive, and keep secrets. I could pretend like everything was normal and nothing bad had ever happened. This pattern would repeat itself all my life surrounding the abuse.

6

Secrets

The sex play began after I turned nine and I acted it out with my plastic horses. The torment lasted for years but I was too scared to say anything. It would affect my entire life. Our encounters of the ugly kind happened in secret when Mother and Father were busy entertaining downstairs or on a vacation. Not until we had our clothes off during strip poker did he ask if he could touch us. First, there was touching my breast and then it was me touching Darin's penis. It was gradual. We were too young to get it. I guess the monster child figured out how to separately seduce us. He had us so brainwashed we had no control over ourselves when he played his manipulative games.

"Bean," Rob said to me one day when no one else was around, "show me your ballet dance."

Why not? I eagerly performed my ballet recital dance for him, but he wanted a different kind of dance. He wanted a sexy strip tease. After he instructed me, I obliged. I had natural rhythm and the sexy dancing didn't bother me. How could I know this was wrong? Maybe it would endear me to my abuser.

But Rob wasn't finished making changes to my choreography.

"Now take off your clothes and swivel your hips," he demanded.

"No," I answered thinking he was kidding.

"If you don't, I'll tell Mother, and she'll be so mad at you that she will send you back to the orphanage," he threatened.

I believed him. He knew Darin and I were afraid of being sent away. Dirty dancing in the nude is where I learned that my body had power. The next time we went into the woods, he brought the girl next door.

"Bean, show Jane how you dance. Remember what I said I would do if you don't."

I began my dance.

"Take off your clothes. Now do a strip tease and stick twigs up there between your legs."

I gyrated around until the tears streamed down my cheeks.

"Please stop," I sobbed after poking a stick up where it hurt me.

He and the neighbor girl laughed and threw my clothes up in a tree leaving me there shaking, naked, and alone deep in the woods. I retrieved my clothes from the tree, put them back on, and followed the path home pretending like nothing happened even though I was trembling in shock.

"Where did you get those chigger bites and those bruises?" asked Joy during my nightly bath.

"Outside playing," I told her.

What a good actress I had become!

Hypersexual

When a particularly debilitating anxiety attack affected my dance performances, mom removed me from ballet class. I was thrilled. Now I could spend more of my free time in my jeans at King's stable with Annie Bertschy, my best friend. She owned her own horse named Candy and I owned Sprinkles. We rode together on Saturdays and played together all the time. My room was eventually covered with ribbons and trophies won in horse shows, and a framed newspaper article with a picture of Annie and me feeding our horses hung on my wall. Both of us loved to ride on the trails and in horse shows. Sprinkles was the only recipient of my hugs and kisses as I shut down emotionally due to my home life. Training, riding, showing and owning one of those elegant and graceful Five-Gaited horses one day was my dream.

Annie and I were inseparable and the stable was a great safe haven from Rob. I loved to be around King Tulles, the owner. He made pinky rings for us out of horseshoe nails, and we screamed with delight when he chased us around with pliers when we had a loose tooth. We were allowed to Roman ride the horses. He even made us tinted green cream cheese onion dip with chips to eat in the tack room. Joe, the six-foot-five tack room giant, watched after us. Without his false teeth his face looked like an old pumpkin.

We rode through the trails in the woods even in the snow and stopped to chip out the snowballs in the horses' hooves so they wouldn't slip and break a leg.

Through horseback riding I met my idol. She was ten years older and a beautiful, blue-eyed, blonde-haired girl who owned an Arabian five-gaited show horse. I wanted to be just like her when I got older. She had pajama parties and we loved to stay up until midnight, eat pickle sandwiches, and watch Frankenstein movies.

Annie taught me how to fantasize and become a horse. We turned into horses and played in her woods. We trotted, cantered, neighed, snorted and pranced around up and down the hills and in and out of the streams on her forest property. We loved being close to nature, and I was lonely when apart from her. She lived in a huge stone Tudor mansion across the woods and I spent as much time there as I could to be away from Rob.

Their Weimaraner's cold, wet nose woke us up in the morning. Then it was off to the formal dining room for breakfast. Mabel their black maid made us the most delicious, thick French toast covered in powdered sugar and warm maple syrup. She poured that warm liquid gold from a beautiful sterling silver pitcher. It always tasted better at her house.

"Tell Linda about our family name," Annie said to her mother excitedly one morning over breakfast.

"The name Bertschy means bear in high German and we come from East Prussia. Isn't your father German, Linda? Do you know what part of Germany his ancestors are from?" she asked me.

"I don't know," I replied, uncomfortable making my adopted status known.

"Our Annie is going to get her own Trakehner, the most noble German horse breed, to train and show. Those East Prussian German bloodlines of the Trakehner make them wonderful for jumping or dressage. Did you know there is a double moose antler brand on the left hindquarter of a true blooded Trakehner? DNA and pedigrees are everything," her mother informed me.

"Horses are in my soul. I'm getting my very own American saddle bred black stallion to train and show in the Olympics when I'm fourteen," I announced not knowing anything more about the bloodlines of the black stallion I dreamed of owning.

Annie and I played with our plastic horses together. They were always mounting each other. She knew about sex too and told me about the f-word. I dared her to say it to her grandmother one time and she did.

"What does fuck mean?" she said softly to her grandmother. Her grandmother was hard of hearing and kept saying, "Was ist fahk?" "Was ist fahk?" louder and louder. We laughed hysterically until her mother found out and sent me home.

One day while playing horse in the woods behind her house, my body threw itself on top of hers. I think I was trying to have sex with her even though I didn't know what it was.

"What are you doing? Get off me," she demanded. I told her I was sorry, but I was never invited to her house again after that.

Rob's Cruelty

The hypersexual switch had been flipped. My fear and distrust of men grew due to the shear violence, threats and terror from Rob's abuse and so did my nightmares. The worst was being kidnapped and pulled into a man's car while I was walking to elementary school. My plan of escape was to open the door and roll out on the pavement at the first stop sign. It always worked, and I got away. Waking up was always a relief.

Rob began to threaten to stab me with his switchblade during one of his sleepwalks. I hid the knife he kept in his desk drawer so he wouldn't murder me in my sleep.

"Bean, look at this," he ordered as he pulled the wings off a fly and trapped it in an upside-down paper cup before lighting the cup on fire. I watched his face contort into a wicked smile.

"You had better keep quiet or you might find a water moccasin or a black widow spider in your bed."

After that, I checked my bed every night to see if he had put a surprise under my sheets.

Our neighbor's noisy and horny black and white fox terrier named Tipsy was always at it with any neighborhood dog that had the misfortune of being in heat. One day, he and another dog were hopelessly attached right on the corner of our dead end street. My girlfriend and I hid behind the bushes.

"Hide, here comes a car. Let's see how the driver will react," I told my friend.

We thought it was funny in a dangerous sort of way to see if the people in their cars would look and they certainly did look. Some even stopped their cars to stare and laugh.

"The neighbor's fox terrier got run over by a car," Mother told us one morning after she returned from a vacation.

I thought nothing of it until one cold autumn Saturday while Annie and I were riding the trails in the woods. We saw a cardboard box ahead of us a bit off the riding trail. Inside was a cut up black and white dog.

"Let's get out of here," I said and we galloped out of there hoping never to speak of it again. I thought to myself that Rob killed Tipsy to scare me into a permanent silence. If so, his ploy worked.

A Natural Artist

In spite of the abuse from Rob, the creative artist in me consistently came to my rescue. Being creative made me forgot about everything. I usually won first prize in the school project competitions for my originality. These talents went unnoticed by my family, as there were no graphic artists in their family tree. My natural artistic talent filled me with joy although Mother ignored this—my most important attribute. The emotional stress of not being validated as an artist exhausted me and often brought me to tears in my room.

Often enough, outsiders noticed my gift, but it was my parents that I wanted to impress. Maybe they didn't appreciate my talent because they didn't understand it. They weren't artistic, so why encourage their adopted child in something they didn't understand? Certainly my real mother would have understood, after all, I inherited all of my talents from someone.

Father Gave Me the Creeps

You would think Mother would have caught on but she was oblivious. She had her own demons. She was too busy trying to keep up her image and her own sanity. Father spent most of his time away and so did she. They managed to come together for cocktails before and after dinner.

"Your father should have married someone who would stay home and darn his socks like his sister! His parents are cold hard-headed Germans and never show affection," she said angrily to me so he would overhear her one night before dinner when she was drunk.

When Dad was home, he played chords and songs on the Hammond organ after dinner while I followed him on my flute. His after dinner drink was on a coaster on top of the organ. He was amazed how I could follow every chord he played. You could have some sort of dialogue with him after he had a few drinks, if you wanted to talk philosophy while choking on his cigar or pipe smoke. I was always trying to outsmart him and make him laugh.

He always waited for me to blow out the flame of the match when he lit a cigar or pipe. The look in his eyes was sinister and gave me the creeps. His parents were Evangelical Christians who were punishers and tried to frighten him with tales of the fires of hell. In church, he sat behind us with his best friend. They either fell asleep, snickered or purposely sang off key. Father made me feel uncomfortable when he was around me and I secretly thought he was weird although I loved to watch him when he was playing his accordion.

At Christmastime, it was easier to nab Father's attention. We engaged in mental and philosophical verbal battles until Mother became jealous and interrupted us. I never discussed being adopted with him because he made me act like his own daughter even though deep down we both knew it was a charade. I didn't know for sure that Father was a womanizer and an alcoholic playboy until after Mother died. Our family had such an amazing façade of normalcy. The image that comes to mind is one of a blind person wearing bifocals. Denial was just a way of life for all of us.

Mother of all Nightmares

When Mother drank she became mean and said insensitive things to hurt my feelings. I never really allowed her to get close to me although I was in awe of her. She was too critical, and I didn't altogether trust or understand her. She thought I was too sensitive. I was eleven years old when she realized we needed a secret hand signal between us for when I was afraid. This was our little secret. I know she thought I was autistic, but in reality I was mute and frozen from Rob's abuse. You can actually see her holding my hand when I was ten and hiding it behind her back in one of our frequent family pictures. Having to pose for the photographer anywhere near Rob caused me to shake with panic.

Mother used time as an excuse not to be with us. The years went by as we watched her go in and out of our front door, dressed and off to some social event. Mother was beautiful, elegant, and always smelled of Woodhue, her favorite perfume. Her social life came first and always had.

Dream Monsters and Real-life Sexual Predators

Monsters began appearing out of nowhere to stalk and hurt me in my dreams. I was being either chased by a bear, by Franckenstein, or by steamrollers. Sometimes I had to run through pools of writhing snakes. When I awoke, my pillow muffled the sounds of my sobs, and fear clutched my chest as a new day meant a new chance to be attacked by Rob, the real monster.

As I entered my teens, Rob developed an obsession with one of my girlfriend's tremendous breasts.

"Invite Jeanette over so I can feel her up. If you don't, you know what will happen," he threatened.

I knew he had hidden a Playboy magazine under his bed because I snuck into his room and looked at it. Because of our sordid history, I had become his accomplice and so I invited Jeannette over at the next opportunity. Rob's interest in sex also extended to me.

"Come into my room and get into bed with me. I want to show you something I learned from Todd," he said to me one night when our parents were at a party and Joy Ella was asleep. I refused and scooted to my own room to lock the door. Having sex with my brother, adopted or not, was certainly not a Christian family tradition.

Rob's friend Todd was one of my girlfriend's older brothers. He was sexually experienced and must have taught Rob everything he knew. One night, I slept over with her and we laughed and giggled in her room until late at night. Her parents went out, leaving Todd to babysit, and that's when Rob came over. The boys invited us into Todd's bedroom where he proceeded to rub his sister between her legs. I didn't understand her motives, but I could see that she enjoyed it. Once, when I was alone with Todd, he showed me how he could hang a hat on his erect penis, and he called me into the bathroom to watch his waterfall. While I watched, he proceeded to show me how he masturbated and made the white water spurt upward. By the time his parents returned it was as if nothing had happened. I felt disgusted and dirty and I never slept over there again.

Uprooted

Just when I thought things couldn't get worse, they did.

A month after my thirteenth birthday I proudly rode in the three-gaited competition and won a blue ribbon and trophy in the big Cincinnati Horse Show. As I was displaying the prizes in my room along with my first formal black riding habit, Mother called me into her room.

"Linda, we're moving to San Francisco Bay in two weeks. Isn't that exciting? Just think; we'll be closer to Nannie, Aunt Carolyn and the beaches! We can even go to Mexico where I lived with Dad," she exclaimed with glee.

I was shocked.

"What did you say?" I asked her in complete disbelief.

For reasons unknown to me, Father went bankrupt around 1960 and we were forced to move to California to start over. Father blamed it on Mother's high lifestyle, but his alcoholism and womanizing was more likely the culprit.

I had just picked out a beautiful, black, American saddle

bred stallion that was to be my very own to train and show. Mother led me to believe they were buying me the horse, but the next day, I discovered we were packing for sunny California. She had betrayed me, too. Maybe it was a blessing in disguise because the sexual abuse from Rob stopped for a while.

7

California or Bust

The fire engine red 1959 Bonneville Pontiac convertible rolled down the driveway of our home as Mother took us on a long cross-country ride to what she called God's country in the Bay area of Northern California. Reaching out of the car window I waved good-bye to our beautiful, empty house and watched my life fade to black. Even though I was losing my best friend, Annie, my beloved Joy Ella, the only person I could talk about Mama to or feel safe with, my flannel security blanket, my horse who was the only object of my affection, my career as a horse trainer and professional competitive rider, and my future, it was supposed to be great. We now had a pool and a beautiful house in sunny Atherton, California, to look forward to and absolutely no snow! I didn't even notice we'd left the hot chocolate, snow ice cream we made every winter with fresh snow and vanilla extract, winter coats and gloves, sleds and skis, my formal riding habit, ballet slippers and pink toe shoes behind.

Mother tried to make the cross-country trip into an exciting adventure by taking us sightseeing. I spent most of the time carsick in the back seat with Rob and Jack. When she drove on the one-lane dirt road high up in the Rocky Mountains to show us the old abandoned silver mine where her father once worked I began to feel sick and wanted out of the car.

"Bean, what's your problem? Do you want your blanket? Mom gave your hamster to a good family, just like you were given to us," Rob said in a low voice just when I was having a panic attack.

"Let me out, let me out!" I screamed as Mother turned the car around on the narrow road 10,000 feet above sea level. On my way to vomit I opened the car door and hit Rob in the balls as hard as I could.

"Stop it! Stop it," Mother yelled until she began to cough, cry, and then sob during an asthma attack. We were all quiet after that. She insisted that I take Dramamine to stop my chronic car sickness which I began chewing like candy because I couldn't swallow pills whole without choking.

On our subsequent travels, there was just no way I would ever ride a donkey on those narrow dirt trails down into the Grand Canyon knowing Rob might try to arrange it so I would fall over the cliffs. The big earthquake at Yellowstone National Park happened two days after we left. No one told me we were right on top of a huge smoldering volcano. I wish Mother had left Rob off in the Bad Lands. The cross-country trip was daunting for a woman alone with four kids. Father was in California preparing and waiting for us in the new house. If only I could go back in time and talk to Mother as an adult. Her life was out of control as was mine. In retrospect, I guess she couldn't have handled any more raw truth, especially what I wanted to tell her about Rob.

By thirteen, I had become the consummate actress, playing more roles that I could keep count. I was Mother's daughter, I was a stripper, Gloria Vanderbilt, and would soon be adding the mythical California girl to the mix.

We finally pulled into the driveway of our new home to see a stunning, sprawling and modern California ranch house made of old gray barn wood. The new house was on one floor except for my room, which was up the stairs right over the kitchen. The rest of the bedrooms were on the other side of the house off the lanai. It was great for me even though my room was really for the help; Rob's bedroom was now on the other side of the house.

We had a heated pool, a pool house, and a lanai, with one acre in the back and one in front. The grounds were filled with olive, lemon, apricot trees and to my dismay there was no place for a horse. Mother was thrilled with the fragrant gardenia bushes, eucalyptus, and acacia trees around the pool. She even had her very own Chinese gardener. Fresh flowers went into her Steuben glass vases in the prettiest floral arrangements, even in the powder room and of course all the Kroehler furniture and antiques were there too. The fragrance from the gardenias wafted through the air like perfume.

We joined a new country club and Father went into a shutter business for himself in a town nearby. Jack went off to college and Mother's asthma attacks became worse from smoking, although she said it was due to the stress of the move and having to start her social life over. Although she must have been extremely depressed over losing Joy Ella and Richard, not to mention her other friends, Mother never showed her emotions. She joined a new social crowd and our life continued as it had before. The earthquakes would come and go, but I never got used to living with the fear of falling down a huge chasm in the earth or being buried alive.

No More Riding

I covered the walls of my room with framed pictures of famous three and five-gaited show horses from the South and rode at a new stable, but it wasn't the same. My new handsome German riding instructor, Bob Schultz, also owned the riding stable. He allowed me to ride his Palomino stallion that performed tricks and had been in the movies. He also showed me how they trained three and five-gaited horses. Although I was impressed that the horses were bred to naturally perform the slow gait and rack, I was horrified to learn of the brutal methods used by the trainers to increase the flash and flair of every step. The high tail was the result of cutting key muscles and caused dock paralysis, requiring the animal to wear a tail set when being ridden. The beautiful animals were required to wear leather shackles designed to painfully slam into the fetlocks with every step to encourage higher leg movement. The bits pinched the proud steed's sensitive lips to force submission and determine a lifted headset. Riding was in my blood, but the cruelty of it gave me nightmares. I just couldn't ride them anymore and quit.

A Bra, Another Secret

The gift of gab and guts made making new friends in junior high school easy. I somehow kept getting confused with another girl with a similar last name. She was a bad girl who broke the rules and got bad grades. Her grades showed up on my report card one semester. When Mother confronted me about it, I told her about the other girl.

"It's a mistake," I said. "Those must be Linda Meyer's grades. She gets C's and D's and has a bad reputation. She rolls her skirt up at school when no one is looking. She smokes in the girl's bathroom and has wild shorty pajama parties."

Mother took me at my word and looked into it. I found Linda Meyer intriguing; after all, she wore a bra.

"Where did you get your bra?" I asked her one day.

"My mother bought it for me at the store."

"My mother would never buy me a bra, and besides, I'd be too afraid to even ask her. I'm as flat as a board," I admitted.

"Why wouldn't your mother buy you something as important as a bra?"

"She doesn't think I need one."

"Maybe you could steal one," she suggested.

I decided that the only solution was to buy a bra myself and hide it on the roof outside my bedroom window. Mother had huge breasts; just one of her bra cups was bigger than my head. The next time I was in the store alone with my friend, I bought one with pink music notes on it and hid it in my pants before I got home.

"This will be our little secret," I told my friend.

Each night, I placed the size 34AAA bra on the roof outside my window and each morning I secretly put my new bra on under my slip. Off I went to school feeling so grown up.

All the girls in my class hid face mirrors in their notebooks so they could primp during class. I snuck mine out one day in History class and secretly watched the girl next to me picking her nose. She kept digging into her nostril until a long piece of snot came out which she wrapped studiously about her finger. When she caught me watching she gave me a dirty look. Still, that didn't stop me from telling my classmates. One morning I was in the school bathroom stall stuffing my bra with toilet paper and looked up to see her standing on the toilet in the next stall looking down at me.

"So that's why you look so good in a sweater," she said and laughed.

"Don't tell anyone please," I begged her.

"Don't worry; it'll be our little secret," she promised, but took her revenge by promptly telling the entire school.

The next time I sat next to her at lunch, I called out her name and as she turned to me I spit an entire chewed hardboiled egg in her face. We were both called to the principal's office. The principal stood there, towering over us, and didn't know what to say.

"What's going on here?" he asked us trying not to laugh.

"She stuffs her bra. I caught her doing it," she revealed.

"So what. She told the entire school when she promised me she wouldn't," I answered.

"Well, get back to your classrooms and don't let it happen again," the principal told us. Thankfully, for some reason, Mother never said a word to me about it.

Waiting for the Swan

I hoped the one boy I had a crush on was going to ask me to the Junior Prom. Instead, he came up to me at school one day and called me Bucky. He must have noticed my confusion because then he clarified: "Your teeth look like the cow catcher on the front of a train."

Mortified, I refused to go to school for a week. Mother made an appointment at the orthodontist. He pulled five of my teeth and fitted me with braces and head gear. In California, image was everything. Being a square, skinny Midwestern girl with buck teeth and a long neck was giving me an inferiority complex.

"One day you'll emerge a swan," Mother said to me. "When all the pretty girls have lost their looks, you'll be a beauty. If you continue marching in the band you might get to march in the Rose Parade in Pasadena. I used to spend hours working on the floats when I was a little girl."

I scrunched up my nose. "I don't like the band uniforms. The pants, the jacket, and the helmet look so retarded and embarrassing."

Mother braved on. "Do you want to continue taking private flute lessons?" she asked, and then took one of my hands into hers. "You are a true virtuoso. You can do anything with those long beautiful fingers."

I did love to play, and I nodded my head. "But you'll have to tell Father to stop smoking his cigars at night. The smoke rises to my room and I can't breathe when I'm practicing."

Afterward, Father agreed to smoke in his office and close the door, but it helped very little. Since my room was at the top of the stairs, his putrid choking smoke invariably rose to my room anyway. I remember tying a handkerchief around my head every time I needed to pass his door.

Mother signed me up for lessons at Dana Morgan's Music store and I continued to play in the school orchestra.

"Who's that?" I asked her when we walked in the door

and I saw a big fat guy with long, wild, bushy black hair and a beard behind the counter.

"That is Jerry Garcia, the guitar teacher," said Mr. Klein my new teacher.

I had no idea that I was in the place where the The Grateful Dead would originate. Jerry, the mammoth-like improvisational musician, freaked me out.

The Bare Tree

By the time I entered high school, I was still a Midwestern classical music snob and knew nothing about acid or jamming. Mother tried to maintain the 'prim and proper' façade with me and hoped that I might join the youth symphony, but I refused. Nannie bought me a pink Princess phone for my room with a private line. This was the beginning of my slow transformation into the mythical sexy California girl who had more identities than an illegal alien.

Father stopped going to church. Mother became an atheist and blamed it on me. She thought I was a witch and would have been burned at the stake in a previous time because of my uncanny ability to know things. Hopefully, she didn't see me sneak into her bedroom and turn off the alarm on her clock every Sunday morning so we would miss Church. I, too, eventually left the church as I thought we weren't all born sinners like Rob. Dogma divided people. Weren't we all Divine Incarnations? It would be up to me to retrieve my soul from the lost and found.

Rob gained weight and began taking diet pills.

"Hey Bean, try one of these. It'll make you look like a model, and you'll look so sexy in a bikini."

I tried one to see what it might feel like. I liked it and started to want to take them all the time.

One day, Rob berated me within Mother's hearing. "Bean," he said, "I have to write down my family tree for a project due in school. Too bad you'll never be able to do one. I'm Mom's real son and you're a bastard. Your family tree might as well be a telephone pole."

"I don't care, and I hate you!" I told him as I spit in his face and left the room. Mother followed me to set things straight.

"You are on our family tree now," she said.

I wasn't consoled. "I can't use your ancestors because they aren't really related to me. I'm not doing one."

The next day my social studies teacher asked me to do a family genealogy.

"I was adopted and don't know my past or my family tree, although there must have been a musician and an artist there somewhere," I told him after class and then burst into tears.

"I understand. You can use your adoptive family," he said.

"No, I can't, because that would be a lie. Can I just draw an oak tree with no leaves on it?"

"Sure," he replied and handed me a Kleenex. Funny how the bare tree gave me more comfort than a lying one filled with Mother's relatives.

Sewing Comes Naturally

I think Nannie felt sorry for me and knew that I was suffering. She had a way of looking deep into my soul and was intuitive enough to buy me a sewing machine. She taught me how to mend my clothes and how to sew badges on my Girl Scout sash with hidden stitches. Miraculously, the high fashion designer inside of me slowly emerged. Rob's pills enabled me to stay up all night into the morning sewing haute couture for my classmates. Vogue was my favorite magazine and a fake beauty mark was delicately placed over my own every morning with a brown eyebrow pencil. Sewing was a creative outlet, and I sewed for hours, higher than a kite to forget how physically and spiritually misplaced I felt in my adoptive family.

My own label hung in every original piece of clothing

and the money came rolling in.

"Like I always say, there's nothing like something made with loving hands at home," Mother reiterated as if sewing was for peasants, and off we'd go to buy designer outfit at Saks or I. Magnin.

She took great pride in the suits, long straight shirts, gold jewelry, fresh water pearls, cashmere sweaters, heels, and matching purses that she wore. My walk-in closet was filled with designer clothes that I never wore. She had no idea her adopted daughter was a gifted high fashion designer herself. How could she know about all my talents when I wasn't a part of her genetic mirror? I could have been Coco Chanel and she still wouldn't have known. She thought sewing so plebian. My fabricated self and my true self were making me confused, lost, disconnected and crazy. My disappointment in my adoptee status and not being understood began to grow into a full blown depression.

My Mask

One Christmas, instead of adhering to the tradition of making sugar cookies with Mother's heirloom cookie cutter, I decide to make a Gingerbread house with Gingerbread men and women.

"I can see the family resemblance, Bean," Rob snickered, as he looked at the cookies. "You don't look like anyone in this family because you're adopted. Did anyone ever tell you that you look like a witch?"

"Too bad you're stupid and aren't as talented as I am," I retorted as he walked away.

"Save some of your cookies for my dinner party tonight," Mother requested.

Dessert time came and we heard, "Oh, dear God," from Mother as she looked down at the polished silver tray on the table to see erect penises and huge bosoms on the gingerbread men and women. Her male guests began to laugh.

"Linda, take the cookies to the kitchen. Now!" she

ordered and followed me into the kitchen.

"Rob did it," I told her.

"He said you did it and I believe him."

Angry and red-faced, I threw the cookies at her and Rob and ran to my room. Locking the door, I flung myself onto the bed and sobbed. They were all living in denial.

After the guests left, Mother came to my room and stood in the door.

"Why don't you have any enthusiasm for anything I care about?"

I wanted to say to her, "Because I don't relate to the things you like to do. I'm not your genetic child, and I have passion for the things that my natural relatives did and do and I am so tired of having to pretend I fit into this family. Why is that so bad? After all, I'm in an arranged family and it isn't my fault we aren't alike. Do you really think it's easy pretending to be your real daughter and being abused by your son?"

But I said nothing.

Perhaps, if I had said such a thing, she might have understood me better, but I couldn't take the chance that she would instead tell me how ridiculous I was behaving. I was never unkind to her to avoid the risk of being rejected, so I remained a compliant but misunderstood daughter. The hurt never went away because I couldn't talk to her about how artificial I felt or that her son was a pervert. We were both hurting. Being adopted and living with Rob was a huge psychological burden. I was the Lone Ranger with a fake beauty mark and false eyelashes instead of a mask.

8

The Perfect Girl

Rob's perversion shifted. I didn't know it until I was fifteen and saw his shoes among my shoes in my walk-in closet one night while I was getting into my shorty pajamas. I pretended he wasn't there and ignored him. Once I was in my bathroom, he disappeared without a sound.

He wouldn't leave me alone and appeared in my room again.

"Put on your short skirt and go-go boots and do a sexy dance for me," my stalker asked.

"No. I'm trying to live a normal life. Now leave me alone or I'll tell Mother."

Sometimes I could hit him and he'd leave; sometimes a kick would do it. Too often, there was nothing I could do to get him to leave me alone.

I loved to throw moonlit pool parties so my friends and I could swim under the stars in the heated pool and dance to the tunes on the jukebox.

"Come on, Bean, invite your friends over for a sleepover so I can watch them get undressed," Rob asked when no one was around. "I'll give you a hundred dollars and all the diet pills you want!"

"You're sick! Now leave me alone or I'll tell," I threatened.

"She'll never believe you," he reminded me.

Ironically, even though her monster child was the one she should have been worried about, Mother set strict dating rules for me. The front door lights flickered on and off at 10pm if I was still in the car with my date.

"When the lights flicker that means come inside now, not ten minutes from now," Mother said.

The boys in high school thought I was frigid because of a rumor that got out saying Rob had raped me. I found myself walking on thousands of snakes in my never-ending nightmares.

Sara, my best friend from New York, told me years later that she woke up one night to wonder why Rob was in the bedroom with us. I wondered if he did sexual things to me while I was sleeping.

Sara and Missing My Old Home

Sara and I had the same big green cat eyes and dark sense of humor. We both had ESP and her mother thought we were good witches. She was having an elegant lunch at Blum's with Mother and me one day and innocently said, "You two look so much alike. Have you ever noticed that Linda's right eye is a bit smaller than her left one?"

Mother and I looked at each other.

"Should we tell her?" Mother asked me.

"I'm adopted," I told her even though I wasn't even aware then that I had a mother that I surely must look like. Talking about Mama was taboo and the conversations about my adoption always stopped as quickly as they started.

I continued to get diet pills from Rob. They not only took away my appetite, but also seemed to take away my bad memories, crazy depressing thoughts while giving me energy to burn. When the dose wore off, I was back in my adoptive family's world and more depressed and lost than before. I needed them to stay sane.

While I was on the pills I didn't think about missing Joy

Ella, my best friend, Annie, horseback riding, my life in Ohio, or wonder about my first mother or the day we left for California that played over and over in my head like a bad movie scene. The sheer grief of it all constantly made me break down and cry. The desire to unlock the mystery of my identity was beginning to emerge as well. Where was Mama, my heart's desire?

Bob Weir, later of The Grateful Dead, went to my high school. Sara called him Bob Weird because he wore baggy ripped jeans, never washed his long greasy hair, and walked around school with his guitar on a shoulder strap.

On my way to the pastry shop to buy the cake I would later gorge myself on, I often walked past the pizza parlor where he was playing to an audience of hippy kids smoking pot. Being a classically-trained musician, I hated their music. It was loud and hurt my ears. To me, the hippies were the great unwashed.

Sixteen was my lucky year because Rob, the pervert, left for college. My buck teeth were now straightened and I could smile without having to cover them with my upper lip. I bleached my hair platinum and dropped out of the band and orchestra. On my eighteenth birthday I decided to come out into high society as a Northern Peninsula debutante with my best friend Sara.

"Mother, I think I want to be called Melinda now. Everyone calls me by our last name, but I want that to change. What does my name mean?"

"It means beautiful in Spanish and is of Greek origin meaning gentle, soft, and kind."

"I was going to name you Natika Wren, a Persian name, because of your big exotic cat eyes. Have you ever noticed how your eyes sometimes look gold, and they have an amazingly beautiful teal colored rim?" Mother asked.

"Yes, but can you tell my right eye is smaller than my left eye?"

"I have noticed that," mother admitted.

"I wonder where that comes from?" I bravely commented to see what she would say.

"Yes, the orthodontist told me that as well," she commented and didn't continue the conversation.

Sara and I decided to make our debut into high society together. Her mother called me Olive Oyl, after Popeye's girlfriend, because I was so tall and skinny. Once she joked that if I cut my hair short, I'd look like a walking Q-tip.

Sara and I had gone through puberty together waiting for our armpits to smell and trying to figure out how to use Tampax. I figured it out with the help of a mirror on her toilet. She even stole a dirty magazine, and we secretly made a tape recording on Rob's recorder containing every bad word we could think of. One night, she caught me throwing up my Hippo chiliburger in my bathroom.

"Please don't tell anyone. I won the modeling competition for Macys and have to model a tennis outfit in front of a big movie star." I wanted to be thin for the actor David McCallum, who played Illya Kuryakin, the Russian spy in *The Man from U.N.C.L.E.*

"I won't, it will be our little secret," she promised.

It was now 1965 and my turn to strut the catwalk before a panel of celebrities. Modeling short white tennis shorts and a white shirt, all I could think about was if anyone there could tell that I had an evil big brother who kept trying to molest me. Why couldn't I be a happy model wearing an exotic sexy outfit like Veruschka? To maintain my composure while modeling, I forced Rob out of my mind and pretended to be a famous German Vogue supermodel.

On the way home in the car I wanted to tell Mother about her evil son, but instead, I talked about my feelings towards some of the other debs I'd met.

"I can't stand some of the girls that are going to be debutantes," I told Mother on the way home from the fashion show at Macys.

"You will never make a good socialite. One has to pretend to like everyone," she instructed.

"I can't tolerate stupid, shallow, or false people and refuse to make small talk and I hate Rob," I thought to myself.

"Make sure you wear your pretty Chanel suit and your lovely flower brooch tomorrow for the mother-daughter tea," Mother said, closing the subject. "Family Services is doing a Who's Who article about us for the San Francisco Sunday Chronicle."

Wearing suits, matching purse and shoes, elegant hats and brooches like Mother who dressed like the Queen of England was not in my genetic code, but I complied and I must say, we really did look like Mother and Daughter. We listened to a lecture and received counseling on how to handle emotional problems in the days of the feminine mystique and the battle of the sexes. Knowing yourself thoroughly was the key of Dr. Gertrude Hengerer's speech to all the debs. The irony here was astounding: How could I possibly know myself without having the details of my real identity?

Debutante

"You have to go out with Steve Skinner. I promised his parents you would. He's a very nice boy and he comes from a good family and maybe he could be your chaperone for the debutante ball," Mother informed me.

It was impossible to say no to Mother as I would never dare hurt her feelings. This is why I first said "no" and later "yes" to a date with him to please her knowing that he was much too short and skinny for me. I was embarrassed to be seen in public with him. He asked me to go see the Monterey Grand Prix car races at Laguna Seca Raceway, and I said I would. Sara and I tried to think up a way for me to get out of it so I tried to fall off a rock and break my ankle. When that didn't work, she threw a rock at it. We put a fake cast on my leg. Unfortunately, Mother made me go, cast and all. I sat there with tears in my eyes and sick to my stomach hating every minute of being with him. How I wished I could say "no" to Mother.

I so envied Sara, who wasn't adopted, and was in love

and dating a handsome swimmer who was training for the Olympics in Tokyo. I had a crush on Greg Buckingham, Lindsey's (of Fleetwood Mac fame) older brother, who was tall and handsome and later won a gold medal at the 1968 Mexico City Olympics. He was the most handsome fellow I had ever seen in my life. I was too afraid to even look up at him. Sara and I sat together after school often to watch them play water polo matches in their sexy Speedos at the high school pool. She borrowed my best green jumper to wear to impress her future Olympian. We teased, flipped, and sprayed our hair until it wouldn't move. Our mothers were friends and we went to all the debutante parties and high teas. I must have bought fifteen party dresses and five long ball gowns. Shirley Temple Black's daughter Linda was in our group. One of the high teas was held in her house. Mother and the aging child star shared a certain love for English elegance, yet Mother outclassed everyone all the time and so did I, being her perfect daughter.

"Why would she put a huge crystal chandelier in her powder room right near the toilet? It could have fallen on us during an earthquake," I told Sara.

"Doesn't her daughter look like an Amazon china doll? She uses her stepfather's last name instead of her biological father's last name," Sara explained. "And did you know Shirley was in eleven films where she played an orphan?

"Linda's so distant and aloof and doesn't seem real," I replied, my mind wandering down those old roads: who was my biological father and where was he?

Mother gave me a present the day before my debut.

"This silver service is yours," she said, as she handed over a used set of Gorham flat silverware from The Family Service consignment shop. The initials inscribed on the silver made it clear it was hardly a family heirloom.

"How beautiful," I said, secretly thinking I would never use it because of those alien initials. It was insulting to me knowing that Rob was going to inherit her good silver. It was hard enough to use my adoptive family's initials and now she wanted me to use another strange family's used silver with their initials? It made me want to find my own family name and initials even more. My initials were MAM but a part of me thought of them as ???.

Sara and I were partners in crime and devised a little wicked plan as we didn't take ourselves as seriously as the other debutantes.

"Let's buy some chocolate covered baby bees and slip them next to the fancy chocolates on the table at the next high tea," she suggested.

"Okay! I think they sell them at the gourmet store," I laughed, knowing that watching the older ladies and pretentious debs crunching the chocolates would be a hoot. We snuck them on the tea table at the next luncheon.

"Are those peanuts inside?" asked one of the older ladies as she inspected the-piece of chocolate. We laughed and laughed as we watched her swallow the bees.

The big Coming Out event was held at the Country Club with an Old English garden theme. Our chaperones wore white gloves, white ties and tails. I wore a long white gown made of white pique and matching sixteen-button kid gloves. The proceeds went to the Family Service Association to which Mother belonged.

"I dare you to fall down after you curtsy," Sara said.

"I will if you will."

"When it's our turn to be introduced to society and dance with our fathers, let's walk out under the vine-covered archway, do the big curtsy, and fall down," she said.

"I'll think about it."

"Do you even know the name of your real mother or father?" Sara asked me.

"No," I told her and changed the subject. My anxiety level rose so fast when the topic of my adoption came up I always redirected the conversation as fast as I could and then proceeded to eat too much and purge it out into the toilet.

Before the Ball, Mother informed me, "You will be expected to dance the first dance with your father." When they announced my name, Father took my hand and we waltzed as everyone clapped. But my mind went back to a time when Father looked in on a strip Poker game where Rob, Darin and I sat naked playing cards. In my vivid memory, Father took in what he saw, snickered, and closed the door. The memory made me so anxious that I tripped on his foot and fell down in front of everyone at the dance.

While I sat on a chair recovering, I watched a free-spirited, beautiful woman with long, dark, wavy hair wearing a red chiffon strapless dress dance with her handsome partner. How I longed to take off my long white straight jacket and be free to look and dance as she did. She was happy, glamorous, and sexy. Mother had made me into a sexless robot, her British reserve successfully drilled into my persona. I was a fraud. As I watched the Ball proceed, I vowed to myself that I would find out the truth, who I was, and I would break free from the lie. I would figure out a way to allow the free and easy Melinda to emerge as she was meant to do.

The music played on, and I thought about the time I danced with Father at one of the Country Club black tie dinner dances to please Mother.

"I will know you have grown up when you finally agree to dance with your father," she said.

He kept trying to lead me and it became a war on the dance floor, especially because I felt so uncomfortable being that close to him. It was becoming impossible for me to keep pretending he was my natural father. I wanted to scream out, "I'm adopted, these people aren't really my parents, and their son, Rob, is a pervert!"

I was sitting next to a Senator at the time and kept wondering and even hoping that he might be my natural father. My false self was still in control and was too afraid to ask him about adoptee issues or if he was in favor of opening the sealed records of adoptees; I missed my big political chance to make a real difference. If only I had asked him the big question, "Are you my real father?" Who knows where that might have led me? Thoughts went through my mind like "even if he was my father, he probably wouldn't tell me," or that "everyone else there knew he was my father but me."

The next morning after the ball Mother said, "Linda, I

think I'll put a dance floor over the pool and float votive lights and gardenias on the water for your wedding reception one day. Did you know that when Nannie was living at The Woods hotel in Guanajuato, Mexico in 1905 with Gaga the pool was covered with gardenias every morning? Don't you think that is wonderful?"

I shrugged. I didn't care about all that stuff, and why didn't she call me Melinda as I had asked her to.

She would have loved to pick a husband for me and plan a big wedding. Father was the last person I wanted to walk me down the aisle and Mexico was very much a part of Mother and her family history, not mine.

Most of the kids at school knew me as the rich tall, skinny, blonde girl called "The Stick," who hosted fun parties and only wore the best brands. No one knew the other me, the one who was lost and popping Rob's diet pills to take away painful thoughts of my real mother and my brother's abuse. The other me was the one driving her mother's red convertible up and down the Pacific Coast Highway screaming, "who am I?" and "help me, Jesus. I want my mommy!"

After my high school graduation, Mother decided I should go to the University of Arizona with Rob.

"Rob loves it there," she rationalized. "And this way, you will have your brother around to keep you company."

Just what I need, I thought, another year with the pervert in the scorching hot desert. I went running to pop another pill.

Sara went off to Berkeley, and I went with my abuser in his red VW Bug to The University of Arizona in Tucson. Everything was peachy. I had everyone fooled; if only I could have fooled myself.

9

Sorority Sisters

Rob was already in a top fraternity at the U of A when I went through rush and was accepted as a pledge into Kappa Alpha Theta, the most elite sorority house on campus. I was Mother's perfect clone, and by this time, I was a master at reinventing myself. The long platinum hair, moss green velvet headband, white flats, white straight skirt, button down cashmere sweater, fresh water cultured pearl necklace, sterling silver charm bracelet, beauty mark and false eyelashes on the outer edges of my lashes and sophisticated lady like behavior enabled me to make it into the sisterhood. Luckily, there wasn't room in the sorority house so I stayed in a dorm. I really didn't like the formality of the House and was still hiding my bulimia.

"You will be a Liberal Arts major," Mother declared and that was that. Shelly, one of my three roommates in the dorm, was an artist and I envied her choice as an Art Major. Her father was also an artist and encouraged her talents, where no one in my family knew or cared about my artistic talent. I was also impressed with how relaxed, young, and handsome Shelly's father looked.

"He's a vegetarian, into juicing, meditation, and yoga," she told me. "His art studio is over our garage."

"Is he adopted?" I asked.

"No, why would you ask that?" she replied.

"I am, and I was just wondering. My adoptive grandfather was a vegetarian," I commented quietly, always searching, even when I didn't realize it.

Shelly's dad didn't smoke or drink and I wanted to look as young and as healthy as he did when I reached my forties. My other Californian roommate was already sexually active and a pot smoker. I thought she was a bad girl and was afraid of her; I knew nothing about intercourse other than it was something to avoid. The fourth roommate was short and her face looked like a pig. I just felt sorry for her.

Shelly was also accepted into the same sorority.

"Here, take this valium during initiation. It'll calm your nerves," she said telling me as she took the pills for her anxiety.

"Why do they have to be so mean to us? What kind of sisters would abuse their own?" I asked her.

"Well, that's just the way it is, so make sure you take the valium I gave you when the going gets too rough. I hope I don't faint," she said nervously.

The hazing turned out to be nothing compared to all the abuse I had gone through from Rob. They herded us in like cattle to spend the night in a room full of metal bunk beds. We slept on the stiff little mattresses with no sheets or blankets only to have them awaken us at 4 a.m. They yelled and ordered us around as if we were in the army and threw some sort of slop from a bucket on us. Most of it is a blur as I did have an anxiety attack and took the valium so I wouldn't cry.

After making it through the initiation, we were ready for the formal secret ceremony. We were to dress in long white togas, adorn our heads with laurel wreaths, and drink the dark syrupy, sacred drink out of a sterling silver chalice. Then we were given Greek names after taking a secret oath of sisterhood in a darkened room in the sorority house decorated like a Greek temple. I thought it rather stupid at the time and wasn't interested in yet another secret name, being Greek, or belonging to another covert society. After all, I was a lifetime member of the secret adoption society triangle.

I ate all my meals in the sorority house and returned to the dorm to live, study, and sleep. Mother decided The Liberal Arts program was to give me room to figure out what direction to go with my education. However, my agenda did not include a career because no one told me that I should even have one. Marriage to a wealthy man was supposed to be at the end of the rainbow for me as it was for my well-connected mother.

"In my day, women from the upper classes didn't work. The only career choices then for women were to be a nurse or a teacher, and who would want to do that," she said.

"What's wrong with that?" I asked her.

"It's too common and there's no money in it," she said with disgust.

She was lucky she didn't have to work. Away from Mother, my inner world began to unravel because she wasn't there telling me what to do and who to be. Without her, I was lost.

Dining with my sorority sisters reminded me of our formal dinners at home. I was once again pretending to be happy and didn't feel like I fit in at all. I ate slowly and was always the last to leave the table, giving me time to secretly go around and eat the leftover desserts. My sweet tooth had a life of its own, especially for my favorite lemon filled cake with buttercream frosting. It gave me comfort and serotonin. I began bingeing and purging more frequently. In fact, I had anorexia too. The problem was a bit more serious than wanting to be thin. My secret trauma-driven compulsions were out of control and I was slowly being sucked into a giant black hole.

I began to wonder why college was necessary. Why would I need to study the mating habits and genetics of the melangaster fruit fly or take advanced French Literature classes? Getting A's was important to me, so I studied for finals high on diet pills. My adoptee self was still in control, although my authentic self was always coming out to save me from total disintegration. A complete identity crisis was on the horizon. What was becoming clear was that I knew more about the genetics of the fruit fly than I did my own. Rob was there triggering my anxiety, and to complicate matters, I was hopelessly attracted to a tall, dark, wildly sexy artist on campus. I knew absolutely nothing about real sex and I devised a secret plan to meet him.

So far, I had remained a virgin, and my best male friend was a homely but nice Jewish intellectual. Because I was adopted and didn't know my origins, I very well could have committed incest with a half-blood brother or any half-blood relative. I was the only person worrying about this as it was a non-issue to everyone around me. This issue was becoming a growing concern. I could be related to anyone I saw on the street and maybe I shouldn't have sex with anyone. The thought of having sex or even kissing a guy frightened me because I associated sex with Rob who made want to throw up.

College Life Continues

Rob drove me home at the end of my freshman year. His fraternity mascots - rattlesnakes and scorpions - lay coiled in boxes on the backseat as we drove home for the summer through the hot desert. I was so unhappy and didn't say a word to him the entire trip.

Luckily I was asked to babysit for a Congressman's five kids at Aptos beach for most of the summer which allowed me to get away from him. Fall arrived and once again we packed up the VW, and I headed back through the hot desert for my sophomore year with Rob and his fraternity brother.

Early into my sophomore year in 1966, I found myself still attracted to Jim, the wild artist, who wore a railroad cap and was a member of the Jet Set. I didn't realize this particular jet set took LSD. I barely knew about pot let alone acid. My Jewish friend knew him and took me to one of their parties.

I couldn't believe my eyes when we walked into what seemed like something out of a Hieronymus Bosch painting. All over the place, people were dancing and drinking in various stages of undress, gyrating under the flashing strobe lights. After sipping the Hawaiian punch, I became nauseous and headed back to the dorm where I promptly bleached my dark roots in the bathroom at midnight with peroxide.

My pot-smoking roommate Janis caught sight of me the next morning and asked, "Linda, did you know they laced the punch with acid at the party last night?"

"What's acid?" I asked her.

"Take a look in the mirror," she said.

"Oh, my God!" I screamed. My hair was bright orange. "Mother will kill me!"

"Acid makes you lose your mind. Didn't you know?" she asked.

"My mother's going to be here tomorrow. I'm in big trouble. Will you cut it all off for me?"

Mother arrived the next day. "What happened to your beautiful hair? Did you light it on fire?" I had an answer ready.

"My roommate played a trick on me and cut it all off when I was asleep, Mother," I told her being an expert liar.

She had been having my hair frosted platinum since I was fourteen. Once away from her, there was no way for me to have it professionally colored.

"It will grow back eventually," she said, but probably thought I had a psychotic episode.

Once she was gone the serious depressions got worse and so did the crying.

"Just get more sleep, dear, you're overly tired," Mother told me when I called her crying.

Insomnia wasn't the problem. It was much deeper and much more complicated than that. I was lost without her controlling me and telling me what to do. The combination of my budding sexual attractions to the best looking guys on campus and being around Rob, along with the diet pills and LSD flowing in my brain sent me deep into a world of high anxiety, fear, stress, trauma and confusion.

Rob called me and asked me to meet him in his room at the frat house. He wanted to set me up on a date with the ugliest fraternity brother on the football team.

"You'll like him. He's sensitive, smart, and nice," he assured me.

"No, thanks, but can I borrow one of your records?" I asked.

"Sure, if you give me one of your sensuous backrubs."

"No! Are you crazy?" I answered and ran all the way back to the dorm, staying in my bed for two days. From that day on, I never went to see him again, deciding I was going to go home.

A sorority sister invited me to her parents' horse ranch in California over Easter break. We went on long trail rides on her horses and even longer drives where I poured my heart out to her. She was on the same wavelength and cared that I wasn't happy. We talked for hours trying to figure out what was wrong with me.

"I think trying to walk in your Mother's footsteps is leading you off a cliff. Everyone thinks you are the biggest snob, but in fact it's your mother who is the snob and is making you one, too. You're nothing like your adoptive mother," said my sorority sister.

"She's not even related to me," I managed to mumble not mentioning the problem went much deeper than Mother.

"I wonder if you are more like your birth mother," she said giving me even more think about.

How could anyone else understand my feelings if I couldn't either? I was being pulled like a piece of taffy in so many crazy directions. The unspeakable and the unspoken were holding me hostage and yet there was a little light of truth flickering in my mind that kept me going toward Mama.

Every time I saw Rob on campus walking with his girlfriend who was a tall, beautiful natural blonde I felt sick. One moment, I was fine, and in a millisecond, was having a major anxiety attack, stuffing my face with sweets and retching my brains out. The only reason I stopped was that I almost choked to death one night throwing up in the garbage shoot at the dorm. The secret sexual relationship between me and Rob, and being unable to control the path of my life triggered my eating disorders and depression.

Being at college with the devilishly handsome Rob was emotionally complicated. Pretending that he was my blood brother and also pretending there was nothing perverted going on between us was stressful. I thought perhaps I had lucked out when my wild pothead roommate got me a date with Jim, the sexy Jet Setter. We went to see James Brown and his dancers. God, was I happy to finally cut loose, dance, and experience some joy.

"If I could only become a dancer for the Godfather of Soul, I could be happy all the time, earn a living and get away from Rob," I fantasized.

The concert got me so excited that Jimmy thought he could get me into bed for a little sex after he saw me dance. He made sure I was high on beer and proceeded to manipulate me into a bed after we went back to the party house.

"Get off me," I demanded while he tried to pin me down to give me a sloppy French kiss.

"Please take me to the dorm, or I'll be locked out. It's past the curfew," I said and spit in his face as hard as I could.

"Come back here, you crazy bitch. Are you frigid like everyone says? They call you The Machine," he said clearly in pain as I ran out the bedroom door with him in hot pursuit.

"Let's see how the Machine will react when I hit her with a beer can," Jim announced to all his friends as the can hit me in the head.

They laughed as I sprinted out the front door in the darkness crying all the way back to the dorm while holding my torn blouse together. Finding another sexual abuser to trigger all the anxiety and more panic attacks hurled me deeper into the black hole of confusion and despair. Even the diet pills couldn't help me now. I was only into the second semester of my sophomore year when all I did was cry and call home sobbing depressed and afraid.

College Aborted, Going Home

Susie, my trusted sorority sister, bought me a plane ticket to the San Francisco airport. I packed my trunk and flew home unannounced. Mother answered the phone when I called from the airport. I began to cry.

"I'm at the airport. Please come and get me," I pleaded.

"Linda, you're running, she said in an angry and mean tone of voice. I called the headmaster of the school and she agrees," and she hung the phone up on me making me feel so ashamed. I called her back.

"Put Father on the phone," I demanded.

"Come home," he told me, but gave me an ultimatum. "Either you go to work, go to secretarial school, or back to college. Nannie will buy you a car so you can go where you need to go."

"I'll go to secretarial school," I promised and picked out a canary yellow Firebird with a black roof thinking they would always be there to rescue and take care of me.

My parents had moved to a smaller house so I stayed in one of the guestrooms. Secretarial school was a bore, so I decided to work for Father. I couldn't stand the cigar smoke and dirty ashtrays in his messy far-from-elegant office. Away from Mother he was a slob.

I was twenty-one and inherited a trust fund from Gaga's estate. Father set me up with my own bank account and MasterCard attached to my stock dividends with strict instructions not to tell anyone. So I had yet another secret to keep.

The interior designer decorated my new bedroom in beautiful shades of soft celadon green. Mother found two prints she had framed and hung them on the walls. One was titled *Transition* and was of a beautiful blonde girl with huge dark eyes. Her shadow was self-painted behind her by the artist MDH Keane who was famous for her big-eyed paintings.

"This painting looks a lot like you," Mother said. "Especially her long neck and big eyes,"

"I guess," I replied. The sad-looking blue shadow behind the girl seemed symbolic of my emerging grief-stricken secret self, the other woman's genetic daughter.

The other print titled *Nina en Azul* was painted by the Mexican artist Gustavo Montoya. The subject was a poor, barefoot Mexican girl sitting on a chair with white daisies forming the shape of a heart in her lap. She, too, had huge almond brown eyes like mine. I assumed the painting must have had deep meaning for Mother and of the days she and her sister spent with their father at the silver mines in Mexico. I had no genetic family connection to Mexico that I knew of so this picture had no meaning for me whatsoever. I hadn't really realized I most likely looked like my natural parents or that they were alive and living somewhere because no one ever brought up the subject. Was Mother haunted as well? Did she wonder what her own genetic daughter might have looked like? Was she angry because she couldn't have her own biological daughter?

10

KAT House

Time marched on, and after a lonely year at home I decided to go back to college at San Jose State University. I didn't know what I was doing there or why I even needed a degree other than to meet a rich husband, but it was better than working as a secretary for some strange man who might turn out to be a pervert.

Moving into the Kappa Alpha Theta house on a campus closer to home seemed like the safest and best idea. My new major, home economics, was my choice as I was already a successful clothes designer. The sixties were in full swing and it was not too long before the black civil rights movement, SDS (Students for a Democratic Society), and the teachers on strike demanding higher pay was brought to my attention. I was now in an ultra-liberal, subversive, and radical left-wing world and had a lot to learn from all the socialists on campus.

Minoring in sociology on this campus was to awaken to social problems I never knew existed. The famous civil rights leader, Harry Edwards, and the comedian and black activist Dick Gregory were on campus speaking about poverty and racism. Lucky for me, the radical group The Black Panthers was way out of my league. I wasn't that hard core or black, but I did empathize with them. The SDS and the Weatherman Underground were demonstrating and recruiting on campus while the Vietnam War raged on. I became a radical, but I was no Patty Hearst.

Making clothing patterns in Home Economics became boring after the freedom of designing high fashion in high school and I changed my major to Creative Design with a Psychology minor. The more I learned in my classes and talking to other students who had no problem at all talking about racism, sexism, and classism the more I began to dislike the establishment and my conservative parents. After all it was the sixties; I was pretty well-known on campus as an artist and well respected for my talent and brains. Selling Rob's diet pills to my sorority sisters for twenty-five cents each helped them to study in order to get good grades while providing me with pocket change for art supplies, gas, and sweets. No one knew I was calling the pharmacist and refilling Rob's prescription. When I went to pick up the Rx I charged it and said Mother had sent me to pick it up. It worked every time because they didn't know he was in Vietnam.

My creative design teacher was a mystic and deeply involved with the occult. He decided to hold a séance on Halloween down by the train tracks in San Jose. We were told to create something to sacrifice and to evoke our dead ancestors' spirits as our project.

"I'm adopted and don't know my ancestors," I said to the teacher.

"You're an artist aren't you? Just do the assignment and pay close attention to your dreams and visions. They may be telling you who you are," he said.

An old red railroad lantern in an antique shop caught my eye. I bought it and put a hollowed out gumball with a wish on a piece of paper inside. My secret wish was to call on the higher spirits to find my lost spiritual connection and to channel my natural parents and ancestors.

It was my first introduction into the occult. We built a huge fire and threw our sacrifices into it as we danced around the hot flames yelling crazy incantations. Sadly, despite our fervent efforts, no spirits appeared.

Majoring in psychology lead me to a strange fellow studying to be a psychiatrist. He told me about the psychoanalytic therapist and philosopher Carl Jung and the anima, animus, the shadow and archetypes. I was interested to find out why, as a child, I had been dreaming of bears, Frankenstein, and homicidal steam rollers.

"Jung's term synchronicity means that we are all connected and that every symbol has meaning," the student said to me during one of our talks. "He says there's a universal connection among all people, which has an effect on the collective unconscious. In other words, what happens to any one of us affects all of us."

"Do you think that my archetypal dreams have anything to do with me or my connection to my natural parents?" I asked him.

"Could be. Why don't you go to the Alan Watts lecture with me. He's really a far out cat," he exclaimed.

Alan Watts, the foremost interpreter of Eastern Philosophies was lecturing on Zen Buddhism, nothingness, the loss of oneself, and the ego.

"Trying to define yourself is like trying to bite your own teeth," he lectured.

I wasn't quite certain how this could help me find Mama; Watts' main interest was trying to figure out the sound of one hand clapping. Didn't I have to find myself first before I could lose myself? He certainly didn't know anything about adoptees. Being an adoptee was the sound of one hand clapping!

Another acquaintance was psychic and experimenting with LSD for an experimental psych class. He told me it was possible for people to communicate telepathically, without any use of sight or hearing, since deep down, our minds are all connected. We talked about the paranormal, cosmic consciousness, and the universal mind, especially psi, ESP, telepathy, cellular memory, meditation, and quieting the mind of all thought.

I confided in him that I was adopted and wanted to access information about Mama, but had no idea how to become telepathic. He invited me to meet his psych teacher, but I decided to steer clear of him in case he was insane or maybe a serial killer. He began to freak me out when he began talking to me and wasn't making any sense. He told me he had been abducted by aliens and invited me to sit in on one of his hypnosis sessions. I declined.

My talent as an abstract artist impressed my teacher and one of my classmates wanted to buy my first painting.

"Linda, your art is so metaphysical and far out. You're a creative genius. The artist's soul is a receptacle for the Divine and honey you've got it," he said.

"I am? I do?" I replied.

"You must have lots of professional artists in your family. Are any of them famous? I am studying to be a meteorologist and this looks very cosmic to me," he exclaimed.

"I don't know who my family is because I'm adopted," I replied once again to a total stranger.

"That's so far out! You blow my mind. I wish I had an abstract mind. You are truly a beautiful soul inside and out," he said as he gazed at my pastel.

The piece contained within spheres or orbs floating in deep purple space pictures of faces. It was cosmic and I happily sold it to him for one hundred dollars. I also won a first prize blue ribbon and trophy for the sorority house by designing and making the UFO Homecoming float. We spent hours making a huge flying saucer and the costumes for the super strong gray alien androids. The production was like something out of a Hollywood set. I proudly received a gold medal on a blue ribbon awarded to me by the fraternity boys next door, but didn't tell anyone I actually thought I might have come from another planet myself. They even had me stand on a wooden pedestal to receive my medal, and like magic I was a star at SJS.

I must have looked like a freak roller skating to class in my own designer dress. My colleagues really must have been confused when they also saw me wearing lederhosen expounding on the Latin name for the white edelweiss flower, leontopodium alpinum, embroidered on the pants. Perhaps they also thought me a bit weird. The validation, for my originality and my talents, and being a Dean's Scholar, filled me with joy and happiness. My identities were diverse and as intertwined as a DNA molecule, and besides the infrequent nightmares, I was free from Rob at last.

The more I learned in my classes the more radical and incensed I became by social injustices. Higher pay for teachers and civil rights for blacks were my pet causes. The farthest thing from my mind was that I was a minority and had no civil rights to my real identity as an adoptee from a closed adoption.

A sociology course led me to tutor Gregory Johnson, an orphaned African-American fifth grader. The tutoring took place in his modest house where he lived with his grandfather. We ate the intestines of hogs, called chitlins, collard greens, and sweet potato pie. I pretended to like their cuisine, but it certainly didn't taste like tomato aspic, or quiche Lorraine. At least he knew he was black and had known his own parents before their deaths.

His grandfather and I spent many hours at his kitchen table discussing racial prejudice, oppression, abuse, illiteracy, and poverty. Gregory unfortunately became too attached to me, and I had to stop seeing him. His teacher told me that he would put his head inside his desk during class. She asked him what he was doing and he replied, "I'm in here with Linda." I ended the relationship and began to realize I couldn't make a dent in their progress for civil rights unless I was going to adopt him. Mother thought she had protected me from such harsh realities about African-Americans, but not anymore.

At Christmas Father always brought out an African-American framed art print painted in the late 1920's of a poor black slave boy smiling on Christmas morning declaring "Oh, Golly"! In the heart-warming picture the Christmas tree had two bulbs and a candle tied on top and the tree stand was a can with an orange label on it. The gift was a little handmade wood wagon.

This was Father's way of reminding us how fortunate we were and how so little could make someone so happy. I thought it was condescending and wondered if the artist, Ancus Max Donall, was a black slave. Did Father know that the black people I knew were smart with spiritual riches and musical talent as good as any white person? I knew he and Mother never socialized with blacks but I adored them.

After observing an emotionally disturbed boy in his school classroom for another class my conclusion was that he would get better during the day then returned just as disturbed the next day. I was convinced his home environment was to blame. The thought never occurred to me that the little boy could have been traumatized like me. Why else would I have such insight?

Moving Out / Dating

The noise in the sorority house became too much for me, and the girls who lived there were such an odd lot. One girl took ten showers a day. Obsessive Compulsive Disorder was not a public word then. My roommate had an obsession with working out to impress her boyfriend. She put on her ski boots and did hundreds of leg lifts so he would stay sexually attracted to her butt. What was that all about? One of the girls was abducted by a group of Hell's Angels and narrowly escaped being raped by slipping through a bathroom window. The sorority housemother slept on her back to avoid face wrinkles and drank gallons of carrot juice.

I packed up my trunk and moved into an apartment with three girls. Here, I would have a room of my own and finally some much-desired privacy.

My new friends at the apartment thought *me* odd as I put up my sleeping bag over my window so the room would be quiet and dark. The window in my room overlooked the street and the noise from the cars made me nuts. I was light and noise sensitive and had great need for silence in order to relax. Thinking deeply about things while alone was something I had done all my life in my own room and found necessary for my sanity.

It wasn't long before I was dating, but this time I never dated the same guy twice to avoid their advances. My sexual self was awakening now that Rob was not around and I began to slowly feel safe enough to take off the charm bracelet, white flats, moss green velvet headband, and let my hair grow long and walk around on campus in shorter skirts, dresses, and shorts. I even bought a string bikini to wear to the beach.

ST was 6'4" and a very handsome black basketball player. He was in the NCAA and played for the San Jose Spartans. I always walked past him on my way to class, and one day when I was walking behind him I stepped on his heel to get his attention as I used to do to Joy Ella. He thought it was funny and we struck up a conversation. Not long after, I invited him to the apartment. He was funny, gentle, smart, caring, quiet, and nice. His smile lit up the room; one romp with him and I was hooked.

No one knew that I associated Rob with every white guy that wanted to be intimate with me. The connection to this San Francisco 49er didn't cause me emotional pain or a traumatic anxiety reaction at all, but instead comfort and joy. His skin was as beautiful and soft as brown velvet, as was his gentle touch. Racism and segregation made it taboo for a black to date a white girl on campus, so we snuck around under the cover of darkness. He snuck into my room in the apartment at night. I was never afraid of blacks and let him touch and nurture me due to my deep love for Joy Ella. I found a black athlete to replace the close bond I shared and missed with her.

I was in shock when my Dutch psychology professor asked me out. He was a bit weird and eccentric with his wild, curly flaxen hair and warm green eyes. Why did he wear a Mexican serape over faded jeans and clomp around in wooden clogs? After a few glasses of carrot juice at the local juice bar, I figured he was smart enough about my issue so I told him I was adopted.

By this time that was about the first thing I told everyone. It was in the name of being honest about it to others right up front.

"I really want to find out who my mother is," I told him.

"You must be pretty angry that you were given away. We have the same color eyes. Maybe we're related," he said without a hint of humor. "My great grandparents on both sides came from Luxembourg. I suppose you don't even know who your great grandparents are."

I shook my head.

"My sister was adopted and she committed suicide because she was clinically depressed. She found out her natural mother was a paranoid schizophrenic and gave birth to her in a mental hospital. I think you should come to my Psychodrama therapy group and get in touch with your grief and infant rage. You should search for your relatives too," he suggested.

I attended once, soon after that, but the angry confrontation and yelling scared me away. I wasn't ready to talk about my problems or give anyone that kind of control over me ever again. Plus, the thought that we might be related was way too much information and it made me turn mean and reject him.

All the while, my depression deepened. The smog was choking me and burning my eyes and once again I began to think about dropping out. My long drives to the ocean, the redwood forest, and Lake Tahoe to ski, get fresh air and feast my eyes on the beauty of nature kept me sane. Nature, soul music, and art were my refuge and my joy. No one ever heard the screaming from the raw pain, growing confusion, and endless loneliness I felt. I just didn't fit in anywhere.

11

The Call

I hadn't seen my adoptive brother Jack since 1966 when he called and asked me to meet him for our favorite hot fudge sundaes at Denny's in Palo Alto. He went off to college in 1960 when we moved to California and then divinity school so I rarely ever saw him. Off I drove to meet him at the diner even though there was something so unpleasant about diners that walking into one made me lose my appetite.

"Linda, I'm going to become a missionary. I fell in love with a German girl from The Church of the Nazarene and am going to get married and live in South Africa," he said with great excitement as we sat across from each other in the diner booth.

"Would you call me Melinda now?" I suggested trying to suppress a laugh as I began thinking about what his friend had told me a few days ago. The story I got from his best friend was that Jack had gotten *The Call* and God had spoken to him one night in his living room. His friend was convinced his wife put a tape recorder under the couch saying, "Jack, this is God!"

"My wife convinced me I was a sinner and needed to be saved. I was drinking too many Singapore Slings at Trader Vics in San Francisco and am an alcoholic like Mom and Dad," he confided.

"How did you get saved? Isn't Africa a bit far to go?"

"I got down on my hands and knees at the altar in her

church and asked Jesus into my heart. Now I am a fundamentalist missionary with Marylou. Her mother is an adoptee who may have been a product of incest. I call Dad my earthly father and God my Heavenly Father," he said.

"What do you call your natural or birth father?" I asked wondering if he had the need to find him.

"My acceptance of Christ and God's call to service is very real to me," he said ignoring my question about adoption as Mother always did. I guess he wasn't ready to talk about his natural father or delve into the reasons why he was going to live a continent away saving Africans. In my mind, the only thing that could save an adoptee was finding their real identity.

While we were talking, I saw an ethereal-looking man in a trench coat walked in the front door of the diner heading toward the counter. This being's radiant crystal clear blue eyes, platinum hair, and porcelain skin left me spellbound.

"Jack, turn around," I muttered barely able to get the words out. By the time he turned around to look, the man had disappeared into thin air.

"Who am I looking for?" Jack inquired.

"He was right there. I think I just saw an angel!" I exclaimed not thinking Jack might think I was hallucinating. When the disdain in his face deepened, I immediately dropped the subject.

"We're going to teach the Zulus Christianity in Durban, South Africa, and I just wanted to say good-bye," he continued like nothing out of the ordinary just happened.

I thought it odd that he was teaching Africans *not* to worship their ancestors when he didn't even know who his ancestors were. I could understand him teaching them to be monogamous, as they were polygamous. Deep down he was trying to help them by teaching them Christian morals, as if he were teaching them to avoid the sinful promiscuity of his birth mother.

"I'm friends with lots of blacks and am dating one on the basketball team," I blurted out as we both stood to leave. "My friend Gail Ward has a black boyfriend and he wants to introduce me to John Carlos the famous track star soon."

Was he trying to regain his lost connection and bond to Joy Ella with an entire African nation? Neither one of us knew that African mothers are thought by some to be the most nurturing in the world. Jack was taking refuge in The Lord and Africans to save himself. I was taking refuge with African Americans, too, but I knew the only thing that could save me was to find Mama.

Guess Who's Coming to the NAACP Meeting

Soon after Jack and I met at Denny's, Mother insisted I go with her to a very important meeting of the National Association for the Advancement of Colored People in San Jose. I think Jack's decision to go to Africa as a missionary was the reason why she was involved with this group. He must have told her I was befriending black athletes because there sat ST, John Carlos, Tommy Smith, and Harry Edwards on the stage, ready to speak.

Mother was dressed like HRH in her Chanel suit, matching purse and pumps, fire engine red nail polish, lipstick and perfect silver sprayed bouffant hair. I wore my yellow linen sun dress from Saks and black patent Ferragamo heels, feeling embarrassed and overdressed under ST's gaze. They spoke about their civil rights struggle as well as the peaceful demonstration at the Mexico City Olympics that tuned into a living nightmare by the end.

When receiving their medals on the victory podium at the 1968 Olympic Games in Mexico City, these men lifted their black-gloved fists in the air to symbolize the Black Power struggle. They looked pretty amazing to me as they sat up there on the stage describing such a passionate subject.

ST's friend Sam was dating my friend Gail who was studying to be a probation officer and was as tough and unconventional as I was.

"Sam told me you're just one of many of ST's gal pals,"

she told me one day over coffee. "He wants you to meet the fastest man on earth. You know, John Carlos."

"The famous track star?" I exclaimed and off we went that night with Sam to the bar where he hung out.

We hit it off instantly, although I didn't know much about him. No one told me about his bad reputation, but I wouldn't have believed it if they had. He was the nicest person I'd ever met and somehow, he instantly knew and respected me for being myself. I was completely color blind and swept away with his many charms. Close friends called him 'Los and I was soon with him as often as possible.

We danced to the Motown music on the jukebox in the bar and I was in seventh heaven. I loved the way he sang and engaged me in a little bump and grind dance on the floor. No one in the past had been able to get so close to me without triggering my panic. With 'Los, I felt as calm as a bird. Plus he was outspoken, funny, and smart.

"I used to dance for money as a kid in Harlem," he told me once. He'd also worked opening car doors for the people who came to the Savoy.

"You have beautiful hands," I exclaimed as I fondled his long brown fingers. "Your fingers are so long and delicate."

"Like yours; I know," he replied and looked me in the eye. "We have artist's hands. How come you don't know you're an artist? Your work looks professional." He'd seen a 6'x 6' framed tie-dye piece that I'd sold to Gail's boyfriend.

I didn't have a good answer.

"I guess because I'm adopted and no one knows," I said in response and the conversation ended.

This world class sprinter was regal and exquisite, powerful and spiritual. He wore two silver bracelets made by one of his artist friends, something I had never seen on a man's wrist. Gail told me that the white racist system had turned him into something less than a person. She also shared that he came from slaves and was brought up the son of a shoemaker in Harlem. He made me feel safe whenever we were together, and he was as sweet and warm as Joy Ella ever was. I was certain that we weren't related which was likely the reason I fell for him so readily. I sensed greatness in him, not knowing anything about his borderline criminal background as a numbers runner and thief in Harlem or the oppression he had experienced as a black. He'd been labeled a dangerous radical socialist and was being tailed by the CIA and the FBI.

In my mind we were both artists on spiritual journeys. He had a cause and was deeply committed to God and the struggle for human rights in America. He was actively involved in helping to organize the Black Student Union and the Black Studies program on campus. Icing on the cake was that he liked me as much as I liked him and he truly appreciated my artwork.

Blacks weren't allowed to live on campus so Gail and I rented a little apartment in the poor part of town so we could have our black boyfriends over. My parents never knew I left the old apartment until it was too late to stop me and I looked forward to the times when he would sprint over in his Adidas shoes and track clothes to see me at the apartment after dark. We talked about our feelings and psychology for hours, but never about his unhappy marriage, the sexual abuse I endured back home, or how disturbed I was about being adopted.

His speech patterns drove me crazy sometimes. "Ax him to go wit' chew," he'd say. Or, "dat's the way I learnt it." I'd invariably correct his grammar and pronunciation as Mother did mine as a child. 'Los would only grin and reply with, "Don't you like my New York accent?"

I continued to create original paintings and eventually, I turned the tiny apartment into an art studio and gallery. I sold abstract paintings, collages, and tie-dye art for extra money and did pretty well. Still, the more serious subjects of the discrimination against Blacks and my depression over being adopted were never far from my mind.

Neither 'Los nor I had any civil rights; I'd been born into a system of slavery just as his people had. One night after we'd had a little more wine than usual, the subjects collided—aloud.

"Baby, you ain't got no more rights than I do," he said.

"The law doesn't allow you to get your personal records. Think about it."

My throat went dry. "What do you mean?" I replied.

"Baby, the government's holding your original birth certificate and adoption decree in secret. You been bought and sold like a slave! They changed your name, too. You got no rights at all."

"I think I'm going to be sick," I said and ran to the bathroom to dry heave. 'Los followed me down the hall, a look of true concern on his face.

"Hon, how could you not know this?"

"Because," I spat out unintentionally forceful. "I'm not allowed to think about it and no one in my family will talk to me about it."

"Don't get so upset," he said trying to calm me down. "Yes, my ancestors were stolen from West Africa, then to Spain where our name was changed from Carlo to Carlos. My mother was from Cuba. *You don't know the trouble I've seen*," he said softly as he sang to me. *"People get ready, there's a train a comin'. You don't need no baggage, you just get on board. All you need is faith to hear the diesel humming. Don't need no ticket, you just thank the Lord,"* he continued to sing softly while I considered our conversation.

"You have lost ancestors and slavery to deal with; I lost my ancestors and my identity at birth. It's like we are both victims of a kind of psychological slavery. We're both being oppressed by the same system. We're outcasts. Second-class citizens," I opined.

"It's a kind of common bondage, isn't it? I get it. Adoptees had their sense of self stolen from them like African Americans did. It's sort of like indentured slavery when you think about it."

The room fell silent and he touched my hair. Finally, he asked, "Didn't your adoptive parents tell you that you're a great artist? That you're brilliant?"

"No," I grumbled. "They don't know or they don't care. They know I play woodwinds, but not that I can write and draw. They barely know me at all."

He began humming his song to me again and I felt peace, touched by the soulful sound of the spiritual song. The lyrics described true faith that transcended racial barriers and welcomed everyone onto the train to the Promised Land. Deep down, as far as I was concerned, the *Promised Land* was the place I would finally reunite with my real people.

"You're famous and have been around the world, and I'm from the white power elite yet we have both lost our original identities and are both treated unfairly." I lowered my head to weep. "God! We've both been rejected. Doomed the minute we were born."

He commiserated with me wholly. We were both minorities and mad at the system that oppressed us.

"The song by Billie Holiday, 'Strange Fruit,' means lynched blacks on trees," he said in a soft, strange voice. "Lynching was a public spectacle, just like beheadings in France."

I was mortified, but followed the thread of the conversation. "I'm definitely strange fruit hanging on the wrong family tree. I have no roots."

He handed me a copy of The Crisis Magazine. "Look at this. It's one of the oldest black periodicals."

"What's it about?" I asked.

"It was founded by a black man named Dubois. The first voice for civil rights, *way* back in 1910."

An idea sparked. "Maybe I could start one for adoptees." It would be decades before the internet would allow adoptees to touch base with each other from all over the world, but it was a need that was a long time in coming.

Sexual Healing

I found myself physically attracted to 'Los, but still had my hurdles to leap in order to have a normal sex life. 'Los plied me with alcohol and weed, in the hopes that I might be able to relax and enjoy sex with him.

"Why are you so mean?" he asked me when the chemical

stimulants were not working fast enough. “Having sex with you is worse than a wrestling match. Have you ever had an orgasm?”

“I don’t know,” I said and burst out laughing to divert him. I wasn’t able to tell him that being abused and stalked by Rob my whole life had made me mean, angry, and afraid of men, and I certainly didn’t have the guts to ask him what an orgasm was. All I could hope was that eventually I’d figure it out without exposing my deepest shameful secrets.

The adoptee part of me felt rootless, powerless, stuck in the veritable vortex of incongruities; my life had no meaning. ‘Los’s validation of my artistic ability was empowering, but practically meaningless since we could not be seen together publically.

Eventually I invited John Carlos to meet Mother and Father thinking they wouldn’t disapprove, especially since Mother was the one who took me to see him at the NAACP meeting. Unfortunately, that I brought a poor, married, infamous, angry black Olympian home for dinner frightened my parents to death.

What I didn’t know was that Father thought he was after my trust fund. I found out after the fact that Father took him aside and threatened to sue him for alienation of affection if he tried to sweet talk a single penny out of me. After the visit, ‘Los was livid.

“What did those crackers want to see? My papers?” he asked after the horrible encounter with Father.

I had no answer for him, but Father’s disapproval didn’t stop me from keeping my apartment in the poor black part of downtown San Jose. Although I admit that coming home to my beautiful room on weekends made the other easier to handle and less depressing.

Mother was civil to me on my visits, until a few cocktails loosened her tongue and revealed her mean-streak. Was she trying to make me feel badly for not being the daughter she wanted? Was she angry with me for being weak and dependent on her? Or was it mostly embarrassment because I liked blacks?

The next morning, after one of our worst fights, I found one of her elegant handwritten notes under my door offering an apology.

My Darling Daughter, Guilt!!! What is guilt? That which was done, which should not have been done—that which was not done which should have been done. How could you castigate yourself when you have seen, done everything which could help me—and done nothing but what was a joy to me? Guilt—you have not! Should not! And never will have!!!!

Your most loving and admiring mother---Me

Mother and Father needn't have stressed over my fling, for soon enough, he moved on. The next time I saw him, the love of my life told me he was leaving to play pro football for the Philadelphia Eagles. Suddenly he was gone and it took a while for the shock to set in.

One of his talented black artist friends helped me to get through my loss. Art was a short, fat professional trumpet player who played in a jazz band and didn't drink or smoke pot. I knew a black man dating a white girl was not socially acceptable, but that didn't stop me from being friends with him. He taught me a few jazz riffs that I played on my flute and he listened to me talk on and on about my lover.

"My good friend is the lead singer for the Motown group The Dells. He's a true artist just like we are. How about going as a present for your twenty-first birthday?" he asked.

"I love the group. They sing the most beautiful and deep love songs," I said.

"They are singing in San Francisco, do you want to go see and meet them?"

"Of course," I happily replied.

We drove in my Firebird to a club in San Francisco to meet his friends. I gladly drove them to their hotel after the performance. They were a bit scary, as they were gang members, but I was in awe of them. This group, my soul brothers, like me were from Chicago, and they sang Happy Birthday to me in the car! Their soulfully sung love songs brought tears to my eyes.

I foolishly thought Father, who supposedly loved black jazz musicians, would approve. He didn't. Blacks were socially taboo in his world. Mother told me long ago that he was a reverse snob. I was given more mixed messages and realized they would always look down on African Americans.

Music for My Soul

Being an intellectual, a musician, as well as an abstract artist, I took my flute with me everywhere. Music and art gave me an immediate way to express myself and keep me in touch with my creative spirit. Mother acknowledged classical music as the only legitimate music form, but I loved to play improvisational jazz, blues, love songs, and black soul music. The music I loved was inherently generated was below the waist and *verboten.*

In an effort to control my musical tastes, Mother toted me to see performances such as Mary Martin in the musical *Peter Pan* and *The Nutcracker* danced by Nureyev and Fonteyn. She brought me to hear Yehudi Menuin play his Stradivarius, and to be entertained by Victor Borga, the comedian. But still, my favorites differed greatly. I liked James Brown, Gladys Knight, and Aretha Franklin. Segovia, the classical Spanish guitarist, was my soul father and most favorite musician of all. Mother and I were from completely different worlds. I was a sensitive artist and had an artist's soul and she didn't even know it.

I forced myself to meet Mother and Darin in San Francisco to see the movie *Camelot.* All was well until the end when I realized King Arthur had an illegitimate son by his half-sister, and that triggered a double flashback which left me crying uncontrollably in the dark theater.

Too often, the topics of incest and adoption loss triggered horrible attacks of disassociation, grief, and panic. There was no stopping the raw pain.

After the *Camelot* episode, Mother studied Christian

Science to help her with her depression. She told me to feel sad for just a little bit and that would help my own negative attitude. She knew I had carried viscous and hidden emotional triggers, but she had no idea of how emotionally crippling the flashbacks had become.

She was very unhappy with me for not fulfilling her expectations as a classical flutist and deeply troubled by the fact that I loved R & B. Mother's worst nightmare was that I might marry a black man or a spaced-out artist.

"Melinda and her dogs," was her favorite put down when she referred to my socially unacceptable boyfriends.

"Jesus, Himself, would not have been good enough for Bean," I overheard Rob say to Mother while they played bridge one night when they were all drunk.

My struggle was indeed a matter for the Heavens. I needed help from on high as I was being pulled in many directions and was completely misunderstood. Why was I so confused and filled with so much pain? My fight was spiritual and only Divine intervention could save me from the madness of it all.

Somewhere out there was my real mother, and all I could think about was finding her. She would *know* me. She'd *understand* me. And I would be *safe* with her. Where was she?

John helped me to understand that I lost my identity, my voice, and my balance, and I was heading for a breakdown. My nightmares always had me abandoned, lost, and paralyzed, trying to call for help, but could make no sound. With thousands of snakes biting my ankles and no one ever came to rescue me.

I grabbed my flute, hopped into my Firebird, turned the music as loud as I could, and sped to the ocean trying to forget that there was another person inside of me that I barely even knew existed. The unknown *me* lay in my brain like an unborn fetus. I had an entire lost history to find. More and more, I put my faith in God, hoping he was listening and would help me find and connect with my blood mother. There I sat like a yogi out on a sand dune playing my flute to God, the crashing waves, Mama, and the glorious blood orange sunset!

Sometimes as an adoptee I was acting-out, projecting anger, chaos, frustration, hostility, and the fear of being controlled by my adopters. At other times I was acting-in, projecting fear of rejection, helplessness, inadequacy, loneliness, confusion, and hopelessness. I had no sense of self or a future. Being adopted hurt like hell, and I was helpless to cure myself.

My entire life had revolved around being controlled by my adoptive parents, Rob, and their family histories. They expected me to believe I was their biological child and I did until now. I began to obsess about who my parents were and about their family history. The more I thought about it the more I began to realize I had an entire family out there somewhere. There were lost great grandparents, grandparents, siblings, aunts, uncles and cousins. Did they know about me? What country did they come from? What were their names, what did they do and what did they look like? Did any of them look or act like me? Did they love me? All these questions and more began to take over my mind.

12

Triggers

It was 1970 when living in the tiny, dingy apartment off campus in the poor part of town became too terrifying without my black lover. He was gone after winning the 1969 NCAA Championship and so were all of the world-class fellow athletes who used to come over to play cards, laugh, dance, listen to music and drink in our little kitchen turned 'speak easy'.

One night after drinking way too much, Gail and I were listening to a collection of my favorite songs on tape. She put in a tape by Brook Benton and as he began to sing "A Rainy Night in Georgia," the words triggered a memory of me waving to the conductors in South Pasadena. I immediately began to cry, then sob, then shake, then moan, unable to come out of it. Neither of us understood what was happening deep down inside of my mind or why trains and losing people I loved make me so uncontrollably sad and afraid.

"She might be schizophrenic, or maybe she's missing John," I overheard Gail say to Mother over the phone as I lay on the moth-eaten couch, drunk and wracked with pain. "I think she's saying 'I want my mama.' I'm moving out and she'll be all alone in this dump. Should I take her to a mental hospital?"

"I'll be okay," I groaned loud enough for her to hear. "Just let me sleep. Hang up the phone; we'll talk about it tomorrow." When she relented and hung up, I slept it off and went off to class the next morning as if nothing happened.

The Artist

I barely got through my Life Drawing class that day. As I began to draw the nude female model, I had a flashback of Rob abusing me in the woods. A panic attack set in and I ran out of the class to hyperventilate. The fears, secrets, and traumas overwhelmed me and once more, I was emotionally out of control. I forced myself to return one more time to get the credit for the class, and my teacher had finished the charcoal drawing for me.

"You're a gifted artist," he said to me as I studied his completion. "None of my students draw this well—so much like the old masters."

"Really?" I said in amazement hiding my puffy eyes behind sunglasses.

"Who else in your family can draw like this?" he asked.

"I'm adopted and it's something I need to find out," my reply.

"Well how can you find out? Do you know who your birth parents are?"

"It's against the law for me to know because I'm from a private and closed adoption." I said leaving out the part about Rob.

"Well, you inherited a talent for drawing that's for certain," he assured. "You have *genius* genes. If you need to talk you can come to me. My father belonged to the Carmel Monterey Peninsula Art Colony. You should come to my studio in Big Sur for private lessons," he offered knowing I was disturbed about something. He had finished my drawing of a woman on the edge of a precipice ready to fall into a deep dark crack in the earth. The nude girl was me, and at that point, I knew he could see that I was on the verge of a nervous breakdown and about to fall into the abyss.

I dropped out and I never went to the lessons.

Re-traumatized

My worst fear came true as Gail broke up with her boyfriend and moved out, leaving me by myself in the empty apartment. Soon after, I ran into an old boyfriend of a classmate I knew in high school. He seemed like a friend and he asked me out for a drink. When we returned to the apartment, we'd both had too much to drink and he tried to kiss on me at the door.

"No. Stop it," I said as he forcefully French kissed me. "Goodnight," I said breaking away from his embrace. I slid through the door and slammed it on his hand. He didn't like being rejected and began to harass me outside the door, cursing and banging on the windows.

"I'm going to kill you, you stupid fucking bitch! You almost broke my fingers. You're nothing but a tease. Who do you think you are? Fuck you!" he yelled and almost knocked the door in.

I ran into the bathroom, locked the door, and hid in the shower stall shaking and whimpering until he finally left. Once again, I'd been traumatized by an angry alcoholic would-be rapist. Reduced to jelly, I determined that I needed to carry a handgun. The next day, I drove downtown and stopped at a pawnshop.

"Who are you planning on killing?" the salesman asked.

"No one; I need it for protection," I told him and left with the gun and ammo in my burlap bag.

The next morning, I drove home to recover and feel safe. My transition into a California surfer girl was almost complete, however the long blonde hair and short mini dress failed to escape Father's lurid gaze when he saw me.

"Linda Lou, come here," he said beckoning me with his hand while he stood by the organ in the living room late that afternoon.

I walked over to him and without warning he grabbed me and pulled my pelvis deep into his crotch with both of his hands.

"Let me show you how a real man kisses," he said as he tried to stick his tongue in my mouth.

"Get off of me," I said in disgust pushing him away. I ran to my bedroom and locked the doors, and then hyperventilated when I realized that he was drunk and we were alone in the house. My left hand clutched my gun as I hid behind the bed ready to shoot him if he came after me.

Why did he do this? Was it meeting John that made him go insane, or was it my long hair and short dress? Telling Mother was out of the question. She would never believe me and would have taken her husband's side. They might even try to have me committed for delusions. What else could I do but permanently leave the only family I had ever known. Living without them and their financial support was something I couldn't even imagine doing until now.

That was it; I had to leave home for good. My escape plan was plotted in my bedroom behind locked doors. Reading books on the philosopher Hegel and issues of the nutty *Mad Magazine* gave me time to think and plan my escape. I wished there was a pair of magical Seven League boots in the closet to help me travel 7 leagues, 21 miles in a step that would take me to Mama.

I created a collage book of models cut from the pages of Vogue magazine and wrote a very dark poem titled *Rage* while I tried to figure out what to do next. Once again I had to play along as if nothing had happened. To temporarily escape my fear and circumstances, I fantasized about being the happy, successful, and independent supermodel actress and artist Veruschka. Where in reality I was that helpless and nude girl falling into the abyss.

Mother left a book on autism on my night table while I was out. Did she actually think I was autistic? The reality was that I had become mute from the traumas. I was protecting her by not telling her the truth about her perverted son and now her husband. The incest had finally emotionally severed me from the only family I had ever known. My precarious safety net was gone and I would have to search for Mama alone or die trying.

Loretta Young's Nose

I told no one about Father's advance on me. Enraged, betrayed, insulted, and frightened, I dropped out of college once again. I took off in my Firebird down the Pacific Coast to think about where to go and what to do next.

Now a college dropout for the second time, I began wearing a little button with the word Apathy printed on it. The rebel with a cause was born. Hanging out at the apartment during the day until the lease was up, and in my room at home with locked doors at night gave me time to figure out my next move.

"Rob's getting married, and you're going to be a bridesmaid," Mother said not realizing anything bad had taken place or that I had dropped out of college again.

"No, I'm not."

"Oh, yes, you are. The fitting is at I. Magnin tomorrow at 2pm. Don't you care?" she asked and looked at me like I was crazy.

"Not really. I don't care if he drops off the edge of the earth. I hate him."

"You don't mean that," she replied.

"I most certainly do," I reiterated, *wishing* he was dead now that he told me that he had dibs on most of the good antiques and silver in their will. Why didn't Mother ask me what I wanted?

Rob's wedding came and went. I began having the snake nightmares again and basically dissociated to get through it wondering if I would ever have a wedding or if my Mama was married to my father. How could she be if I was born out-of-wedlock? Knowing how sick Rob was and now my father too made me feel sorry for Rob's wife and for Mother.

They were clueless about their perverted loved ones and I wasn't about to tell either one of them.

While sunning on the beach I figured out my next move. The life of luxury in Ohio and Atherton was but a distant memory. My MasterCard gave me some sense of security even though I was now homeless, but I knew one thing for certain, and that was I had to see John again before I went totally crazy.

I ran into Beth, an old high school friend, while shopping at Saks who told me she was living in a condo next to the Stanford Linear Particle Accelerator near Stanford University.

"We have an extra room. Do you want to see if Susie will rent it to you?" Beth asked.

"Yes," I said trying not to cry.

Susie was a graduate of the all-girls prestigious school near Stanford and could take care of herself. She was an art major who just returned from school in Germany thanks to the encouragement of her Francophile grandfather. You could hear her coming because of the clacking of the Dr. Scholl's wooden clogs she wore. She and two friends were buyers for Saks Fifth Avenue and living in the condo. I rented a room and moved a mattress in on the floor of my newly-purchased empty bedroom. One night, Susie and I stayed up and talked for hours.

"My mother had five children and they all had different fathers. She gave up one of her daughters for adoption and will not tell me who my father is," she told me after a few drinks.

"So you don't know your last name either?" I asked her in disbelief.

"My stepfather thinks he knows and told me that my biological father's son was the father of my younger sister. So that makes us both sisters, half-sisters and my sister is my niece. How messed up is that? My lost sister was born in Carmel and that's all I know."

"I'm adopted. We could be long lost sisters for all we know," I surmised.

"Maybe," she laughed.

"How old is your lost sister?" I asked her.

"Ten. I was fifteen when she was born."

"How absolutely sad," I said as our eyes filled with tears.

"I remember that my mother didn't wear maternity clothes and used to split the elastic in her pants."

"Did you ever say anything to her about it?"

"No, I was too afraid of her to say anything. I do remember the night she left to go away and have the baby. It was ugly. She even used a fictitious name."

Susie was German on her mother's side, smart and so funny. She had long, beautiful hair, as I did, and we enjoyed its power over men. Never did she think of herself as a slut. She was brilliant and sexually liberated.

She knew more about herself than I knew of myself and was more stable, not having been adopted or abused, and yet she was highly dysfunctional due to her hatred towards her mother. Her creativity and artistic abilities enabled her to make money by working at a local needlepoint store painting her original designs on the needlepoint canvas to sell to the celebrity clientele.

The second roommate, Beth, was the daughter of an alcoholic adoptee whose family owned a national newspaper. We used to hang out at her grandmother's huge mansion and dance in the mirrored ballroom although we were never close enough to talk about her father's adoption. The San Francisco Ballet performed in the back yard, Merv Griffin sang there, and Beth's grandmother had one of the first Waring blenders and made fruit smoothies for all her friends. Betty, her grandmother, wore only blue and had blue tinted windows in the rooms where she spent time. Her grandfather had a wine cellar in the smoking room/card playing room where he spent time with his gentleman friends. He had one leg and gave a yacht to the Coast Guard during WWII.

The third roommate was a buyer for Saks Fifth Avenue and was very scary looking. Roseanne had stringy, coarse, black witch's hair with a face to match.

We were quite an odd bunch of highly dysfunctional

characters and three of us had been touched by adoption. Susie told me that folk legend Joan Baez used to come into Saks after it closed and buy and buy and buy.

"She was such a clothes horse," they all agreed.

Susie ran into Neil Young all the time at the post office. He loved the acoustics inside a silo at a ranch commune in Woodside owned by one of Mother's friends.

Women's liberation, drugs, and free love were in full swing. We weren't hippies but were right in the middle of the movement. Susie worked as a volunteer at the Haight Asbury Medical Clinic helping the druggies even though she smoked pot.

"What are you doing in your room for so long?" she asked me.

"I'm writing a letter to The Cradle Adoption Agency asking for non-identifying information about my natural parents and my true identity," I told her. "My real father or his father may be rich, too. I think my mother is a concert pianist and my father is an electrical engineer."

"It's criminal the way they won't tell an adoptee who their parents are, don't you think? I'll probably never know who my lost sister is or how to find her," Susie said looking down at the floor taking a deep drag on a cigarette. "Thanks to my bitch of a mother."

"Let's go to Carmel tomorrow and look for your lost sister," I suggested trying to cheer her up.

"I shouldn't tell you this, but that singer, Andy Williams, meets his girlfriend in the room next to yours," she confided. I wasn't too impressed.

We drove to Carmel the next day looking hopelessly on the streets for her ten-year-old sister.

"Now look and see if you see anyone who might look at all like someone related to you," I suggested.

"I don't even know what to look for," she said crossing her eyes.

"This is crazy, don't you think? Let's buy some ice-cream. I have a letter to mail."

Susie cracked up laughing as I pulled the letter to The

Cradle out of my purse with one hand and put the cone in the mail box and licked the letter!

"I don't think I will ever know who my lost sister is. Isn't baby selling by law slavery?" she asked me as I put the letter into another mailbox. I didn't like her question, but more, I didn't have an answer.

Back at the condo, she cooked a gourmet dinner. Her mother was not about to tell her anything about her natural father, her deep dark sexual secrets, or the reasons why she was so promiscuous.

"'People are fools,' my mother always told me," Susie said as she lit another cigarette.

"Well to hell with our mothers! My mother loves my ugly witch's nose, but it has to go no matter how aristocratic," I said to Susie.

"So that's why you spend hours cutting out the noses of Vogue models and paste them on your face!" Susie said laughing.

"Yes, I made an appointment with Dr. Burner who is going to do mine so I can look more like a Vogue model," I answered which made her laugh harder and harder until she was rolling around on the floor in hysterics.

"You do look like a model. Did you know that Loretta's love child with Clark Gable was given up for adoption? She gave it up in 1936 and adopted it again not even telling the child."

"Why?"

"She did it to keep her good reputation and career. You know how they shame you for getting pregnant out-of-wedlock."

My appointment landed me in the plastic surgeon's office sitting next to a girl who had a nose like an anteater. I stared at it in amazement out of the corner of my eye.

"I think you would look nice with Loretta Young's nose," he said and showed me a picture of her nose. "Your nose does look like a beak. How are you going to pay for it?" he asked.

"It's beautiful," I said after looking at the glamorous

movie star's nose. "I am paying with my trust fund money if that's okay."

The operation went perfectly. I called Darin to come over to see me at Susie's and tell him I had begun my secret search for my birth mother. He was shocked to see my eyes swollen, black and blue hidden behind the sunglasses that were holding the bridge of my nose together.

"You look like an alien. Did you know that Mother used to tell people right in front of me that when I was born, she saw my black hair and wondered where I came from? She thought I was a Mexican and called me Pedro when she was drunk," he admitted.

"How did you find out?" I asked him.

"Rob's wife told me," he said with tears in his eyes.

"She isn't very sensitive, is she? I also think she tells lies when she drinks," I replied not revealing that our brother Rob was a pervert and our father was too.

Whenever Darin and I were alone together, the tears always began to fall from my eyes and he just sat there in silence pretending like nothing was wrong.

"I don't even think of you as adopted," he blurted out.

"My problem isn't about what you think now; it's about the reality that I have other parents and I want to find them. It is about me and what I think. I don't know who I am. No one in this family understands me, looks like or even thinks like me. You are like Father and Rob is like Mother and her father. I am like no one in the family. You can tell Mother that I had my nose done and my ears pierced if you want, but don't tell her I'm searching for my mother."

"I won't," he promised.

No way was I going to ask Mother's permission to have my nose done or search for my own mother. She didn't know until after the fact. I had the money and the days of listening to and obeying her were over for good. By this time I was furious and looked at her as the enemy for not protecting me from the abusers in her own house. She was devastated after spending a fortune on a commission to her artist friend for painting my portrait in oil, but I didn't care. The sundress she bought for me to wear was blue corduroy from Lanz and fashioned after an Austrian dirndl without the blouse under it. She loved my old aristocratic nose and went into mourning over my new cute little pug nose that made me look like a model and movie star. Well, too bad! I didn't want to look ugly any longer or be called a witch by Rob. I was so happy I cried.

"How does it feel to be just another pretty face Linda?" Susie's current boyfriend said to me.

"Wonderful, now I look as pretty on the outside as I feel on the inside. My first name is really Melinda and I'm going to use it from now on. I finally feel beautiful," I proudly stated as if being beautiful would wipe away all my troubles.

13

On My Own With No Direction Home

The fastest man on earth left for Philadelphia to play pro football after one last night at the condo. I clung to him as I had to Joy Ella and my flannel security blanket in Kettering as long as I could until I finally had to let him go. Two weeks after he was gone I flew to Philadelphia to beg him to leave his wife and kids to marry me.

"The FBI and CIA are following me everywhere. I have a wife and children. You have to go home," he said and left me there in his friend's row house all alone.

This great man was my sunshine on a cloudy day and I cried in the cab all the way back to the airport unaware that he was being photographed with various girls by the FBI and the photos were being blown up and sent to his wife.

Years later, I heard that his wife committed suicide which left him with two children to take care of. Years after that he went on the talk show circuit, wrote the book, *Why*, remarried a wonderful and educated beautiful African American, became a teacher, a humanitarian, a counselor and a coach, and received an honorary Doctorate from SJSU. I later learned of the statue done by the artist Rigo that stands at San Jose State in honor of he and his friend.

Susie knew how devastated I was.

"I heard his bracelets early in the morning as he was leaving your room when he came to visit before he left for Philly," she said and in her next breath uttered, "I know how sad you are, but life goes on. Don't ever get involved with a married man again. I have someone I think you might like. By the way has the letter arrived from The Cradle?"

"Not yet and who is this guy?" I asked wishing I didn't need a man for anything.

"I can't tell you because I want it to be a surprise, but his first name is Larry. I'm inviting him over for dinner and you'll see. He's husband material," she said.

He was a Scotch-Irish intellectual who looked like a Kennedy. He drove us in his Mercedes to a San Francisco Irish pub for coffee after one of Susie's famous dinner parties.

"Larry's father is a personal friend of the poet Robert Frost. Loss is a recurrent theme in his poetry," Susie informed me after a few too many Irish coffees at the pub.

"Oh, was he an adoptee?" I asked.

"No. Frost lost loved ones in his real family," she said without realizing how much that statement hurt me as I didn't even know who my real parents were.

I brought him to meet Mother and she loved him as he was the only intellectual I had ever dated. In other words, the only boy she approved of. It didn't last. He studied at Stanford University and lived in the pool house on his parents' property in Atherton, which he called the black hole. We hung out there listening to music and sang the jazz lyric "Trying to make it real compared to what?" His mother showed up at midnight to find us both drunk in his little garage bungalow.

"Have you shown Melinda the Bruce Clan tartan?" she asked.

"No, Mother, but I will now," he said obediently.

"Larry comes from a long line of Scotsmen," she said proudly as he brought out the family plaid kilt from the closet.

"How nice," I answered as they disappeared into another room together.

"Please go to the guest house, my mother wants to talk to me privately," he told me upon his return.

Perhaps she was trying to protect him from me. No wonder I ended up in Frost's bed wondering if I might be Scottish or maybe even related to Robert Frost. I composed a poem for him before I went to sleep that night. His favorite line when I read it to him was the one about my alcoholic parents.

"Take their cigarettes and alcohol away and just watch those skeletons dance," I said to him with disgust.

Making love to him was like having sex with a mannequin as I had no feeling whatsoever. He was in love with a girl from Berkeley, and once again I had to let him go leaving me again wondering why I couldn't find a husband.

My newfound beauty attracted guys and girls. I was now a blonde bomb shell with a killer body and had to beat them off with a stick. While I was waiting for the letter from the Cradle, Susie's friend who was dating the quarterback for the 49er's introduced me to a handsome black defensive tackle from the team who lived with some of his teammates in a behemoth estate near Stanford University. Earl the Pearl was six feet seven inches and weighed 260 pounds. There were no words to describe how amazing he looked dressed in golf clothes and hat. The amount of food this gentle giant ate was mind-boggling. I had to stand on a chair just to reach his face.

"You look like Ann Margaret. Do you know that? Your sexy eyes 'grrrrrrrrrrrrrrrrrr' and those long legs drive me wild," he said.

It was funny because the white football players lived in the Carriage house while the black ones lived in the mansion. They even had a black lawn jockey in the front yard. They had turned it into a playboy mansion where it was rumored that Ray Charles stayed with his lovers.

We both loved to listen and sing soul music. He sang like Levi Stubbs, the lead singer for The Four Tops. I blew his mind when we were all out for dinner and after too many

White Russian drinks I pulled out my handgun and said, "I need this in case my Olympian's wife finds out about me and comes to kill us all." He thought I'd lost my mind, not knowing I had been with a famous athlete before him.

"You look like a stupid gladiator playboy to me, all football players do," I said to him bombed out of my mind and he didn't like me after that. Everyone I met was boring compared to my ex.

I always managed to alienate any guy who tried to get too close to me. My next attempt at a relationship was with a white running back who was a player for the 49'ers. He tried to have sex with me on the first date and I panicked and shot a hole in the ceiling of the apartment right there in Susie's bed watching the Saturday Night Special blue movie. He thought I was crazy and I thought he was trying to rape me. These players mistook me for a sexy playgirl, but what they didn't know was I had also grown a set of fangs which came out glistening and ready to bite when an unsuspecting guy tried to get intimate with me.

The gun gave me courage and protection from predators during the lonely investigation that lay ahead of me in search of Mama. The "book smarts" were on the back burner, as I needed "street smarts" to survive.

Everyone in the condo was smoking pot, doing LSD and having sex. We all came from wealthy families and free love was in vogue. All of us were liberated and sleeping around. I noticed one of Susie's friends who slept over with her boyfriend was a shorter version of me. She and her boyfriend looked like movie stars. She was short with waist length straight, flaxen blonde hair like mine and her name was Linda. Her parents owned a big food seasoning company.

Everyone called me Meyer, the only name I had ever known to be me. I always tried to fit in but never really did and Susie knew it.

Susie comforted me by saying I was not just getting my feet wet in life, I was getting my knees wet! I passed myself off as a writer to justify my escapades to everyone which would explain why I was so different.

In fact, I was so afraid and lost that it is a miracle that I didn't lose my mind entirely. No one there knew what I was really up to or why I moved in with only a mattress except Susie who kept trying to help me.

"I have an adopted girlfriend you have to meet. You miss your friend, I know, but remember he has a family to take care of and a depressed wife," Susie told me.

"How do you know about that?" I asked her.

"I heard about it from one of the 49ers," she answered. "He has quite a reputation you know."

Susie took me to visit her adopted friend who wouldn't leave her bedroom because she was waiting for her biological mother to call her on the phone. Her behavior was terribly distressing because she was delusional and didn't know who her mother was and was wasting her life waiting for a call that never came.

She ended up in a mental hospital. We were all in such terrible pain and in varying degrees of denial. I didn't want to end up like her.

"Look what came in the mail for you," Susie said.

"It's from the adoption agency, isn't it?" I said tearing open the envelope to read the letter.

"Damn them. They only gave me unidentifying information about my parents." I said and threw the letter down on the floor.

"So what does it say?" she asked and handed it back to me.

"Hold on, I feel dizzy like I'm going to fall."

"Are you okay? Maybe you have vertigo. Sit down before you faint!" Susie ordered.

"I feel better now, that was weird. The social worker says my natural parents live within a 100-mile radius of Chicago and I'm northern European. My father is tall, funny, a teacher with a master's degree in math and science and my mother is five foot eight with big blue eyes and fine, mousy brown, curly hair who worked for the Board of Education somewhere."

"That's so unfair. They are committing ancestricide. You

should be able to know their names and where they live. I wonder if there are any writers, artists, or musicians in your family. How cruel," Susie said in disgust.

"Well, it's against the law. I feel so exploited. They're treating me like a criminal and like I don't even exist. My God, how can they permit this and just ignore the fact that I have a real identity and that it doesn't even matter to me if I ever know the truth about myself. Have you even heard of such a thing? They are forcing me to live in denial. How sick is that?"

"Let's have a drink," Susie suggested and we toasted to a very sick world and got totally bombed on Kahlua.

Every night I cried myself to sleep in that empty room on the bare mattress feeling so lost and alone, yet waking up every morning even more determined to find her.

"Let's go to the stationery store and buy each other a condolence card and then you need to buy some sheets for your mattress and a pillow," Susie suggested probably thinking I was insane." I mean who in their right mind slept on a mattress on the floor??

That night, we made a special dinner, made toasts, lit candles and said special prayers for our lost family members and stolen identities.

"Sometimes I wake up at four in the morning out of my mind with grief that I can't control or stop," I told Susie.

"Was that the time you were born?" she asked.

"As a matter of fact, it was," I answered remembering Mother told me that much about myself.

"Maybe you're experiencing the separation trauma from your mother over and over," she said.

"Do you think I remember it?"

"Yes, I do. Your cells remember because they are your biology. Birthdays must be really painful for you," she stated.

"What a horrible thing to have to remember," I agreed.

Melinda, Magazine Editor

Susie was the only one I was close to in the condo. I thought Rob's evil spirit must have possessed the ugly roommate at the condo because she looked like a monstrous, wicked witch. It was the morning after Susie's Bastille Day party. We were all pretty hung over from the liquor-laced crepe filling, in her famous handmade crepes. Susie actually passed out on the kitchen floor just tasting the fillings I made.

I was in my car when Roseanne pulled her car up beside mine at a stoplight. She locked onto my eyes with a long, soul piercing, hungry, sexual look slithering her tongue between her lips at me as I managed a little wave to her and then hit the foot pedal taking a sharp left to escape her. I hid in an empty parking lot and began to hyperventilate. Not a word was said about the incident by either of us.

I was so spooked and almost glad Susie was getting married. She gave me two months' notice before she was moving out. Like in the past with Rob and Father, I remained scared silent and as always kept protecting the sexual predators. My method was to remove myself from their presence and never to confront because my worst fear was that my fragile world would permanently break apart. Years later I found out that after I moved out, Roseanne physically tried to rape Beth.

My trust fund enabled me the luxury of not having to work so I began to write educational stories for parents to teach their children. I was meeting interesting intellectuals at Susie's who contributed stories and artwork for my new literary career.

Putting up an ad on the Stanford University campus near the condo for writers brought a trained engineer and famous Hollywood horror writer Curt Siodmak, into my life. He wrote the sci-fi thriller *Donovan's Brain* later to be made into a movie in which Nancy Davis Reagan played the love interest. He became my friend and mentor. Both our lives resembled a horror movie, but I didn't know it until 2005 when I read his memoir *Wolf Man's Maker*.

"People are lazy and like stones. You can push them and they will stop. If you didn't keep pushing them, they remain inert. You are the echo of your energies," he told me.

We wrote to each other, but I didn't know that this writer was a German Jew and that he was married to a woman who emigrated from Germany to escape the Nazis. His memoir stated that he based his stories on scientific research. His novel *The Third Ear* was about telepathy based on biochemical substances. He was invited by Stanford University to talk to students about science fiction and fantasy. He never told me he was being visited by Nobel Prize winners or that he lived in Germany until the beginning of the 20th Century, before Hitler destroyed it and left it an artistic wasteland. His brother Robert was a famous Hollywood director of Film Noir movies. A psychologist friend of his said in his memoir that he was always writing about people who want to climb to the top of the mountain and never get there. I was climbing my own Mt. Everest and I would get there eventually or die trying.

A nice, single, Jewish writer who had his own advertising firm in Toronto called me from the ad for writers I left on the kiosk in the campus bookstore. I was away from my WASP family and could befriend anyone I wanted. He lived in Toronto and was visiting a friend on campus. We exchanged phone numbers and I said I would come to visit if my travels took me to Canada. I didn't know that my loss of kin as an adoptee was similar to the losses of the Jews in the holocaust.

Everyone I met and bonded with was traumatized by loss burdened with a deep, lifelong grief.

"Susie, have you seen the tall guy who goes to Stanford and drives a yellow Jaguar?" I inquired.

"I think I've seen him in Kepler's book store," she replied.

"He's so hot! I have to meet him. I think we have ESP together because our paths always cross. Isn't that strange? Maybe he's my soul mate," I told her.

I devised a plan to meet him by writing an ad on a piece of paper stating what I was looking for in a guy and wrote Susie's phone number on it hoping that he was the one. I boldly put it under the windshield wiper of his canary yellow Jaguar XKE and hoped he would call me for a date. A week went by and there was a Mark Moore on the phone asking for me.

"Hi," I said.

"This is Mark Moore. Did you put your phone number on my windshield?"

"Yes, I did. I love your Jaguar."

"I have to meet you because I don't know anyone who would be so bold as to do what you did to meet me."

He was tall, handsome, artistic, intellectual, wealthy, sexy and an Episcopalian like me. I thought for sure we would get married eventually. We dated and I was the only girl he ever let drive his sports car. I drove as well as a race car driver he told me. His sports car and I were inseparable and I drove it up and down the Pacific highway as often as I could.

Mark and I did have a kind of strange ESP together. We had a very strong connection, and we were always crossing paths. He looked like a tall, handsome prince out of a German fairytale. I thought he was the one. We had the exact same initials M.A.M and we even looked alike with our statuesque Nordic looks. He could have been my real brother easily. His fraternity brothers nicknamed him BJ because of his love of blowjobs, something I found out all too soon.

"Why don't you come to summer school with me and take the class on Nabokov?"

"Ok, sure, why not. Who's Nabokov?"

"He's a Russian born American novelist and lepidopterist who also lived in pre Nazi Germany."

I found myself in the Russian Literature class reading the novel *Lolita* clueless about the perverted relationship in the book between a little abducted 12-year-old sex-slave of a middle-aged man. My sexual unawareness and ladylike looks kept me from understanding the abuse from Rob and Father was almost the same thing. I missed the point completely not knowing anything about being sexy, perverts, or pedophilia even though I instinctively knew it was wrong.

"The butterfly is the human soul. There was a law in 17th-century Ireland banning the killing of white butterflies because they were children's souls," the professor told us. Nabokov's obsession with butterflies reminded me of Rob.

I kept picturing myself as a white butterfly on one of Rob's dissecting tables as he was carefully pinning my body and wings down for one of his wall mountings and dropped out of the class.

"Why did you drop out?" Mark asked.

"Meet me at The Beer Garden, and we'll talk about it, ok?"

I met him at the local hangout near Stanford where Hell's Angels, Stanford PhD's and undercover FBI agents spying on subversives mixed company. The more beers he drank, the more his obsession with the Russian writer grew.

"Nabokov was living in Berlin, as was Heinz von Lichberg, who wrote a short story *Ur Lolita* in 1916. Some think Vlad plagiarized from Heinz for his story *Lolita*," he rambled on ad nauseam.

"Why do you care so much about a man who would write a book about a pervert? Who cares what the German professor Maar thought or that Vladimir may have plagiarized from *Ur Lolita* or that Heinz von whatever's gay brother died in a Nazi concentration camp?" I lashed out at him high on beer.

"Well, because I'm German, Austrian to be exact. I love Pabst beer. Have you ever been to the Pabst Mansion in Milwaukee and do you castrate every guy you like?" he retorted.

"I have no idea what I am, and as a result of losing my identity, have no real history of my own. The adoption agency will only tell me I'm Northern European. Do I look German to you?" I asked and struck a pose.

"You could be, I suppose. Captain Pabst was German. Why did you drop out of the class?" he asked.

I couldn't tell him I was identifying with Nabokov and having flashbacks to Rob, the horny evil lepidopterist, whose abuse was leaving me stuck in a prison of terrible memories and feelings that I was too terrified to discuss or that I had developed back pain that was constantly killing me.

"I have no rights as an adoptee. The only solution to my problem is to find my mother and that is all that matters to me now. What I really am curious about is why I had 'bear dreams' as a kid. I see bears in cloud formations all the time and trains really make me cry. It's driving me nuts. I want to know my name and who I really am. Wouldn't you want to meet your own flesh and blood mother? For all I know you and I could be related," I snapped.

Bad Company

Moore was an intellectual and a sensitive artist, too. His father wanted him to take over the family cattle ranch in Oregon but all he wanted to do was take photographs like Ansel Adams. He went crazy when I finally did kiss him.

"If I had known you could kiss like that…." he exclaimed after I let loose one night in his friend's car after drinking at the local bar.

The only climax to that evening was a head-on car collision going 60 mph. I was the only one that didn't land in the hospital.

I dropped out of the acting class that summer at Stanford University as pretending to be a big fluffy white cloud didn't cut it for me.

My life, in reality, had assumed the form of a cloud, a very dark mushroom cloud, pretending to be someone I wasn't for a career was not on my list of priorities. My false self was already an actress in real life; in fact, I should have won an Oscar. *Bad Parenting 101* was not on the academic list of courses at Stanford unfortunately or I would have gladly signed up to teach it.

"Why are you so obsessive about being adopted? I know an adoptee who doesn't care to search for his parents. He thinks of his adoptive parents as his real parents," Moore said after he got out of the hospital from the accident.

"I want to know who I was before I became adopted. That's why. You just don't get it. Your friend is either in denial or brain-dead. Have you ever heard of genetics or genealogies?" I asked him coming to the realization that he wasn't sympathetic to my plight as an adoptee.

"My father is going to disinherit me if I don't get married and take over his cattle business in Oregon. He doesn't understand my artistic side," he told me.

"No one in my family understands my artistic side either, but if you think I'm going to marry you so you'll inherit your father's business, you're nuts. I don't even know who my father is for God's sakes and nothing's going to stop me from finding out, not even getting married to you," I informed him.

"Please come out to dinner and meet my parents," he pleaded.

I managed to say mean things and alienate his parents during our first meeting. My rage at Rob and all four of my parents was misplaced. Mark was mortified when I spoke so rudely to them. Thank God he didn't hold it against me and let me rent the cottage he was staying in on a big estate after he left to study abroad for the summer.

The thought that we weren't getting married and that I was going to be alone again without a husband to take care of me or a place to stay made me almost lose my mind. My world kept shrinking and shrinking, and once again time was running out.

It was evident then that most people didn't understand my trauma and loss issues. Most thought me a dilettante and a snob. I hadn't met any other adoptees or abuse victims, so it was really a singular mission. I bounced from stranger to stranger looking for safety, shelter and understanding.

Out of desperation, I befriended some radical and far out characters I met through The Free University in Palo Alto. The curriculum consisted of a wide range of classes from

Acid Yoga to French Symbolist Poetry. Through the Free U pool party, I met a group of science and engineering dropouts from Stanford who lived in a huge estate in what they called a commune in Atherton near our first house. They were all brains taking LSD who believed in free love, free sex, and all the New Age philosophies. The dark and dangerous mystery surrounding this place intrigued me, and I would soon be in need of a home when Mark returned.

I heard about a guy named Lee from the commune who started the first hot tub business in Santa Cruz. He loved LSD, orgies, S & M and he liked pins stuck into his testicles. This I had to see to believe so the befriending began. He and his friends were making porno movies, trying to elevate pornography into high art. These guys were even crazier than Rob and Father.

"You're so sexy and such a goddess. Your green eyes are so seductive. I want you to sleep with my wife, my Saint Bernard, and my kids," Lee said to me high on LSD.

"What? No way! You're a zoophile too?" I replied in disgust.

What kind of dark distorted reality was I vulnerable to? It seemed so perverted and sick. The sex education I was getting was a far cry from Roy Kepler's Free University dream of a new and freer kind of education. Kepler's bookstore was one of my hangouts along with Gerry Garcia, Joan Baez and her boyfriend, Ira. I often sat by myself reading an underground book while drinking coffee to listen and learn. There was still so much I needed to learn about the real world.

I wondered why so many of the people I was intellectually "in tune" with were German. What was it with Germans? I was English like Mother, wasn't I? However, it was really a dark, sensual, sexual energy operating and a sort of spontaneous gravity at work pulling me into these people's lives.

Besides, I really was terrified and homeless. All I knew was that I was supposed to get married so I kept looking for a husband to take care of me.

A few acid trips with Lee left me stuck with these sex crazed geniuses from the commune. Taking LSD was testing your soul against all the Devils in Hell according to Alan Watts. I didn't need acid for that! The only good thing that came out of it was meeting the ex-wife of the mayor of San Francisco's rebellious son who was secretly and illegally producing porn.

"You look like a movie star. I think you should try out for this S&M porn movie I'm directing," he said.

"What's S & M?" I asked him.

I wasn't wearing underpants and refused to take off my designer dress for the audition and clowned around as he pretended to dominate and hurt me with a whip. When he turned into Rob, I began to cry and stopped the audition cold.

"What's wrong?" he asked.

"This is ridiculous; you keep turning into my brother. I can't do this. I'm really trying to write and publish a children's magazine. I don't know what I'm doing here really. I'm completely freaked out and I need to be with and talk to my real mother."

"I can't help you find your mother, but my ex-wife is a writer and might help you with your magazine. She's a manic depressive and takes Lithium. So many creative people are hypo-manic. She went off her meds and tried to kill herself. Here's her number. What did your brother do to you to make you so afraid?" he asked.

"I can't talk about it, but he hurt me," I replied.

He introduced me to his ex-wife who was recovering from shooting herself in the stomach in a botched suicide attempt after their divorce. She was happy to help me finish and named my little children's literary magazine "The Pet Elephant."

"I'm home schooling my son and maybe we could use the magazine as a teaching tool," she offered and took me to meet her long haired, artist, hippie friend who lived in a VW bus in a park who did all the artwork for my magazine for only $200.

She showed me *The Free You* magazine published by the

Free University and the Realist pulp magazine written by Paul Krassner who wrote satire, attacked establishment values and was considered “The Father of the Underground Press.”

“You can get your magazine published at an underground press too,” she assured me.

The Pet Elephant

Many times when I did what came naturally, my adoptive parents just didn’t get it. Mother would invalidate my originality and innate talents because they didn’t mirror her own or anyone in her very aristocratic conventional family. This was another example of the fallout from the total disconnect from my natural identity. In my case, it was total chaos leaving me misunderstood, crippled mentally, unstable and a lost soul again and again. This is what was holding me back; leading me down dark and dangerous roads with all the wrong people.

“The Pet Elephant” was going to print at an underground comic book press in San Francisco paid for with my trust fund money. I was with my socialist co-writer and her one-year-old, mulatto son negotiating a deal, looked down and saw this smiling child pointing my loaded handgun at us.

“Johnny, give Mommy the gun,” she said to him after he had gone into my purse and taken the handgun out while we were talking. The safety switch was on, thank God. I slowly walked up to him and gingerly took it out of his hand. Yes, we definitely had dodged a real bullet. I sold the magazine to Keplers and bookstores in the Bay Area. Mother later called it “The Pink Elephant” as it contained radical leftist ideas coming from drugged out subversive hippies whom she despised.

“I hope you don’t think you can write. Mary Mapes Dodge, the author of St. Nicholas Magazine for Children and the famous children’s story Hans Brinker, was a writer,” and informed me she threw them all away. ‘The Pet Elephant’ would have been named 'The Pet Adoptee' if I had known or had a voice to address my many issues as an adoptee from a closed adoption. My memory flashed back on Dubois's magazine The Crisis and civil rights but I didn't make the connection that I could have started one like it for adoptees and their civil rights or that I was identifying with everyone else who had a cause but my own.

"You're twenty-three and need to get a real job. You can't rely on your looks forever," Mother reminded me as she handed me a gold chain to wear around my neck for my birthday, totally unaware that I was leading such a crazy secret life.

"I love it. It's the latest status symbol. How much did it cost?" I asked.

"Don't be gauche dear," she reminded me.

She really would have been shocked if I asked her how much I cost?

Neither one of us had a clue why I had even cared about producing and publishing the magazine. I hadn't written one of the stories contained within its pages. It was some deep love of educating children and art to me. The letter from the adoption agency did say that my father was a teacher. I wasn't looking to win a Pulitzer Prize. The most natural and real DNA part of me was in some sort of underground hidden ghost realm and went unrecognized by my adoptive parents and brothers. They thought I was crazy because I wasn't like them and had no desire to play golf, bridge or have aspirations to be a bank teller or an airline stewardess.

Rob was in Vietnam as a forward observer for the artillery, unaware what was going on back in California during the 60's. When he came home, he called me crazy and a communist and wouldn't talk to me because I was so against the war. We went to the country club for the Fourth of July after he returned home and the loud booms of the fireworks gave him flashbacks. Rob began to cry and went home. Many of his buddies were blown apart and he had traumatic memories of bloody body parts flying through the air. He brought home films of it and said that one guy was in a bunker and looked up and saw an unexploded bombshell lodged between his legs. Was he getting some form of karmic payback? At least we had Post Traumatic Stress Disorder in common. What goes around comes around I thought to myself and was almost glad he was suffering.

14

The Astrologist, the Medium, and the Elephant

It was becoming quite apparent to me that the only way to heal my psychic split and stabilize was to discover my genetic roots. In order to go forward, I needed to look back.

"Mother I want to know who my mother is," I said to her one day, surprising myself with my courage. "Lots of people tell me I'm a genius. Was my mother a genius? The folks at The Cradle won't tell me her name. Could anyone, even a human from a test tube, understand himself without understanding his own ancestors?" Mother's face filled with an expression I didn't immediately recognize.

"You wrote to The Cradle?" she asked after a few seconds.

I had my answer; her incredulity was proof that my question went over her head. When I nodded, yes, she sighed resignedly.

"I don't know where your mother is or if you are a genius. My father was a genius," Mother said, her eyes going soft. "Nannie almost left him because he drank too much wine."

I suppressed a growl. What did that have to do with anything I just asked? I monitored my tone and tried again.

"Why is it illegal for me to find out who I am? The people in power locked up my original birth certificate (OBC) for ninety-nine years. How can they do that? I have no rights as an adoptee and am forbidden to understand myself." Mother's expression did not change and I forged ahead. "Can't you see how abusive this is? It's mentally cruel! Are you sure you don't know?"

Without a smidge of understanding dawning in her eyes, Mother touched my shoulder and shook her head sadly. "I'm sorry, but no."

When I tried to continue the thread of conversation, Mother launched into another subject and closed my questions off completely. Deep down, my frustration grew into rage coupled with an obsession to uncover the truth—at any cost.

Soon after, Mother pretended to be helpful by having her friend do my horoscope. I learned that I was an Aries with no planets in earth signs, with Gemini rising, a Sagittarius moon, a grand triune and a YOD. The YOD signifying The Finger of God was present, where even the astrologers didn't know what that really meant.

"You have Gemini as your Ascendant which will keep you looking for your twin until you realize the twin is really you, in you, part of you," the astrologer said to me. "Your Aries Sun will probably keep you running, never stopping... You could be the next Mary Roberts Reinhart (the famous murder mystery writer), but don't run for political office as you would probably be assassinated."

"You should write for *True Confessions,* or better yet, *True Romance*," Mother said sarcastically and laughed. I didn't see the humor. My Sagittarius Moon held me back from my career and public recognition while the planets were to blame for my unstable relationships. The elephant in the room was totally ignored: that I was adopted and my invented heritage not only abused and crippled me, but also led me astray daily. Bottom line: the skeletons in my closet were holding me hostage.

When I developed Raynaud's Syndrome, back problems, and eye trouble, Mother took me to Transcendental Meditation meetings. After a complete physical, I learned that

Raynaud's was idiopathic which meant it was from unknown origins, the story of my life. Every time I got cold and extremely stressed my ring fingers would turn white from the total loss of circulation.

"Do you suppose my natural mother had Raynauds?" I asked the doctor during a complete physical.

"Perhaps," he replied. "Do you know who she is?"

"No, it was a closed adoption and I'm not allowed to know. Isn't that insane?" I challenged.

There were times I had to run to put my extremities under hot water or jump into a hot shower to get the circulation back. Sometimes it felt like I was watching myself die.

"I'm taking you to a famous tarot card reader in Carmel," Mother informed me after a shopping session for herself and a two martini lunch.

She drove me to meet the famous clairvoyant Tarquin in his little seaside cottage in Carmel. He dressed in an exotic red silk Chinese robe with a black velvet turban on his head.

"Come and sit at the table," he beckoned as the golden light from the scarf-covered lamp illuminated the tarot cards and made the room glow as if from an enormous harvest moon.

"You have an amazing root system," he said, as he read the cards. "You were an Indian Princess in a past life."

"What good is a past life? I want to know who I am in this life," I barked with unexpected venom, and jumped up from the table to leave.

"I'm sorry, I can't help you with that," he replied.

Mom paid him and we left. I turned my head away from Mother as we drove home so she wouldn't see me crying. She had to know who and where my parents were, and it was infuriating to know she was a straight-faced liar just like Rob.

"Perhaps you should see a psychiatrist," she proposed.

"Okay, make an appointment if you think it might help," I said to please her even though I was beginning to hate her more and more with every breath I took.

Shrinking My Head

Once in his office the doctor asked, "Do you think you need to be here?"

"No," I replied in a low, angry tone. "I'm not even allowed to know who my real parents are or to know if I have inherited something bad or good from them."

"Tell me what you mean," he said in his perfect psychiatrist monotone. I decided to give it to him straight.

"Adoption is a *pretend* world with *real* people who have real feelings, but have to pretend those feelings aren't real." He nodded his head thoughtfully.

"Have you heard of post adoption separation trauma?"

With my shameful past history with Rob and Father, and then my more current lost episodes, I sat silent. The doctor lowered his chin and said with finality. "If you don't want to talk about it, then my advice is to get out of here and go live your life."

And that was that; I left having no idea what he was talking about and without any more comfort that I'd had going in.

Back at home, Mother told me that I needed to get a job as she was completely oblivious to what I was all about.

"I will, just give me time," I promised her thinking if she knew the truth she would understand why I was emotionally shutdown and dysfunctional.

Beth was working in the Infectious Disease Lab at Stanford Hospital and after a call to her she got me a job collecting diseased specimens and answering the phone.

"You're too talented to be stuck in here," the head of the lab kept telling me.

Labeling cancerous tissue and stool samples wasn't exciting and neither was dating the head doctor in the department, but I tried. His lab coat impressed me, but he was in love with his microscope. The doctors I dated were so damn boring and clueless about adoption issues. One psychiatrist told me he was treating a homosexual who tried to eat glass, and another who planned to kill himself. No thanks. Then I met some real brains from the Stanford Research Institute (SRI) who were working on artificial intelligence. No one told me that the CIA at SRI was studying remote viewing, a top-secret project for the military. They considered psychic phenomena a science, which would have given me hope if I'd known it at the time.

Remote viewing interested me the most. If remote viewing allowed a person to bring something which lies hidden in the subconscious mind to the surface and objectify it by describing or drawing details about a place, person, or thing without prior knowledge of that person, place, or thing, then they might have located Mama for me. Or perhaps they could have taught me how to become a psychic spy and remote view to locate her. I would have been a natural at it being left-handed and totally right-brained.

Germans and Angel Dust

Many nights I spent drinking too much beer and dancing alone at the local smoky jazz club "In Your Ear." I met Vince Gueraldi, Mose Allison and Cal Tjader, one of the "Fathers of Acid Jazz" who played there regularly. Susie met me there one night and we had a joint with Vince in the back of his van.

Father's sexual advance freaked me out so much that I began to wear a patchwork granny dress with a skirt down to my ankles. I wore it everywhere as not to attract another attacker. It made me feel protected although it made me look like a hippie.

Was there such a thing as a preppie hippie with a credit card? My flute stayed in its case as female jazz flutists were unheard of. It was a man's world and my talent meant nothing in their *cool* music scene.

I loved jazz and R&B music because it made me happy. The musicians expressed their feelings, something I was never allowed or able to do. The words and melodies in the songs about romance, love, and loss always made me smile as they put words to my grief and spoke to my broken heart. While dancing in my long granny dress at the jazz club one night, this nerdy genius from Stanford came up to me after watching me do my Watusi head twirl. The group Fafnir was playing and I had my eye on the sexy saxophone playing leader of the band.

"I'd give you the world if I could," he told me as I gazed into the coke bottle lenses of his glasses.

"Thanks," I said and laughed to myself and approached the leader of the band as he finished his set.

"What does Fafnir mean?" I boldly asked him.

"Fafnir is a character from the German Old Norse mythology of Sigurd who kills the dragon Fafnir."

"Oh," I said as I admired his long flaxen hair and gazed into his big blue eyes.

"I'm also studying German opera in Berlin. I'm going to be in Wagner's *The Ring of the Nibelung*. My girlfriend is gone so why don't you come for a visit. We live in Santa Cruz," he told me and I paid him a visit the next day.

He and his hippie actress girlfriend were living in a little gingerbread house that looked like something out of an old German medieval epic tucked in the Santa Cruz hills. When I saw all her theatrical dresses in their tiny cottage it was obvious he only wanted a one nighter. My response was to engage him in conversation instead.

"I was adopted and just found out I'm from northern Europe."

"Have you heard of the pagan religion Asatru?" he asked me.

"No, what is it?" I asked.

"I don't have time to get into it now, but my girlfriend and I are from Scandinavia and are really involved with our Old German Norse heritage and German paganism. Did you know that the Germans originally came from Scandinavia and the women were soothsayers?"

"Do I look Scandinavian to you?" I asked him.

"You look a lot like my sister." He said politely and started moving off. "I have to go to the gig now. It was nice meeting you."

They took off for Germany the next day and I was lost and alone again. Yet, my unconscious had a life of its own and soon it lead me to another German.

Gary was a mime at the Renaissance Fair in San Francisco. His smile managed to captivate my attention as he performed his act.

"Hi, do I know you?" he asked, as I sat and watched him mime.

"No, but I really like your act," I said noticing his fine bone structure and chiseled features.

"Tell me, my fair lady, just what do you do?" he asked.

"I'm lost and in need of a prince," I replied amazed at his graceful movements as he juggled six fireballs in the air.

"My folks hail from The Isle of Wight in Great Britain and it would be an honor to hear from you," he said and handed me his phone number on a piece of paper.

"I wish I knew where my folks came from," I said to myself.

"Would you like to sniff some snuff? I do it all the time," he offered.

"Sure. I always wanted to be a snuff sniffer." I laughed, took a sniff and sneezed all over him.

He was much too young for me and lived in a lower middle class neighborhood in Oakland with his parents. But I didn't care; he was not only a gifted artist, but a writer too. Mother would never approve of him, but our artistic similarities attracted me in a huge way.

Gary was far from conventional. He was using various mind expanding drugs and had an obsession with Ambrose Bierce. He told me when he was younger he walked around as a warlock in a black cape with a pet crow on his shoulder. His penchant for Satanism and eagerness to conjure up the dead turned me off. My quest was to find the living. I tried to overlook the fact that his best friend was a paranoid schizophrenic and that he was still living with his parents. For the time being, I was happy to be with another gifted artist who cared about helping me with my children's stories. The pull was natural and part of my hidden genetic design.

Night and Day

Mother never understood my non-conformist behavior and bizarre attractions. We were as different as night and day. She never would have approved of this eccentric weirdo and I knew it but I was terrified of being alone as it always triggered the fear and depression from the trauma of my original abandonment.

I often drove to Carmel to wander and think. In fact I took trips everywhere by myself as often as I could. My next trip to Carmel took me to an art gallery where I fell in love with two fascinating oil paintings and carried them in my car to show Mother.

"Why did you buy these hideous oil portraits of two ugly Germans?" Mother asked me when I brought them home for her to keep for me.

"I like them. Look how interesting they are and how they change from vegetables to people. Some of my friends have told me I look German," I replied with great enthusiasm wishing she could get excited about art as I was.

This was the first time I actually saw the duality in a painting and was fascinated by it. The optical illusion and the two different perceptions of the same subject were magical. On some subconscious level, I was aware that I had lost relatives who held the key to my secret identity and that art played a major part in the reality of who I was as well. I had no way to tell her that I wasn't a "tabula rosa" (blank slate) and that these vegetable people represented my first parents and the dual nature of my reality as an artist and adoptee. The fact that I had another set of parents with other genes and talents than hers was never discussed. My buying the paintings was a silent scream to her for help. As usual, Mother didn't get it.

The awareness of my secret identity began to grow and the knowledge that I had other parents and relatives grew. Gary's parents started to pressure us to get married. His intellect, artistic ability, and creative genius attracted me but he was a freak from Oakland, low class and a hard-core drug addict. His parents thought he had hit pay dirt finding a classy girl with money, and I had to tell him I wasn't in love with him on my last visit to his room in his parents' basement.

"Melinda I have this amazing new kind of snuff. Here sniff some before you leave," he offered and poured some white powder in the palm of my hand. Without trepidation, I took a snort.

"This will help your creative process and will expand your mind so that you might be able to psychically access your lost mother's spirit," he assured me. "When the doors of perception are cleansed, everything appears as it truly is – infinite," he mentioned as if Mama's spirit was going to suddenly materialize.

Just as I was leaving to drive back to Mark's cottage, Gary said, "You have just sniffed PCP which is a very potent psychedelic. Don't drive because you'll hallucinate and lose control of your car." With the slight warning, Gary turned and went back into the house.

"I'll be fine," I assured myself and began the drive back as a nuclear explosion began to slowly go off in my brain, throwing me into a surreal scene of confusion.

I suddenly became disconnected from my body as my car began to drive itself into an impoverished black section in downtown Oakland. I was scared to death I might get raped or killed, but I bravely checked into a seedy motel until the drug wore off. Once I was safely in the room I proceeded to lose total control of my mind as I entered a psychedelic state.

Safely in the motel room, I looked at myself in the mirror as my reflection turned into a florescent red, blue, and green neon sign. I turned and looked at the oil painting of a vase with flowers over the bed and the vase turned into a human skull. This powder took me into another dimension. The feeling was worse than being stuck inside a Salvador Dali painting; I thought I was going to die.

My parents would never understand why I was in a dive in the most dangerous part of Oakland, home of the Black Panther Party, telling them I was lost and had turned into a neon sign. It was bad enough that I brought those strange paintings for her to see, and now after this I was afraid Mother would send the men in the white coats to come to take me away. I decided to call the rebellious porn producer for help.

"I'm busy," he told me. "But call this number. This guy will come and get you."

It was the number of the biggest porn producer in San Francisco. I was calling the devil to ask him if one of his friends could help me out. In fact, I trusted a sexual predator just like Rob once again. Rob was psychologically attached to me like my Siamese twin from Hell and this guy was from Hell, too. I called him against my better judgment. He arrived at the hotel door and drove my car to his apartment where he tried to guide me through it.

"I don't want to live anymore. If I can't find my mother there's no point in me living any longer? I can't invent my heritage. The stupid adoption agency won't give me any information about where she is or who she is. I'm tired of having to live such a convoluted life," I sobbed. "Have you ever been stuck in a veritable vortex of incongruities?"

His apartment was decorated like something out of The Arabian Nights. I fended him off on his king-size waterbed, which was next to an enormous water pipe. He sat in the yoga position on top of a huge pillow, water pipe in hand, looking more like the fat, ugly caterpillar in Alice in Wonderland than a sultan. He sat there puffing on his pipe.

"Why don't you write to ALMA - the Adoptee Liberty Movement Association? They might be able to find your mother for you. Did you know that Alma means soul in Spanish and that all adoptees have been hurt in the same way?"

"How do you know that?" I asked half out of my mind from the drug.

"I'm adopted and ALMA found my mother for me. Not to change the subject but if you don't want to do porn you should get breast implants and become a Playboy bunny. I have connections and there's lots of money in it for you," he told me as I began to fall asleep, clutching my handgun at the bottom of my purse, on his Persian rug wishing it would turn into a magic carpet and fly me right to Mama.

The next morning the horrific episode left me so paranoid to drive on the freeway that I called Susie, my beacon of light in the darkness, to come and drive my car and me back to the cottage.

My life was a spiraling secret inside a secret inside a secret. The journey, an Arabian nightmare that caused me to wonder if I would make it out alive.

The drugs were loosening my hold on reality which was spinning out of control and I began to feel like my head was screwed on wrong. I was pretty sure it was over with Moore although I did feel loved and special being the only female ever to be allowed to drive his beloved Jaguar and stay in his cottage. Eventually, I read a love letter that arrived in the mailbox addressed to him from some girl in Hawaii. Mark was in love with someone else and informed me that I had two months to find another place.

I felt like a trapped rat and began to pace around in the small room at the cottage, panic-stricken until I noticed some books in a bookcase about telepathy, ESP, clairvoyance and mediums. Maybe achieving cosmic consciousness might help me to obtain the higher awareness and find Mama. I read and read trying to understand that a genuine spirituality, like art, was open and dynamic.

Mark, too, had a big-eyed Keane print in his cottage of the same tall, thin, blonde-haired, brown-eyed girl standing next to her surfboard –the same one that Mother bought for my room. Something very strange began to awaken within me as my eyes studied her. Who was I and whom did I resemble? In reality, I had four parents, and I needed to find my biological mother and father to see who I looked like. Knowledge is power and I pursued it like a girl possessed.

Wanting to find my natural parents wasn't mere curiosity on my part, it was a necessity. I needed my genetic mirrors to piece together my lost identity.

Psychically Homeless

The weirdo artists were attracted to me like the paparazzi to the hottest celebrity. My new nose went to my head as I was finally attracting the right guys. It was exhilarating, empowering, and intoxicating. Mark wasn't the only fish in the sea.

The African American bohemian conga drummer who played with the Latin vibe jazz musician, Cal Tjader, came over to talk to me after another night of dancing. He wore a dashiki and talked me into driving to see his house which stood on stilts in an artist colony in Sausalito. Once I was there, he and his roommate tried to get me to snort cocaine and seduce me, but it didn't work. I shared with him my plight and we became friends. He wrote a story about a little African boy named Malik for me and let me into his world as a professional musician.

Life on the road with this group of jazz musicians was rough as they were always high on drugs and using prostitutes. We drove to gigs smoking pot in his van while listening to Marvin Gaye, Miles Davis, John Coltrane and Dvorak's New World Symphony on his 8-track. The tables were turned, and I felt real racism from whites. It was a revelation for me, and I didn't like it. This coke-snorting, acid-dropping musician thought he was the archangel Michael, and as a Gemini, was identifying with the twin Gods, Castor and Pollex, who are supposedly a sort of cosmic stabilizer in Pagan Religions. He was also a Scientologist and tried to no avail to get me to join the group in San Francisco.

"I think knowing one's identity, name, and biological parents is considered essential to personality and psychological development, don't you?" I asked him.

"You got that right, baby girl. It's no joke being

psychically homeless," he replied.

There was something seriously wrong with Michael, the love angel, when he began to soak his hands in lye to toughen up the skin for his conga drumming gigs with Tjader, as the skin on the palm of his big hands was being eaten away and he didn't even care. What was it about California that did this to people?

"I landed in a psychiatric ward during a very bad acid trip after turning into a frog," he admitted.

I thought he was crazy until it dawned on me that after an acid trip I too was driving my car to Santa Cruz and turned into a water droplet dripping down the side of a giant icicle. I was really way off track with this nut. How many frogs was I going to have to kiss? How could a female jazz flutist survive in their crazy world?

Now that I was on my own without Mother and Father to take care of me or my brothers to help me I was forced to keep hooking up and trying to bond with total strangers, as I bravely continued alone on my forbidden journey to find Mama.

One day while roaming around Carmel on one of my many day trips, I met Sam, a real live WASP while sitting on the beach. Perhaps this tall, blonde, green-eyed, handsome artist and master carpenter would have some answers. He was living in Carmel Valley after dropping out of an advertising agency on Madison Avenue in New York. We met often at The No Name Bar to drink and talk. He loved the casual lifestyle as I did and dressed in old, faded jeans and a denim shirt. I learned that his wealthy ex-wife lived in Napa Valley with their two sons and Mongoloid daughter.

"What is your real name?" he asked.

"I don't know, but I'm going to find out if it kills me. I'm going to write to ALMA to see if they can get my Adoption Decree," which I did the next day.

We met at a bar in Carmel and sat underneath a huge oil painting of Kim Novak to talk and drink for hours every Friday. His pain was not my pain, but we were friends.

"God is a woman. I can't imagine what it's like not

knowing who your own mother is. Did you know you have the most beautiful eyes I have ever seen?" he said before taking my hand and licking it.

"It's so painful being adopted. It's like being caught in a giant twisted web of lies," I tried to explain to him after a few martinis before I drove back to Mark's cottage.

Baby Girl Lumsley

I was on my secret search and nothing would deter me. We were all on some strange mobius curve. ALMA, the advocate group for open records for adoptees founded in 1971, wrote me back telling me they had no problem going underground to help adoptees get their Adoption Decrees and the woman who wrote the letter said she was trying to get mine for me. I was holed up in Mark's cottage waiting for the letter to arrive with my decree in it. My days at Mark's were numbered and soon I would have to find another place to live.

Finally a letter came to the cottage addressed to me from ALMA. I anxiously opened it and there was my Adoption Decree stating I was Baby Girl Lumsley! My mother's name was Dorothy Lumsley and I was born in Chicago. I quickly wrote to the hospital for more information, but they wouldn't release any to me. Out of desperation, I wrote to Jean Paton, an adoptee and the originator of Orphan Voyage which was an open records movement she started in 1953. She wrote back to inform me that it was a miracle that ALMA had gotten my decree. Those fighting for adoptees' rights had their own underground railroad.

I was so mad and sad because it meant more searching. The Cradle wouldn't allow me access to any of my birth or medical records either, so how was I going to find out where she lived or if I inherited some dreadful condition? I was up against the powers of darkness, their lies, and the law. They criminalized, including fines and imprisonment, anyone who received any information with unauthorized disclosure from a sealed adoption file. This insane law was recommended by

The Uniform Adoption Act and such an insult to my intelligence. These law makers weren't concerned at all that they were treating me like a criminal for wanting to know my name and my genetic heritage. Keeping this kind of a secret was hurting me and could lead to incest with a blood relative or there could be cancer, insanity, or genius in the family. I wondered how many adoptees married a half-sibling or cousin unknowingly, or even committed suicide or ended up in a mental hospital due to the insanity of closed adoptions. All I wanted was to know about and hopefully meet my own mother and father. Why was that a crime?

Others were getting married or going off to medical and law school, but I was paralyzed and in need of finding my genetic self. The truth was something I was ready to die for and it was the only thing that could set me free. With new determination, I bravely pressed on with my search.

15

Black Magic

The spirit world beckoned and it wasn't long before I was dancing in sartorial splendor at the jazz club, wondering how I was going to survive and where I was going to live. Out of nowhere, a charming tall, dark, and handsome rock 'n roll musician appeared who sang and played the electric piano in his own rock band called Robin and the Four Hoods. He dressed in white oozing charisma as we danced the night away. We smoked pot and I let him seduce me in my car outside the club that night.

"I'm living in a little cottage and need to find another place to live soon or I'll be homeless," I told him high on pot after our romp in the back seat of my car. "By the way what's your name?" I asked him high on mysticism, love and the weed.

"My name is Casey and you have just met the right person," he reassured me.

"I'm a musician, too, and I love jazz and the blues. Maybe you could teach me how to play some jazz tunes on my flute, but what I'm really about is searching for my natural mother and the laws have kept me from finding her. Her name is Dorothy Lumsley." I rambled on wondering why this person had come into my life.

"Really? You were adopted? Lumsley is English and I'm Scotch-Irish. What are you?" he asked forgetting I was adopted.

"I don't know but maybe I'm English," I replied.

"I can channel information from the spirit world," he said.

This white musician was more than good-looking; he was beautifully angelic and might even have the power to find Mama, I thought and I found myself falling under his spell.

"Yeah, I'm Robin Hood and I steal from the rich to give to the poor," he said laughing.

"Can you channel my mother and tell me where she lives?" I begged him hoping he would find her for me.

"Sure, I will try, but tell me where do your adoptive parents live?" he asked unable to keep still as he bobbed his head back and forth to some imaginary music in his head.

"They live right outside of town. My father came on to me and I ran away," I admitted.

"I'm sorry. My father lives with my grandmother here in our nursing home. He plays the guitar and owns the home. Would you like to meet him?"

"Sure, why not," I answered thinking it would never come to anything.

I had nothing to lose and couldn't go home again. Lord knows I was trying to get to the source of my being! His father was just as talented and handsome as his son and played the blues on his electric guitar like a pro. We walked around the nursing home which I found depressing. How could anyone live in this home with all these old, poor people?

"I'm going back home where my mother, sister, and half-brother live, north of here. Could you drive me to the airport tomorrow?" he asked me back at the cottage.

The next evening, I dropped him off at the airport and was about to get on the thruway when I panicked and proceeded to dissociate and have a major melt down. Cars were zooming past me at top speed as I got out of the car and ran in my flip flops, then barefoot all the way back to the airport in tears to beg him not to leave me and to drive me back to the cottage. I told him about my bad drug experience and opened up about what Rob and Father had done to me as he drove me back to Mark's place.

"Do you want to come and see where I live? I could drive you," he said.

Off we went the next day to his log cabin up on the rugged north coast of the Pacific in the incredibly beautiful redwood forest for the weekend. I couldn't handle being alone and definitely couldn't drive anymore on the thruway after that terrible drug experience. We pulled up to an adorable log cabin that he built himself which was nestled deep among the majestic redwood pine trees. A fabulous six foot long redwood dining table that he crafted by hand stood in the kitchen and a king size bed six feet off the ground took up his entire bedroom. He called it The King's Bed. It didn't take long for me to realize he wasn't very talented and it was then I wished an enchanted castle would appear in the depths of the giant trees where Mama might be waiting for me.

My rose colored glasses remained in place after he informed me that his father was a big-time criminal, apparently rehabilitated and owned Lefties, the first topless bar in San Francisco. I ignored all the flapping red flags and fell madly in lust with him.

"Let's drive back and you can meet my parents. Do you think your father might know how to get my birth records out of the hospital for me?" I asked thinking his father might know some illegal way to get my records.

The fact that his Irish father was a criminal should have been a big warning for me, but I needed shelter in order to continue my search for Dorothy. Perhaps Casey Sr. knew some way to break the law to get my records out of the hospital in Chicago. I had to find her no matter what. Trusting strangers was a necessity now. The spirit and criminal world were my last resorts for information as the closed record system, Father and Mother failed me.

I took Casey to meet my parents, packed my things in my

red suitcase with my monogrammed initials on it from Mark's cottage and off we drove North together to my new home.

Mark, Susie and my parents were history. The road less traveled morphed into life in the utility lane and off I went with the channeler to the spirit world.

Trusting strangers was my fate. There was no turning back. From now on, my life was to resemble The Flight of the Bumblebee. Rob and Father had made sure of that. I was a homeless beauty, living on a wing and a prayer, on some invisible strange magnetic, yet sacred, journey to Dorothy and my secret personal history. Gambling wasn't in my blood, but I had to risk it all to find her or die.

Casey, the gorgeous and charismatic woodsman, musician, carpenter and I began to live together among the world's tallest redwood trees in what he called nature's cathedral. Living at the cabin was peaceful and charming at first, as well as somehow cozy and familiar. I was comfortable there in the quiet, natural beauty of the woodlands living among the animals as the artist in residence at our little forest home away from my insane family. Drawing botanicals, nature, taking field notes, and playing my flute in the quiet, pristine wilderness kept me relaxed, happy and busy.

Casey's half-brother had a beautiful house on a hillside where he operated a redwood burl business and sold various pieces of wood sculpture and other items in a cute little store right off the highway.

"What's a burl?" I asked him when Casey took me to his house to meet him and his wife.

"Redwood trees are stump-sprouters and develop masses of dormant buds around the base of the tree or they sometimes protrude on the trunk called burls. The grain is very complex and interesting looking and people love to buy them after I make them into table tops, chairs and clocks. I'm just trying to keep busy until I die," his older brother told me.

"My grandfather was a famous botanist, my grandmother carved wood and my father worked for a famous furniture company," I told him, but he didn't seem to care.

"Do you want to go for dinner at The Benbow Inn? It's right down the road. Clark Gable, Spencer Tracy and even Eleanor Roosevelt used to go there. It's famous you know and looks like a touch of Old England," he said to impress me.

"No thanks, I want to get to the cabin," Casey told him and we sped away in his truck to his little cabin in the middle of nowhere at the end of a very long dark, dirt road.

"My half-brother has a different father, but it's a long and complicated story," he said half asleep.

"What's a half-brother? Oh, I get it. You have different fathers, but the same mother."

"You might be a half-sister or have a half-sister or half-brother you know," Casey muttered leaving me very confused and unable to process what he was telling me. It didn't compute in my head at all so I dropped the subject.

I knew Mother and Father would love to stay in the famous Inn but they wouldn't approve of these pot smoking, ill-bred artists, and I would never want them to see me living in a three-room log cabin.

"Mother, don't you know why I'm here? It's because I have been abused by Rob and Father,' I needed to tell her but never could.

Casey sweet-talked me into getting married in secret at the Justice of the Peace. We said, "I do," and flew to Kauai for our honeymoon.

"Let's rent a little sailboat and go sailing. I know how to sail," he said confidently.

Once we were far out in the ocean he intentionally tipped the sailboat over and I fell into the deep, water and he didn't even try to help me swim back to the boat. Luckily, I was a strong swimmer and crawled back in over the bow of the little sailboat. It occurred to me then that he might be trying to kill me, but I quickly dismissed the idea.

"My brother might be here on the big island. He runs with Steve McQueen and a group of wealthy homosexuals who use women as masochistic tools," Casey mumbled.

"What's that?" I asked clueless about what he was talking about.

"They like to use and hurt women," he said.

"Why?" I asked.

"They use women as sex objects and think they're stupid. That's why," he said in a mean tone. "You're so naïve. Don't you know that your adoptive parents know who your real parents are? I'm sure they're not telling you on purpose and are just pretending they don't know. How stupid can you get?" Casey explained on the plane back from Hawaii as he eyed the sexy stewardess that brought us drinks.

"When we get back let's go and tell my parents we got married and get all the rest of my things," I said to show him if he was trying to kill me at least my parents would know where to look for a suspect. The honeymoon ended and we returned to the cabin to begin married life.

Practical Basketball

We took one last short trip back to Mother and Father's to tell them we were married and to stop to see Casey's father. We practically ran in and out to avoid their disapproval and in no time were on our way back to his cabin as man and wife. Wedding gifts arrived at the cabin from some of Mother's friends and I tried to settle in.

"Your father is spending your stock money for himself, ya know. I don't trust him and neither should you. You need to cash in your stocks and keep the money in your own bank account," Casey told me after he got me stoned on pot and gained my trust.

"I don't think he would do that."

"I'm your husband now and you should have control of your money, not your father. He's not to be trusted. Call the stock broker and tell him you want the money. It's in your name isn't it?"

"Yes, but I don't know how to open a bank account," I answered not knowing anything about finances at all.

"I'll help you," he said and drove me all the way to the stock broker so I would sign the papers and take control of my stocks.

"Smoke some of this pot. It's the best stuff in the world!" Casey said as if he had struck gold and handed me a joint as he drove me back North to his place.

"I feel like I'm floating out of my body. This is so weird. I don't like it."

The new hippie life style was okay at first, but as the days passed I became unhappy and began to feel trapped again.

"Here's the check from your stocks, but you have to sign it over to me because I'm your husband and must have control of the money. You don't have a clue how to handle it. I'll open an account in both our names," he said trying to kiss me.

I foolishly trusted him and stupidly endorsed the check over to him and he took off in his truck to open an account in his name. When I found out he tricked me and took control of all my money, I got mad. As a result, he began to drink and to beat me. He told me he was deeply involved in the occult, that he channeled for Lucifer.

"Let me tell you something, you idiot. I hung out at the jazz club on purpose to find a stupid rich girl like you with lots of money. I purposely got you on pot so I could control your mind, take your money, and then kill you. My brother also married for money and is planning to kill his rich wife for her money. Our father has done hard time for drug dealing and has ties to the mafia," he told me now that I was hopelessly caught in his web.

"I'll kill you and cut you into little pieces and no one will ever find out if you leave. Your parents don't give a damn about you. I'm Lucifer and have magical evil powers over you," he threatened.

It's so nice to meet you, Lucifer. The question is, do you know who I am? I secretly thought feeling empowered as my gun was tucked into the waistband of my jeans.

"Yeah, you're up a creek without a paddle," he laughed and had the phone disconnected so I couldn't call out for help. "Don't tell anyone that I'm dealing drugs in San Francisco. Give me your gun and stay here until I get back and don't go to the mailbox," he threatened and drove off in his truck leaving me too afraid to make a move.

He intercepted my letters to my parents for help. I outsmarted him and called Gary to ask him if he would kill my husband for me. It was a desperate and sick situation. I couldn't even look into the fire in the fireplace without seeing the devil's face in the flames laughing back at me. Casey tricked me like Rob had done and once more I was being terrorized by another dangerous psychopath.

Casey used my money to buy himself an organ, and plenty of equipment to start his own redwood burl business. He bought a flatbed truck, big chainsaws, a truck, a water tower and whatever he wanted. Perhaps he thought he could support himself on the little burl business. He made a shed which he converted into a sauna with a wooden stove inside and installed speakers for his music. We took hot saunas that winter listening to The Allman Brothers Band Live at Filmore East and jumped out naked into the snow. Casey was very talented and had his good points when he was sober.

He often took my car keys leaving me all alone in that cabin in the middle of nowhere after I threatened to leave him. Sometimes when he returned at one or two in the morning he was wired on coke, drunk and abusive. When the dark side of his personality emerged he demanded sex. If I refused he put his hands around my neck and hit my head on the headboard of the big wooden bed until I complied. I had no idea that rough sex turned him on as I didn't know what rough sex was.

Casey began to play loud heavy metal music to Black Sabbath on the Hammond organ that he bought with my money, hung bone mobiles from the ceiling, and lit black candles to scare and control me. This so-called sorcerer threw the bones mixed with his blood and held séances to conjure up the devil, not my mother, Dorothy. When he told me they were human bones I realized I was married to a satanic psychotic out to steal all my money and then possibly kill me.

He made me act normal when we went into town together and never let me out of his sight. There was a general store that carried sets of cheap watercolors and I bought one. Back at the cabin I began to draw and paint while plotting yet another escape plan. Houdini was an amateur compared to me. Hours went by as I drew and painted the beautiful vast snow covered redwood trees and forests that surrounded his log cabin. These became Christmas cards for my parents and brothers that year. My art saved me again and again from the darkness and this demon. On the inside, I was freaking out, but I acted as if nothing was wrong.

Casey's voluptuous and beautiful mother looked like Liz Taylor and so did his sister. His mother was an amateur artist, recognized my talent, and gave me a set of her old pastels, a drawing pad, and a huge art history book. She told me about the time she saw the devil in her bed as she referred to her ex-husband, Casey's father. How could she allow her daughter to dance topless at her own father's bar? I had to get the hell away from these pathetic ill-bred people.

While flipping through the pages of the book, *The History of Art*, the picture by Michelangelo of The Creation of Adam fascinated me. Adam was on earth receiving the Divine Spark—the soul—from God in the heavens. This painting was symbolic of me on earth trying to reach God to give me the hidden knowledge of where Mama was and to reconnect our separated worlds, i.e. *my* world to *her* world. I was certain she would save me. This famous painting was the inspiration for my first pastel of our sleeping cat curled up inside a giant cell-like sphere. The bright pink, blue, and green pastel sticks had a life of their own, as if someone else was moving them in my hand. The final masterpiece went into a frame I found in one of Casey's closets.

When he was gone, I was free to play my flute, draw and paint, feeling so free and a part the grand design, but sad that I had to yet again plot another escape from a dangerous, controlling person to continue my search.

One day I was alone and sat on Casey's basketball thinking of a way to escape. I began to roll back and forth on it and this amazing warm and tingling feeling began to rise and rise until it exploded inside of me.

"Oh, oh, awww," I muttered in sheer ecstasy after having my first rolling orgasm. Casey never made me feel like this and I proceeded to roll back and forth on that ball every time he was away.

He bought two Indian trail motor bikes which we used to ride on logging trails, in the fields, and along the streams and into town. I liked to hang out at the town's old train depot that looked like an old Swiss chalet. I would sit in the engine as if I was the conductor of the train. Casey thought my behavior very odd, but I did it anyway.

When he was sober, he took me to see his brother tie flies and then fly-fish in the Eel River. He would also take me to Lake Alminor near Mt. Shasta to ski and watch his band perform.

When he *wasn't* sober, drinking or drugging, the redwood forest became the evil Black Forest. No one would have guessed that I was hiding such dark secrets as I tried to look as normal as apple pie.

His handsome brother came over one day when he was away and flashed a gorgeous Hollywood bad boy superstar's AMX Gold card in my face.

"Casey says you are *way* too quiet a person for him. Do you want to go on a trip to the Bahamas with me on this? I could also get you a job as a bunny at a playboy club or as a showgirl in Vegas," he said with a huge grin.

"How did you get his card?" I asked in amazement.

"All I had to do was f… him in the ass. What are you doing with my crazy brother anyway?"

I couldn't say, "He's holding me hostage and has taken all my money," so I said that he was teaching me to channel my birth mother.

"He told you he could channel? What a joke. Don't you know the guy's nuts?" he asked.

"I know you're trying to kill your wife for her money and your crazy half-brother is planning on killing me too," was what I wanted to say. He left shaking his head in disbelief and I didn't trust either one of them knowing they might be killers.

My escape was well-planned. I waited until Casey took his truck to town, hid my gun under a redwood log so he wouldn't shoot me, packed up my bags, pastels, flute, Adoption Decree, basketball, art books, and paintings, and put them in the Firebird. Then I waited for him to come home drunk. Once he was in the bathroom, I grabbed the car keys from his jacket pocket, ran to my car. I locked the car doors just as he appeared at the front door and came charging out to stop me.

"I'll have my father put a contract out on you. You're dead!" he yelled as he leapt onto the hood of the car. He held onto the windshield wipers while I sped up and jammed on the brakes several times to throw him off.

His face contorted in anger as growls came out of his mouth and his spit flew all over the windshield. Finally, he slid off and I drove like a bat out of hell to town. I sold the car for $200 in Eureka, and went to the airport with suitcase in hand.

My survival hinged on being quick; if not, I would be dead. Here I was, alone again, running away from an abuser, running back to my parents. This time, I arrived so traumatized and drunk they had to wheel me off the plane in my dirty bell bottoms and t-shirt. Through my drunken delirium I heard Mother say to Father as I sat slumped over in a wheel chair, "What's that basketball doing in her lap?"

Home Again… Naturally

Mother was livid. She was mean and abusive, and I disheartened and furious with her because she wasn't protecting me from yet another abuser. When we arrived at their condo, my eye caught the *The Scarlet Letter* by

Hawthorne sitting right on the bookshelf in plain sight. My triggers went off like an AK- 47 and I focused on a print of The Girl With A Flute that hung over the crystal decanters to calm myself. Why would this bitch be so insensitive as to have this book about a woman who was shamed for giving birth to a little girl out-of-wedlock as a result of an affair, on her bookshelf in her own home for me and everyone to see?

Blinded by fear and rage, all I could think of to do was to tell Mother I was going to Canada and to call Chris, my writer friend in Toronto, for help. I managed to tell him my husband had beaten me and was going to have me killed by the Mafia and that I couldn't trust my parents to protect me.

"Come on up, I'll take care of you. Do you have a passport?" he offered.

"Yes from a trip to Mexico I took," I answered remembering Mother had it in her desk.

I surreptitiously called a cab to pick me up, and Mother grabbed my arm when she realized I was leaving.

"You're running again," she said.

"Where is my passport?" I asked as she ran into her room to hide it from me.

"Get away from me," I mumbled to Mother and grabbed it from her hand. She wasn't giving up very easily so I bolted out the front door. She tried again to grab my arm, but I reacted by hitting her in the face. As her glasses flew off, I hopped into the waiting cab.

Still, with my comings and goings from her house, my biggest fear remained: that she would have me committed. No doubt, she thought I was insane, and maybe I was. But it wasn't from a mental disorder. No, it was from hating them and the fear of being killed!

By this time, I didn't know the good guys from the bad. Nothing could have stopped me, as I was in survival mode, emotional hyper-drive, afraid and sprinting for dear life knowing I'd search for Mama even if it killed me.

They all were to blame and yet it was always my fault. Someone would have to pay for this in the end. I was mad at the world for betraying me over and over again.

No one ever told me much about the history of my adoptive family or that Kroehler, where Father and his father made all their money, originated in Ontario. There, the company made furniture for Princess Elizabeth and The Duke of Edinburgh in the 1940's. In fact, I wasn't told that in 1941, Kroehler had three factories in Toronto. I also didn't know that Gaga bought the mineral rights to land somewhere in Canada. No one in that family ever talked about money or taught me how to make it so I could take care of myself. The deep bond and connectedness that guided and held my adopters together and gave their lives purpose and meaning just wasn't there for me. I was totally on my own, relying on strangers, and my raw talent and wits to survive or die.

Photo Album

My first home, The Cradle, Evanston, IL.

From The Cradle Website:

Famous Cradle Families

In the early years, adoptive families from all over the country applied to The Cradle to adopt children. Some of the more famous adoptive parents include entertainers George Burns and Gracie Allen, Bob Hope, Al Jolson, Donna Reed, Pearl Buck and Gale Sayers. Today, The Cradle continues Mrs. Walrath's legacy by creating families through adoption and finding families for children from not only the U.S, but from all over the world.

Me and Gaga.

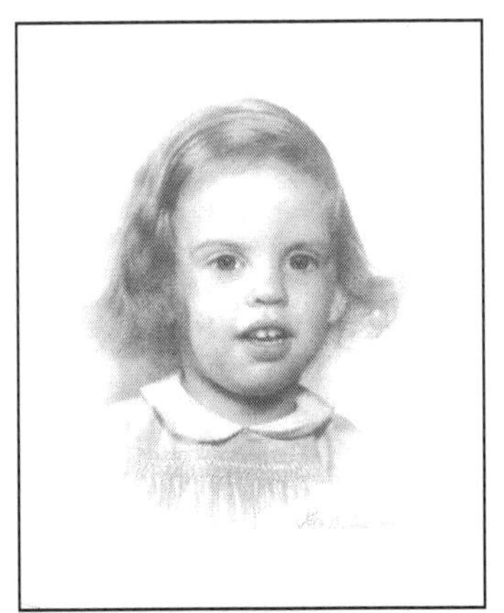

Me as a baby.

The house I grew up in.

My youngest brother and I with the Easter Bunny.

Me on Santa's lap.

Mother, proper as always.

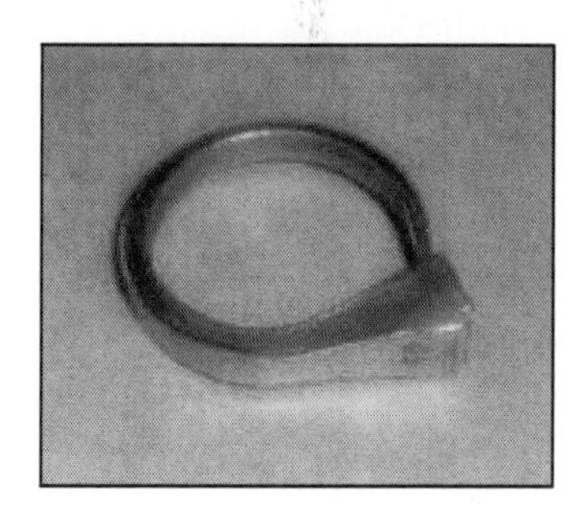

Pinky ring King Tullis made for us at King's Riding Stable in Dayton, OH.

The "Meyer" Family, note Mother holding my hand to calm my nerves.

WHO'S WHO — SAN FRANCISCO SUNDAY CHRONICLE

Frances Moffat: Counseling for a Curtsy

• Don't be afraid to be different and to let others be different.

• Be aware of your emotions and have the ability to direct them.

• Learn to understand and control your anger.

• Do not blindly accept or blindly lash out at authority.

DR. GERTRUDE HENGERER
"Let others be different"

LINDA MEYER AND MRS. ROBERT MEYER

Always in the papers, an aristocratic girl.

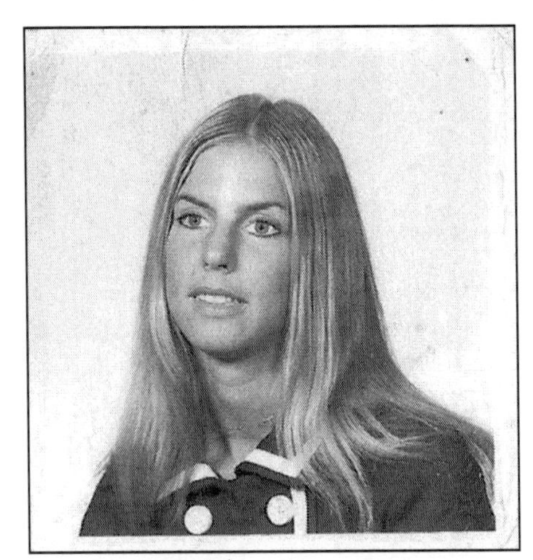

Me as a young woman, pre-nose job.

2—S. F. Examiner

WOMEN TODAY

The Peninsula Ball

Peninsula Ball debutantes danced in an English garden setting at the Palo Alto Hills Golf and Country Club last Saturday night at the first Peninsula Ball to be held in the summertime. Frederick Sherman presented each of the 21 debs, who then danced with their fathers and their escorts to the music of Walt Tolleson's orchestra. At left, deb Kathryn Kiely whirls around the floor with Sam Felix III, and at right, Linda Moyer dances with her father, Robert R. Moyer of Atherton. Ball proceeds will go to the Family Service Association of Palo Alto.

The Debutante Ball, dancing with Father, 1965.

Me at 21; new nose, new life.

My first oil painting.

This is my pastel of "Silent Witness" with Dorothy's baby cup and spoon.

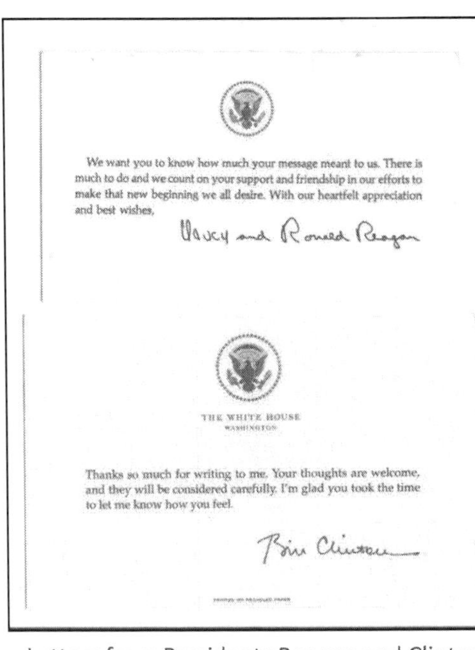
We want you to know how much your message meant to us. There is much to do and we count on your support and friendship in our efforts to make that new beginning we all desire. With our heartfelt appreciation and best wishes,

Nancy and Ronald Reagan

THE WHITE HOUSE
WASHINGTON

Thanks so much for writing to me. Your thoughts are welcome, and they will be considered carefully. I'm glad you took the time to let me know how you feel.

Bill Clinton

Letters from Presidents Reagan and Clinton regarding Adoptee rights.

Photo Amy Carter sent with her thank you note.

Thank you for writing to me. It's fun living in the White House, and I'm glad you are my friend.

Amy Carter

P.S. And thank you for sending the picture.

Ms. Melinda Meyer
2d0 Sand Hill Circle
Menlo Park, Ca.

My portrait of Amy Carter and her response.

Flutist Melinda shares her

By FOXY GWYNNE

Melinda, like Madonna, goes by her first name. When I met her at a party a couple of years ago, she played a little flute solo that impressed me. As I learned more about her, I knew that the flute has been part of her life wherever she went.

Soon after birth she was delivered to the Cradle, a private adoption agency in Evanston, Ill., the same agency from which Bob Hope had adopted his children. Baby Melinda was chosen by a rich socialite California mother and her handsome, alcoholic husband, a salesman for the prominent Kroehler Furniture Co. She went to live with her adoptive parents in a four-story mansion overlooking Mr. Kettering's (of Sloan-Kettering cancer hospital) estate in Kettering, Ohio. Two boys and a third natural son comprised the family, yet the only person Melinda felt truly honest with was Ardella, the black maid.

"I had to grow up," she said, "without ever seeing myself reflected back; in other words, mirrored back by my birth mother or any birth relatives." It was an anxiety that plagued her always.

Ellie Moyer collected children as one might china. I gathered that she was a person agreeable enough with her friends, but not a loving mother. In Melinda she saw a continuation of herself, and was delighted to find the child even higher achieving than she could have imagined.

By third grade, Melinda was taking classical lessons on the flute. "My adoptive mother bought me a nickel silver Manhattan band flute made by Selmer," she said. "I have kept it always because I have put my soul into it. I think the sound is as good as a $10,000 flute, which I have also played."

She spoke of her admiration for James Galway, who plays a gold flute, and flutist Jean Pierre Rampal.

By fifth grade, Melinda had a perfect score when she played the "Pipes of Pan" before judges, and rose to level five out of six.

Debussy was her favorite composer, although Melinda is no stranger to Bach and Beethoven. In 1960, when she was 13 and had picked out a three-gaited black stallion to train, her adoptive family went bankrupt and moved to Atherton, Calif., into a house across from the Shah of Iran. "I was heartbroken to leave, and I still had no idea who I was without the genetic clues," she said. "My mother — even though I was prepped endlessly for the rich WASP world — told me I could never be a socialite because I was way too frank."

'I went to high school with Bob Weir, leader of the band Warlock and later the Dead. We called him "Bob Weird."'

Melinda played first chair flute in the high school orchestra and marched with the band while making straight A's academically. "My mother insisted I try out for the youth symphony orchestra or go to Juilliard," she said. "I had terrible anxiety problems, and she was so controlling

Melinda

I felt like I was being put in a straitjacket. I resisted. I put down the flute. Off came the white flats, velvet ribbon headband, long straight skirts, pearls, and flipped platinum hair sprayed stiff as a board. Up went the skirt length, down came the long blond hair, and on went the bikini. I dropped out of the orchestra and the marching band."

Drawn again by the flute, she took lessons at Dana Morgan's music store, the original musical home of the Grateful Dead. Jerry Garcia played and worked there. "I went to high school with Bob Weir, leader of the band Warlock and later the Dead," she said. "We called him 'Bob Weird.' I remember when Warlock played for free at Magoo's Pizza Parlor in Palo Alto. The place was filled with hippies, and the smell of pot was in the air. I was a classically trained flutist and a music snob. The hippies were the 'great unwashed,' I thought."

She went to Arizona U and was tapped for the fancy sorority Kappa Alpha Theta. "My artist adoptive grandmother bought me a sewing machine, and I made clothes for myself and designed high fashion under my own label for friends and actually made money," she said. "I allowed my mother to push me into being a debutante, and because of it, could enter a Macy's modeling contest. I won, but modeling felt stupid to me."

At a sorority high tea Melinda met Shirley Temple Black's daughter. "Shirley was a movie star, but her daughter looked Oriental and like

Foxy Gwynne (actor Fred Gwynne's first wife) had a popular newspaper column in Bedford, NY, and here she interviews me.

Me and friend Debbie Lang (she was a jazz singer with the Glenn Miller Orchestra) at Foxy's annual Halloween party, 2003.

This is a signed photo Frank sent to me after I mailed him a pen sketched portrait.

The first cards I made, printed baskets with hand painted flowers.

Pastel birthday cake.

A pastel of an apple on papers.

Card I created and marketed for searching adoptees; it reads, "Every Search is Worth the Journey."

Sketch of a nude from an art class.

Mama Dorothy with her parents, 1915.

Mama as a toddler.

Mama at Oktoberfest, Wisconsin, 1961.

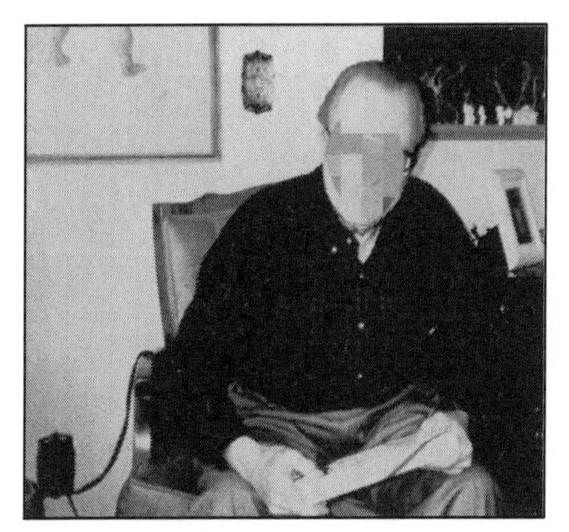

My half-brother, and behind him is a sketch he did that is similar to the sketches I did of Peanuts, the Afghan hound I adopted.

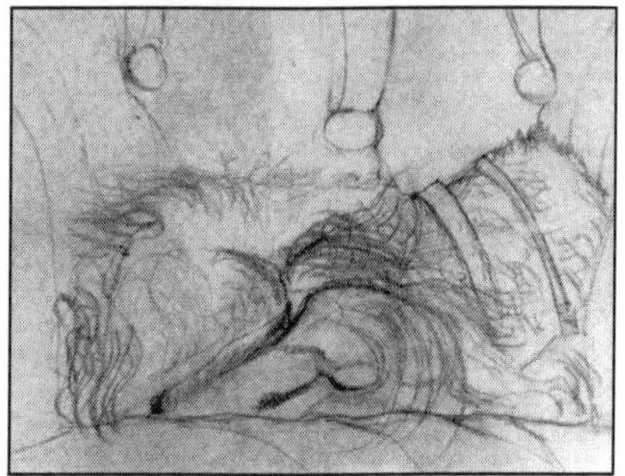

My sketches of Peanuts.

Mama in her 80s, with my brother's wife.

Mama in Numberg, Germany, 1983. This is the arch from my pastel.

The trains my "Franck" Uncle and Grandfather conducted from Wisconsin.

Pioneer Zephyr Dawn to Dusk Club.

FIRST MEMBERS OF EARLY CATHOLIC KNIGHTS OF WISCONSIN
BRANCH No. 42

Back Row: Left to Right—Frank Haser, John Fahey, Andrew Kaltenbach, James Kelly, Peter Bliudert, Jacob Duve, John Gerhards, Henry Wallenhorst, Charles Weber, Geo. Baumler, Frank Daser.

Middle Row: Left to Right—Henry Stohlmeyer, Joseph Langkamp, Henry Uppena, Jos. Gerhardts Sr., Jos. Gunther.

First Row: John Furc, John Tobin, John Stelpflug, Anicet Maurer, August, Franke, Henry Flogel.

CATHOLIC KNIGHTS OF WISCONSIN: Later in 1885, leaders of the Catholic Knights of America in Wisconsin saw fit to separate from the mother organization. Hence the original and subsequent members were called Catholic Knights of Wisconsin. Pastors usually saw the need of Catholic fraternals more clearly than others. It was in 1885 that Father Joseph Dries (1880-1886) sought to establish the Catholic Knights of Wisconsin here. Potosi Branch 41 was established in Saint Thomas Parish. Potosi Branch 42 was established at St. Andrew's. The original charter, issued December 14th, 1885, bears the following names: Father Joseph Dries, Henry Brake, John Jacob Duve, Joseph Gerhard, Frank Henry Flogel, John Celestine Herber, Joseph Langkamp, Anicet Mauer, John Philip Stelpflug, Henry Stohlmeyer, Henry B. Uppena, Mathias Wagner, John Weber, Charles Theodore Weber, and Andrew Wilhelm. These men were hard workers, honest, and thrifty. It seems amusing to us now to read how in one meeting there was considerable debate before a motion was carried to spend sixty cents for stationary. Some, trained by necessity to get along on little, felt that a nickel tablet would do.

SAINT ANDREW'S BENEVOLENT SOCIETY: Since benevolent cooperation proved happy in the matter of life insurance, members of the Catholic Knights next formed a Saint Andrew's Benevolent Society, the purpose of which was to mutually supply insurance against sickness and injury. In the case of each sickness or each accident all members contributed a certain portion of the total sum allowed. All went well for a time, until some of the members became a little too free in asking for compensation, sometimes when they were not strictly entitled to it. As a result, the Saint Andrew's Benevolent Society did not long survive.

UNDER THE CHARITY SYSTEM: The Catholic Knights of Wisconsin, as a state organization was also destined to see hard days. In 1885,

73

My great grandfather, August "Franck", born 1836 Gunthersdorf Silesia, East Prussia. Died Dec. 9, 1914. He was a tailor.

My great-aunt, Hannah "Franck".

This is me, Melinda A. Warshaw, today.

16

Manure and Religion

While boarding the plane to Toronto, I tried not to look terrified as I hung onto my sanity, my suitcase of earthly goods, including my two favorite Lanz sundresses, my flute, my letter from The Cradle, and my Adoption Decree while carrying the framed abstract pastel painting of Casey's sleeping cat.

Chris Levine was waiting for me as I arrived in Toronto half-dead, beaten, black and blue. He took me to get a massage and nursed me back to health while I stayed with him in a seedy downtown apartment.

"You remind me of a wandering Jew," he said and handed me a copy of the children's story The Velveteen Rabbit to soothe my battered orphan soul.

"God, could I be Jewish and no one ever told me?" I said and skimmed the book and the story which made me feel even worse.

"I have an adopted friend. She's a minority as an adoptee like you. Her natural mother is Jewish and her natural father is a Greek Orthodox Catholic. She was brought up by her adoptive family as an Atheist. She and her natural parents are reunited, but she is permanently scarred from it. When she comes to visit I want you to hear her play the guitar. I've never heard such haunting and sad songs in my life. Her natural mother is a musician, too. I wonder if your mother is just like you. Did you know you can take a blindfolded newborn and put it to five women's breasts and it will only nurse from its own mother? Now, that is amazing," he said.

He was a student of Kabbala, which contained mystical and ethical Jewish writings, and gave me his copy to read. I read about the Zohar which contained formulas by means of which the adept could enter into direct communication with invisible powers and exercise authority over demons, nature, and diseases. But why was it exclusively for orthodox Jewish men over forty? I was pretty sure I wasn't a Jewish man, but I *was* interested in direct communication with the invisible to obtain the truth about Mama's location.

"*Yod* means 'sperm of God' in Hebrew and is the smallest of all the Hebrew letters. Yod also means 'Hand'—the same hand in which the Hermit holds the light for everyone else on the spiritual path of life," Chris informed me.

"Perhaps that is what the Yod, the 'Hand of God' in my astrology chart means," I said.

"I just read about a study done on child Holocaust survivors who did not know their true identity. They have post-traumatic stress disorder symptoms and psychological distress. Maybe you do, too." He tried explaining further, but I just didn't get it.

The Jews belief in good luck charms for protection like The Star of David to ward off the Evil Eye seemed so superstitious. Chris told me there was a Jewish soul and that excluded anyone who wasn't Jewish according to Jewish law. Catholics also were exclusive with their rules and used the Cross as their protection. Did one soul go to Jewish heaven and another to Catholic heaven? It made no sense to me. No one group of people owns God even if they think they do. I could never give the power of my soul to another group of strangers even though strangers had taken care of me all my life. This is why my study of all religious thought began. My soul searched high and low for a protector, the truth, and a place to belong. It seemed my birthright to study the Kabbala if I wanted to. I would study manure if I thought it would help me find Dorothy. There were many paths to the Absolute and I guess being in Toronto was one of them.

Chris, of course was like any other man, but I really needed him for protection. While I was staying with him in his hotel room, I met so many shady people. Why he was staying in such a place I will never know. He was a serious pot head and the hotel where he lived was filled with Toronto Mafia characters. They told me they would look out for any American hit man that was out to kill me. One day, I followed Chris into the room where he bought his pot only to see bloodstains on the shower curtain. It freaked me out because I read about a murder that had taken place there the night before and surmised my new found friend might be a drug dealer.

My next channeled pastel began that night in his room when I was alone. The same face of a blonde-haired, blue-eyed man in the clouds with a streak of yellow lightning through the dark sky appeared on the paper as if it drew itself. The face looked similar to the man or angel I saw with Jack in the diner. Heaven kept breaking through the veil just enough to keep me guessing. Was I getting help from the other side? Jack told me once that the Holy Spirit guides us gently to the truth.

Looking for Love in All the Wrong Places

I began playing my flute at a Toronto coffeehouse at night. The first time, I played slow sultry tunes that excited two gays who came over to me and couldn't stop shaking my hand. After a set another night, a handsome gentlemen with slicked-down blonde hair, magnetic big, blue eyes, dressed in a banker's suit walked up to me as I left the stage.

"You're great," he said. "Would you like to have a drink?"

I gladly went out with this handsome tow-headed stockbroker and after a few dates, said goodbye to my Jewish friend and went to live with Stephen Powell in a beautifully decorated rented house thinking he was the one. His father was an attorney and his mother a lovely English aristocrat like Mother. He wore starched white shirts with French cuffs and suspenders like Father used to do.

Steve piloted his biplane and flew me to his family's house on their private island in Perry Sound every weekend. I loved to canoe in the lakes and take steam baths with him after a few games of tennis, but I didn't like having to eat formal dinners with his family every night.

It was a stormy afternoon after too much wine, when I secretly paddled out in their canoe to read Canterbury Tales by flashlight, feeling quite happy to get away from his family. The tales of these 14th century pilgrims on their way to the shrine of a saint at Canterbury Cathedral were like me on my pilgrimage to Dorothy. I was so engrossed in the stories that I barely noticed him when he came out in his boat and motioned for me to follow him back to the dock.

"Why did you disappear like that? Don't you know you could have been struck by lightning and killed?" he screamed.

"Sorry, I just wanted to commune with nature. I love the feeling and sound of the wind and the rain. It soothes me."

"I'm going to St. Cloud, Minnesota, to hunt and fish with my friends next weekend. Is that ok with you?"

"Sure, I'll be fine alone at your house," I replied hoping Rob wouldn't appear in my dreams or Casey banging on the front door of his house to scare me to death.

I had no idea where Minnesota was, nor did I care. In fact, I couldn't see the forest for the trees as I was trying to love him and fit into his family. He was funny like me, an outdoorsman, extrovert, a Leo, a heavy drinker, social and very conventional like my parents. I knew I would have a great life with him, but he didn't care at all about my search for Dorothy Lumsley and now Baby Girl Lumsley, too. No matter, I could not give up my quest for answers.

When he was away on his trip, I took my first train ride

from Toronto to Oregon and back to Toronto. I rode across Canada alone, just for the love of it. Trains felt safe, giving me good memories of my favorite conductors in South Pasadena that passed by Gaga's house where I loved to wave to them as a little girl.

I really liked Steve, but it became evident that his alcoholism was not a mere trifle. He had an explosive temper, and could be controlling, too formal and uptight. He had three bad habits—a fondness for prostitutes, Stilton cheese, and alcohol. Funnily, it was his breath that finally drove me away.

"If you marry me, it will be so perfect," he would say wistfully. "We'll have four towheads with blue eyes. I'll buy a big house, and a yacht in Florida and a house in the Canary Islands."

He had our life all planned out, but it felt like another prison to me. What about what I wanted? To my horror, he came back from the hunting trip with his yellow coveralls caked with animal blood. It sickened me as he proudly filleted his kills and had them for dinner.

"Take that disgusting deer outside. I can't stand the sight of blood," I ordered.

I knew our relationship was doomed; it just didn't feel right. He wasn't spiritual, sensitive, or artistic, but he was very much in love with me. Love wasn't enough. I remained strangely detached and began to plan my departure.

The Gorgeous Alien

My next male friend was a 74-year-old Viennese chemical engineer. He came over to wine and dine me when Steve was away. We waltzed and waltzed until I waltzed him right out of my life.

There is a saying in Alcoholics Anonymous: Alcoholics don't take prisoners, they take hostages. I was drawn to alcoholics like a magnet and kept becoming the hostage of one after another.

Steve's best friend, a scion of Canada's blue-blooded retail chain of Department stores, avid horse breeder and outdoorsman, told me about Madame Blavatsky, the Russian Noble clairvoyant, who believed in the astral plane and the spirit world.

"My mother is a member of the Theosophy Society and has invited you to a meeting."

"I'd love to go and learn more about the spirit world. M. Blavatsky has the most beautiful mystical eyes I had ever seen. They look like moonstones."

"She wrote *The Secret Doctrine* and *The Voice of the Silence* and brought reincarnation to the west from the teachings of the Tibetans,. Compassion is the law of laws," he said.

My attendance at the meetings gave me more insight and awareness into the knowledge of the Divine. My quest for the truth from the spirit world continued even if I got stuck in the astral plane and couldn't get back.

"Do you want to be in a movie?" Steve asked.

"Really, you want me to be in a movie? Sure," I said with great excitement.

"The movie is called *The Priest, the Rabbi, and the Minister* who turn out to be dealing drugs. One of the stars in it is Mia Farrow's little sister."

We were in a formal dinner party scene, sitting around a table. When the movie was released and I saw myself on the screen, it was as if I was looking at a zombie. The truth of the matter was that I was a tall, thin, beautiful, big-eyed blonde girl who possessed no identity of her own. Who was I? I didn't even recognize myself. How could I with no genetic mirror?

"I look like a freak, I told Steve, "I think I'm an alien from another planet."

"Are you crazy? Don't you know you're gorgeous? You look like a movie star."

I had no answer for him. My boyfriends were all victims of my unfulfilled secret needs. I left behind a trail of abandoned beaus and failed relationships as I nomadically forged onward toward Mama. Empathy was not in my vocabulary. What none of us really knew was that intimacy was exclusively reserved for Dorothy. No amount of alcohol, drugs, or sex could fill the void that was left from my total separation from her. There was only one person I wanted to bond with and that was Mama, my blood tie.

If I stuck around Toronto, I would never find her. She held the key to my real identity and my sanity. Finding her was now a life or death matter. The mother-child bond is the strongest bond there is, and the force pulling me to her was unstoppable. I abandoned Steve and hid from him at a posh local hotel. He searched and searched for me until I finally called to tell him I wasn't coming back.

During dinner in the hotel restaurant dining on truffles, a gorgeous man-boy named Michal who was dressed in linen slacks and a blue polo shirt came over to my table and introduced himself.

"Come sit down," I offered.

"I noticed you sitting all by yourzelf. Are your alright?" he asked in a heavy foreign accent.

"I'm not alright. My life is a mess right now and you probably wouldn't want to hear about it," I said and watched him hand roll a cigarette and light up at the table.

One look at him and I was once again totally smitten. He invited me to come and see his glamorous penthouse art gallery filled with abstract art. The white walls were covered with original lithographs, prints, etchings, linocuts, aquatints done by the modern masters. He sold original lithographs by Picasso, Chagall, Miro, Dali, Calder, Franckenthaler, plus ancient Russian Icons. Steve was history and off I went to live in a rarified contemporary fine art gallery penthouse with this exotic and sexy creature who loved art. Perhaps this was where I belonged.

He was not an artist, but an art dealer. His big, blue eyes, sparkled and his light brown curly hair, smooth baby skin, and European accent captured me right off. He had that unmistakable fine European bone structure I couldn't resist. The letter from The Cradle said that Dorothy Lumsley had huge blue eyes and fine mousey brown curly hair. Was this why I found him so irresistible because he resembled her? I left Steve, the British fisherman, woodsman, hunter, trapper, pilot, broker, and alcoholic, to live with the stunning big blue-eyed, chain-smoking, and alcoholic Jewish Czech art salesman from what once was part of Silesia, Prussia. Prussia could have been on Mars for all I knew. Everyone I met knew their heritage and where they came from, but me.

This elegant and exquisite being taught me how to roll my own cigarettes, taught me about modern art, bought me beautiful clothes from his friend's boutique and dressed me like a sophisticated, sexy European model. I learned about communism in his country, an evil he had escaped while his family was still captive. He told me his parents had nervous breakdowns when the communists came in and took all their money and ruined their business. The secret police were everywhere. His own brother was not allowed to talk to him. He had terrible loss issues; we both had.

"Don't you want me to help you learn proper English?" I asked him.

"I don't zinc zo. Let me tell you zomezink. Art iz zo mysteriouz and zo zacred. Don't you zinc zo? Your pastel is amazink," he said as he took a deep drag on his cigarette.

"Yes. Especially because I'm a fine artist and nobody cares," I retorted.

"I know a man who owns an art gallery who might vant to buy your sleeping cat paztel. How much are you azkink for thiz abstract masterpieze?"

"A thousand dollars in American money," I said to him shocked that anyone would want to buy it, let alone the owner of an art gallery.

A week later I had ten one hundred dollar bills in my hand.

"Look at thiz picture of my parentz. I get zo lonely for zhem," he admitted to me one night.

"Why don't you call them?" I asked him.

"Talking to zhem makes me cry," he replied.

"You have your mother's eyes and your father's facial

features," I noticed.

"Who do you look like?" he asked innocently.

"I don't know because I was adopted. The only reason I'm here is the fact that I'm searching for my mother so I can get answers to all those kind of questions."

"You do look like you could be my zister. How did you end up here?" he inquired.

"It's a long story and too painful for me to talk about it right now."

"I understand," he said hugging me and kissing away my tears.

What a strange journey I was on.

We went out on the town, smoked and drank bottles of Pilsner, a Czech beer. I felt like a Vogue model dressed in the clothes he bought for me. He was a style genius and we were both in love with the mystery and sacredness of art. My genes had a mind of their own. Michal was so glamorous, sophisticated, and worldly. His eyes drew me to him like some are drawn to a bedazzling gemstone. The art drew just as strongly. I felt I belonged in Europe, not America, for some reason.

He took me to a friend's bat mitzvah and they wouldn't let him in because I wasn't Jewish.

"Don't bring that shicksa in here," the mother of the party said to him.

"A shicksa? What in the world is she talking about?" I said feeling humiliated.

"Oh don't listen to her. It just means you aren't Jewish," he said on our way out of the party.

This was the fourth time I felt discriminated against. The first time was while befriending black men and the second was while traveling around with the black conga drummer and the third being an adoptee.

I, Baby girl Lumsley, was wandering from man to man and family to family. Goldilocks and Cinderella could have been good friends of mine. I can only describe what had happened to me by saying it was sort of like Dorothy in the Wizard of Oz encountering the Tin Man, The Scarecrow, and

The Cowardly Lion. That is as close to how it was for me as I can describe it. It was like being stuck living in a fantasy world where I was in a fractured fairy tale or like I took a bite out of the poison apple and was in a coma waiting to wake up and be rescued by Mama. Each of my boyfriends held a portion of my unknown genetic mirror, but the denial and deceit was so deep I didn't consciously recognize it.

Looking into a mirror was insane. I either saw myself as pretty or as *who am I*? There was no in between, and I was clueless.

Michal was keeping secrets from me. He had two handsome gay German friends whom I liked very much. One of them had dark, brown hair with brown eyes and the other was another blonde with big blue eyes. The blonde danced with me at a disco and could have been my twin brother. He was supplying me with diet pills and brotherly love. I loved to lose myself in his beautiful seductive blue eyes as we danced. He and his partner had a pet monkey and together they looked like Seigfried and Roy. It didn't dawn on me Michal might be bisexual. Someone told me he was not only bisexual, but also a prostitute. If this wasn't bad enough, I caught him sleeping with another girl in our bed, and later the same day, met someone who I surmised was his secret pregnant wife who didn't speak any English. His crazy antics and betrayals infuriated me to the point that I put a tab of acid in a strawberry and let him eat it.

"I feel zo strange. Zomezing iz wrong wiz me," he said.

He needed to be punished because he had betrayed me. By this time, I wasn't going to tolerate any more tricksters. He was just another con artist and I must have seemed like a sociopath. I was so depressed that I took a steak knife from his kitchen drawer to my stomach and almost plunged it in. Once I felt the prick of the knife tip on my skin and saw a droplet of blood, I put the knife away and cried until I was a mass on his kitchen floor not wanting to be alive anymore.

The next day I moved out of the penthouse into a dark and dingy basement apartment on the University of Toronto campus to regroup. I took a poetry class and met many

American boys who had run away from the Vietnam War. On the weekends, I played my flute at coffeehouses, drank gallons of beer, rolled my own cigarettes, and chain-smoked. My two selves were bouncing back and forth in my mind like a ping pong ball. Mother and Father called to tell me the date for the annulment with Casey was set. I managed to muster enough courage to buy my plane ticket knowing I had to fly back, give a deposition, and go to court.

My wakeup call came from Tom, another tall, dark brown-haired, brown eyed handsome married German I was having a fling with. He told me that I was drinking too much beer and turning into a lush like Gail Garland.

"I know you are a part of the sexual revolution and women's lib, but if you keep up such self-destructive behaviors, you'll end up dead," he said in a very serious tone of voice as if he was my father or something.

He made me take a look at myself. After being in the sauna and smelling burnt lung and it was mine, my smoking ceased for good. I had to say good-bye to his Harley and him.

"Do you realize we could be related? I could be related to anyone and never know it until I find out the names of the people who I really am related to. I think I'm going to take a vow of poverty and become a nun," I said and proceeded to throw up all over him before I passed out in his arms.

Lovely.

17

Broken Dreams

It took all my strength to board a plane back to my parents' from Toronto for the deposition and annulment from my eight month marriage to Casey. Father hired the Little Caesar of San Francisco as my lawyer. Mother wanted to hire a famous San Francisco lawyer, also known as The King of Torts who was the ex-husband of her best friend, but Father didn't want the bad press or to pay his high fee.

"See what I mean about checking out a man and his family for good background and breeding?" Mother said angrily at the deposition.

I don't know my background or breeding, Mother, remember? Yours isn't that great, either, circled round and round in my mind, but as always, I couldn't get the words out.

Our lawyer managed to put a lien on Casey's father's nursing home. I only received $4,000 back because Casey put my money in other people's names. He walked away with all my money, plus a redwood burl business, an organ, a flatbed truck, chain saws, a water tower, and all of our wedding gifts.

Once on the stand in the courtroom, panic set in as I looked at Casey. I froze and couldn't swallow, completely losing my ability to answer the judge's questions at the trial. Martin coached me through it telling me what to say, and somehow the marriage annulment was granted and an Order of Protection was issued to me. The entire ordeal was surreal.

I reluctantly returned to Toronto, still terrified and afraid for my life. Customs interrogated and strip-searched me thinking I was a drug runner because I went back and forth so many times. The United States authorities should have put me in a witness protection program, but I'm glad they didn't as I would have to assume yet another false identity and would never have found my mother. The men at customs confiscated my diet pills, let me go, and I returned to the dark and dungeon-like basement apartment on campus. I was afraid to live in the United States for fear of getting killed. Casey did indeed threaten to put a contract out on my life, and I knew he could and would do it.

A very drunk Michal kept breaking in through the window of my apartment at 3 AM, ending up in my bed clinging to me.

"Don't go. Don't leavz me," he cried and cried as he held onto me like a baby. "Vat iz diz?" he asked as he picked up a beer stein I saved from a Hops in Humboldt festival I went to with Casey in Fortuna, California.

"I love beer and it's what I like to drink beer from," I answered knowing he loved Pilsner beer from his homeland.

I had to escape another crazy alcoholic? As I kneeled alone, praying for help at St. James Cathedral near my little dungeon apartment, the tears dropped like rain.

"Please, God, help me. I'll go to Lourdes to pray to Our Lady for a miracle if I must. St. Anthony save me, please. I feel so betrayed and am so lost. Where's Mama? Help me Jesus, help me," I pleaded and I wasn't even Catholic.

Howard, a blue eyed curly haired student in my poetry class, caught me crying after class one day.

"What's wrong? Are you ok?" he asked.

"No. I'm so depressed. My ex-husband from the states stole all my money and wants to have me killed for leaving him. I'm hiding from him up here. It all seems futile. I'm so frightened and alone and I just want to die." The confessions flowed out of my mouth like the words to a song.

"Have you heard of The Urantia Foundation? You can borrow my book, and it will help you," he told me.

"What's it about?"

"The Urantia book is about Machiventa, AKA Melchizedic, The Sage of Salem, who came to Earth before Jesus on a bestowal mission similar to Jesus. He came because the concept of God had become very hazy in the minds of men."

"You mean that this was written by ET's?" I asked.

"The information was channeled by ET's," he replied.

"Well being adopted has made me feel like an ET."

I read and read this tome to see if I could learn more about how God works. It was 1,973 years before the birth of Jesus that he was bestowed upon the human races of earth. I read that Salem became the City of Jebus subsequently being called Jerusalem. Melchizedic chose Abraham's family to spread the teachings to the world at that time.

Days turned into nights while I learned all I could holed up in my little basement apartment hoping for some answers. The book mentioned angels, archangels, thought adjusters and all sorts of higher orders of spiritual beings. I read about the life of Jesus. Jesus said, "Where there is truth, there is liberty." This statement furthered my resolve and gave me hope. How lucky Jesus was to have known his own mother.

How was I ever going to access the Akashic Field, a repository for all knowledge in the universe? I prayed and prayed for help wondering why the world was so insane. Would I ever find Mama?

Searching for Clues

The number 44 size tag from the French jacket Michal bought especially for me fell off into my hand as I sat fully dressed, drunk and dizzy in the empty tub after a depressing night barely able to take the loneliness or the fact that I was single and broke. I held it in my hand and thought about numerology, synchronicity, and about the personal significance of this number. Perhaps there was something to The Kabbala and the Bible Code. My spiritual education was opening my inner eyes to the eternal that was happening here and now. It was telling me that the ego sees separation, and I was trying to rid myself of it and become a realized master to obtain higher states of consciousness and enlightenment. I would have done anything to get to the truth. This number 44 stuck in my mind. Was it a link or clue to my secret identity?

The only thing I could think to do was call my old friend, Sam, the ex-New York ad exec, artist, carpenter, and builder who lived in Carmel to see if he would come and rescue me. I had to get back to California.

"Sam, I need your help. Could you come and pick me up in Toronto? I need to leave in the middle of the night to escape my ex-boyfriend who's a crazy alcoholic," I pleaded with him over the phone.

"I'll be there in two days and we'll go and visit my brother and son in New York."

His VW van pulled up in the middle of the night and the journey continued. I had to hope that some higher source and my instincts were now orchestrating the entire search. I had to let go of everything familiar, go with the universe, and live in the moment. The abundance I sought was not in affluence and wealth, but in spiritual terms. I was seeking access to the essence of what all things are. I was seeking communion with that essence inside of me and I had to let go of my ego. Would the truth be revealed in time?

My search and my fear left me so tired, drained, and dysfunctional. I couldn't talk to Mother because she was punishing and called me "an operator" after the annulment to Casey. She thought I was a con artist and was using my looks and sex to lure men for their money.

"You know, my beautiful sister was the one the boys wanted to sleep with, and I was the one they wanted to play tennis with. I envy your sexual experiences as I have only known your father," she finally admitted the last time I saw her.

She was way off the mark about me. This forbidden journey was taking so much energy and years out of my life. Mother thought I was having a party running with all these different men. The toxic secrets were slowly killing me and many times I did not want to live anymore. Did she know I was the family secret keeper and running scared because they threw me to the wolves?

Sam drove me all over the United States. After he picked me up in the middle of the night in Toronto, we went to see his brother, a very successful stockbroker living in New York City, and spent the day at the New York Stock Exchange. I met his old boss at the ad agency on Madison Avenue and we all went to the 21 Club for dinner. We then traveled to Cooperstown to see his family plot, and I learned about his family history. What I was really after was my own family history, not his. We had high tea with Rose Kennedy, stopped at the Anheuser Busch estate, who are famous for their beer, petted their Clydesdales, and traveled on to see Sam's son at West Point. We met a famous writer and left for Westport, CT, where I met Steven Dohanos, the famous artist, whose paintings were featured on stamps. From Westport, we spent the night at Sam's friend's house in the woods in Pound Ridge, an upscale town in New York. Then we ventured south where I met his sister and visited all the plantations in the area. Finally, it was back to Carmel.

"Did you see that UFO in the sky?" he asked me as we rode alone in his VW bus through the desert.

"No, but if you did I believe you," I told him, hoping he wasn't crazy.

He was a surreal artist and way out there after lots of peyote, Quaaludes, and anything else he could put in his mouth. We were headed right for the free-loving artists and intellectuals of Carmel.

I hated staying in campgrounds and living in his VW bus, but I felt safe again. He seemed to understand my genealogical bewilderment and driving need to find my mother. If the ET's did exist, I was hoping they would help me telepathically find Dorothy, as nothing was out of the realm of possibility. I had come full circle and was back in California.

Living with Sam was okay at first until I realized he was just another crazy drugged-out old alcoholic.

"Why would you have a marijuana plant growing right on your front porch? Aren't you afraid the police will see it and arrest you?" I inquired.

"I know the police. They could care less," he replied.

His obsession with the granddaughter of the founder of I. Magnin clothing stores, a conspiracy theorist, drove me crazy. The day didn't begin until he listened to her speak on a local radio station. Didn't he know that I was the pawn in a big governmental "conspiracy of silence" to keep me from knowing who I was?

Sam called me over to look at one of his paintings that hung above his bed.

"Take a good look at the sensuous Santa Lucia mountain range I painted and tell me what you see," he requested.

"I see that the top of the mountain ridge changes into a reclining woman's beautiful nude body. Wow, how did you see that?"

"A friend of mine who owns a metaphysical art gallery in town taught me how to paint from two realities. It's called cognitive illusion. Do you want to meet her?"

"Sure, I would like a job there and maybe she could channel my mother." I hoped.

The beautiful woman with black wavy hair and haunting blue eyes owned the gallery. She was a clairvoyant and was sponsoring a guru named Baba G who never cut his hair or spoke. His devotees from the ashram in Santa Cruz sat around him in the yoga position at *sat sang* (sitting with a saintly person) to ask him questions which he answered by writing on a chalkboard. Baba G invited me to a gathering of the group. When it was my turn to ask him a question, I took the chalk right out of his hand and drew a big question mark on his little chalkboard.

"You have very sad eyes," he wrote on the chalkboard, looking as confused as I felt.

The black-haired beauty hired me and gave me a job selling the art. Unfortunately, it was incredibly boring. I brought my record albums to play on her stereo system while I sat in the gallery hoping for a miracle to happen. The song Time in a Bottle by Jim Croce was one of my favorites.

"I know another lady you need to meet," he said.

"This is Mary. She's a Primal Scream therapist."

"Melinda," she said to me when we met, "I want you to get in touch with your rage. Pretend this pillow is a person you are angry at and start hitting it like it is that person."

"This is ridiculous I can't do it," I told her after punching the pillow a couple of times.

One hour of that just touched the tip of the iceberg. If I had really let loose, I would have destroyed her room and possibly her, too.

In an attempt to make me feel better about myself, Sam took me to see a girl he knew who was mentally ill and on medication. It didn't work.

The New Age Think Tank

Sam wasn't helping me to get any closer to my mother so, after about four months, I moved into a little pension owned by a girl named Jane. Sam freaked out and hated me afterwards for abandoning him, but he was too crazy for me. This New Age bed and breakfast was a safe place surrounded by many people all the time.

Jane was a New Age type who served health foods, taught meditation, and was a devotee and follower of the Indian yogi, Baba G, who believed in reincarnation. She served tahini and freshly-baked whole grain bread for breakfast and various raw foods and juices to her guests. Every night at sunset, she would ring Tibetan bells and stand with her palms spread to get the last energy rays of the sun, and she slept in a sleeping bag on the grass under the stars that seemed close enough to touch. There was magic in the air in Carmel-by-the-Sea. Jane had been spiritually enlightened. I was certain her third eye must be stuck open.

While I stayed there like a Zen master living in the moment, I wrote children's stories and played improvisational music on my flute. It was annoying listening to all the love making going on in the room across from me. Every time a new couple would check in, the noise and head banging made me hold my ears or bury my head in my pillow. I felt totally out of place and hated being so lost, alone and homeless.

One day at lunch I sat at a table with a couple.

"I have just written a screen play and I think you might be perfect for the lead role," the man said to me.

"Really?" I replied.

"Yes, you have the patrician look I'm after. The screenplay is about a famous orchestra conductor who has an affair with the first violinist. Would you like to read for the part?" he asked.

"Sure, may I read the script?" I asked and began to read.

"Well, will you play the part?" he asked as my eyes scanned the pages. I closed it and handed it back.

"No, the lines are stupid. I refuse to be used as a sex object. Could you make a movie about an adoptee from a closed adoption secretly searching for her natural parents? I would play the part in a movie like that," I told him as he turned and left.

Carmel was like paradise. The stores, art galleries, and sightseers gave it a festive atmosphere during the day. I bumped into my friend Sara's mother on a crowded sidewalk one afternoon. She and her husband were living in Monterey and once more welcomed me into their family. It was a lifesaver even though she had no idea about all the craziness in my life until I told her some of it over lunch. She didn't understand how I could exist on nuts and carrot juice and referred to my haute New Age cuisine as rabbit food. Still, it was nice to know she was around.

Enlightenment through Taoism became the big thing. I tried to become one with the Tao, the home of spirit, the field of ideals and manifest forms. My favorite phrase was "don't push the river." I should have been writing *The Tao of Closed Adoption* or *How to Get in Touch with Your Inner Orphan* instead of pointless children's stories.

My first mystical experience on hash happened while I was taking a bath in a huge marble tub in the communal bathroom at Jane's. While taking a long bath, I had a vision of the head of a yogi master in a turban. It freaked me out. Had my third eye been opened? Later I played my flute at *sat sang* for Baba G and his devotees in Jane's living room. A woman came up to me after and said, "You are so lucky because your spirit has been cleared for eternity."

"How nice," I said, and thought to myself, how would that help me find Dorothy?

The woman who owned the metaphysical art gallery in Carmel told me I was a sensitive and clairvoyant. It still wasn't what I wanted to hear. I wanted to know who I was as a non-adopted person. My biological name and identity were still unknown and she was sorry she couldn't help me figure it all out. Could my clairvoyance help me find Dorothy? Where on earth was she and who was I?

A famous psychoanalyst-turned-mystic, was a friend of Jane's and rented the room across from mine. He had his invention, the isolation tank, in her living room. Being unorthodox and somewhat of a New Age icon, he used psychedelics to achieve altered states of consciousness inside the totally dark tank full of water. He also was communicating with dolphins, studying schizophrenia, neurobiology, and the inner realms. I wasn't interested at all as I had been in an unwanted altered state since birth.

I was hoping the wiry haired Dutch channeler, a friend of Jane's, who walked around Carmel talking into a tape machine for a book he was writing called "Conversations with God," could help me. We used the I Ching, the Chinese divination book of changes, daily. He thought I was an oracle and an Old Dutch soul. He stole my Birkenstock sandals and rode off on Jane's bike never to be seen again. All I had done was to draw a face on a seaweed pod and left it down on the Carmel beach. He must have been spying on me or eating too many hashish and mushroom canapés at Jane's. My hope was that the mind-altering drugs would act like truth serum and give me the information I needed to find out who and where Dorothy was living.

Even though I taught flute it never occurred to me that I could have a career teaching it to others. Mother would have looked down on such a thing as too common unless I was a graduate of Juilliard. I couldn't settle down anywhere because my life was on the line for what seemed like mission impossible. One little act of lust by Mama had created such a mind-boggling mess for me. I wasn't even allowed to know my own name.

To complicate matters, Jane's best friend thought I was her reincarnated Indian brother from a past life. She left me her entire collection of books on reincarnation and made me read them, but I remained a skeptic. *Hello, people, I want to know who I am in this life!*

The Sufi group told me to surrender and let go of my ego. Their mystic Islamic tradition and idea of higher consciousness through meditation and poetry was very alien to me. Even the radical and controversial psychotherapist R.D. Laing's books "Knots" and "The Divided Self" didn't address my adoption issues. I was angry and my head felt like it was tied in a knot. No one told me to look for a book about adoption, and it never occurred to me to do so on my own.

Meeting a Familiar Stranger

One day a beautiful big blue-eyed blonde-haired woman came into the Metaphysical Art Gallery and we began to talk.

"What are you doing here?" she asked.

"I'm on my search for my natural mother."

"Really, where did you grow up?"

"In Kettering, Ohio," I told her.

"Oh, I grew up there, too. Where did you live?"

"We lived on Sunny View Lane."

"My parent's house was right down the hill from yours."

"Did you ride at King's Stables?" I asked her.

"Yes, I owned a horse there," she answered.

"You were the beautiful girl on the Arabian stallion," I said in amazement.

"I won him in a contest," she confirmed.

"What are you doing here?" I asked her.

"I'm here spying on my granddaughter, my daughter's secret love-child who has been adopted by a wealthy family in Big Sur."

"Have you found her yet?"

"Not yet," she said.

Free love did have a dark side, as I was proof of that. It had been going on even in the 40's!

"That's amazing that both of us are on a secret search for lost natural relatives through closed adoptions. What a small world," I exclaimed.

"I see you are interested in the metaphysical," she said.

"I'm a musician and an artist and looking for the deeper answers to life. Do you believe in reincarnation?"

"Well, to tell you the truth, I was a horse in a past life," she said with a very straight face.

We liked to meet at a Hollywood star's restaurant The Hog's Breath Inn. We hung out at the bar and I used to see him in the shadows. He was shy and managed a smile when we were introduced and then sunk back into the shadows behind the beautiful wooden bar. I was sitting at the bar at the restaurant with Janet, the aspiring actress, and spy when a woman named Rose, the local psychic who was sitting to my left began to talk to me.

"Why don't you join Mensa?" she suggested after we chatted for a few minutes.

"I'm an orphan and on a search to find my stolen identity. I can't settle down until I find my mother. My adoptive mother doesn't think I'm a genius. I know my real mother will know who I am."

"Did you know the more spiritual you become, the more psychic you get? I understand your need for validation," she said and wished me luck.

Eventually, I moved out of Jane's for more privacy and I settled into a little one bedroom cottage. It was now 1974. I hoped my crazy ex would never find me in Carmel. I rented the daybed in the living room from my roommate who was an ex-Navy Seal from Fort Ord. Deep sea diving had given him a kidney disease that turned his urine dark green. When his illness forced him to move out, in moved a friend of Janet's named Chris, a ginseng, pot-smoking, chain-smoking, mayonnaise-addicted, ex-Buddhist Monk, enlightened Bodhisattva, and artist who played the flute.

"I'm Norwegian, and I have an IQ over 170," he bragged.

He showed me some of his chants and was a great iron sculptor. Neither of us had any money so we lived like spiritually enlightened Monks and played improv on our flutes together. His friend was the daughter of a Whitney of the Whitney Museum in NYC family. He brought her into his room under the cover of darkness and there was never a peep out of them. I never met her, but he told me she had befriended a legendary musician in a park and his underwear was green and his fingernails and toenails were dirty and long. They wanted me to meet him, but the thought grossed me out even though I was feeling like a rolling stone, a complete unknown, with no direction home, and that my answer was blowing in the wind somewhere. I declined the invitation. Yes, there was that mysterious pull of mine toward professional musicians, but not this one!

My mantra wasn't *ommm*, it was *MOMmmmmmmmm!*

I had no phone, no car, no television and was about to get food stamps. Caffeine pills, M & M's, carrot juice, and fear of my ex coming after me kept me hyper-aroused, hyper-vigilant, and too thin.

Wandering around enchanting Carmel barefoot at night, feeling like a ghost, kept me going. I was in awe of the artists that painted the beautiful oil paintings of seascapes in the gallery windows. My dream was to retire there, join the artist colony Carmel-by-the-Sea, and paint the waves on the beach at night that glowed fluorescent green against the sparkling stars in the velvet black sky. When I played my flute to The First Time Ever I Saw Your Face by Roberta Flack, all I could think about was Mama's face. I had a primal craving so strong it completely overwhelmed me. There was so much I wanted to tell her and so much love I had to give to her. The classical piano pieces that Michal had given to me also soothed my aching soul.

My parents and their richer and more elegant friends from Illinois came to take me out to dinner for my twenty-seventh birthday. They arrived in their Cadillac and took me to a very elegant restaurant. I was out of money, living on rabbit food, a broken wing, and a prayer, pretending to be happy.

"It is just so cute that you are living as a bohemian and are so intellectual," Mother said in front of her au courant friend whose daughters she idolized as if they should have been her own.

"Good-bye, dear," she said as they drove off.

She had no idea I was completely dysfunctional, penniless and on the verge of suicide. Father and Rob didn't give a damn about me. It was because of my fear of them that I was homeless since 1970 moving from place to place for five long years. "Who was my father and what was my family name? Was I from an important family with money?" I wondered.

Sam's nudist girlfriend, the current mistress of the famous writer Henry Miller, the Monkish Sage of Big Sur, brought over some primrose plants and planted them on the front porch of the cottage after I moved out of Jane's. I thanked her with a fern and Sam told me she had named it Melinda, after me. Someone told me that she was bi-sexual, so I kept my distance. Sam's friends were a strange and a very far-out group. She thought I was a female Truman Capote, also an orphan. I thought I was way out of my league, but was pleased to be acknowledged by and around famous intellectuals and artists.

Miller wrote his first story *Clipped Wings* about gentle

souls insulted and injured who ran amok or suffered violence that ended in murder or suicide. He could have been writing about me. My liminal (genetic) self was mysteriously in charge, and no one else was going to deceive or lead me down the primrose path again. I had to stay alive and in control no matter what happened.

There was a fork in the road to my future and my sanity. California was not for me. I needed to go to The Cradle in Illinois in person to find the truth.

"My famous movie star friend, Clint Eastwood, is having a party and you're invited," Chris informed me.

"Chris, I just bought a plane ticket to go to my aunt's so I can go to the adoption agency in person. You'll have to find another place to live. I've been looking for myself and my mother in all the wrong places for five long years," I said to him.

I knew if I met this gorgeous star, I might fall in love with him and never get away from Carmel. My decision was to go to Illinois, the place of my birth and say good-bye to my friends and the land of fruits and nuts.

18

Social Wreckers

I gained the courage to call Mother's best friend, Jean Alice Little, who lived near The Cradle in Illinois. Her husband's father was a senator in 1902 and then the Governor of Illinois from 1921-29. She married into a newspaper empire and I was hoping she would let me stay with her while I visited The Cradle.

Their oldest son stayed with our family in California and had fraternity parties at our house while he was attending Stanford University. Mother kept him out of jail during a hazing incident when one of the pledges almost died from being tarred, feathered, and left for dead on the side of a remote road during the initiation ritual. Jean Alice owed Mother a favor. She was delighted and said yes! I flew to O'Hare where their limo driver met me and drove me to their home in Moline.

Jean Alice's son Jed was my age and I knew that Mother hoped we would marry. The fact that he wasn't my blood cousin or really related was never mentioned even though I called his mother Aunt. Mother desperately wanted me to marry into the right family with old money. He wanted to help me and was nice enough to drive me to The Cradle adoption agency so I could talk to the social worker who I was sure would tell me everything about my blood mother and father.

"It's against the law for you to know anything other than unidentifying information," the social worker informed me.

"I need to know my real identity or I'll die. You don't know what it's like not being allowed to know what my name is or who I am so I can stand on my own two feet and be a real person. You are forcing me to live a lie," I replied on the verge of hysteria.

She watched me sob and said, "I'm sorry, dear. I'm just not allowed to tell you. The Kleenex is on the desk," she said with a blank look on her face.

"You know what you are? You're social wreckers, not social workers. You are making me feel like a monstrous Frankenbaby. It's you who have taken normal human beings and turned us into schizophrenic freaks with dual identities after adoption and brainwashed us to think we can live a fictionalized life with no real access to our true blood identity. How do you look yourself in the mirror and sleep at night? I have no idea who I even look like and maybe have a dual personality because of this closed adoption," I managed to tell her and left.

"Those idiots and abusers probably think I'm maladjusted. Don't they know that I was someone else when I was born? I was another person then and the crazy laws changed my name and turned me into someone else. God! They are totally insane to do this to adoptees and think it doesn't matter to us when we are adults," I muttered to Jed who tried to cheer me up.

"Mother is having a big ham for Thanksgiving," he said to change the subject.

"I really don't care if she has the Queen of England for Thanksgiving," I said through my tears.

Looking for Dorothy

The social worker from The Cradle wrote me another letter after my visit. It arrived January 28, 1976. She once again danced around the issues and told me she would help me get therapy if I wanted it. She reminded me that I had written to her in 1970, 1971, and again in 1973. I wanted real names and places, not more unidentifying information or therapy. Therapy didn't work and couldn't fix my problems. I knew their lies were the cause of my dysfunction and couldn't comprehend why this woman didn't understand or care.

I wrote to the Department of Health, Education, and Welfare in Chicago and asked them to find all available data on my biological mother. They wrote back telling me they were sorry they couldn't help me locate her. By law and Social Security Regulations, they were not able to divulge any information about any individual without his or her written consent, and in some cases not even with their written consent.

"Now I get it why you are so screwed up," Jed said to me.

"How would they like it if they had their identity taken away from them? It should be against the law and I'm going to fight for my 'right to know' if it kills me. They are messing with my mind and it's insane what they have done to me. It's abusive and it's identity theft."

We flew out to Los Angeles for Jed's brother's wedding held at the Beverly Wilshire Hotel. The reception was held at Eric von Stroheim's widow's estate. Jed showed me a music video he made at Stanford as a film student on their TV. He idolized the von Stroheims. Unfortunately they meant nothing to me, as I wanted to know my own name. Everyone else knew who he or she was but me, and it left me an outsider, off balance, and without a true family background or purpose always. No one cared about who I was or that I was distraught because I didn't fit in anywhere. Most of the time I felt like a ghost.

"Stroheim wanted to create a false identity and was really the son of a Viennese Jewish haberdasher. Isn't that crazy that you really do have a hidden secret identity?" Jed said to me.

"Yes, it's mental torture and sheer madness."

Sleeping on French Portault sheets, meeting famous people, being a hostess with the mostest, and having everything money could buy still wasn't enough for me to marry him. Beer and pot were the loves of his life as was music and his acoustic guitar. He played the guitar and composed a beautiful etude for flute called Melinda's Song. Requiem for a Lost Soul or Looney Tunes would have been more appropriate compositions. I tried to make the relationship work, but it was useless. He had no idea the pain I was in as an adoptee. My aunt made sure I was on the runway modeling for a local fundraiser and I found a black vocal teacher to teach me how to sing soul music like Gladys Knight.

"You play such beautiful music on your flute," Ardella, their southern black maid, told me. "I know you're lonely," she admitted in a southern drawl.

"All I want to do is find my mother. I have this person inside of me that has important things to say yet isn't allowed to talk," I told her thinking she would never tell anyone.

I was really up against my last wall. Jean Alice wanted to help me get an apartment in Chicago and become a stockbroker, but that was out of the question. She was all excited about buying and restoring an old historic working farm. Their family practically owned the entire town.

"What would you do with $100,000? Do you want to know about options?" she kept asking me.

I was heartbroken and losing all hope. It wasn't money I wanted or to live alone in Chicago, it was finding my identity and going home to meet my own Mama. Living in Chicago alone was *way* too triggering for me and the thought scared me to death. I felt like my head was a helium balloon tied to a string hovering high above my body because most of the time my life was an out of body experience.

Out of sheer desperation I wrote to my old friend, the conga drummer, to tell him what happened at the adoption agency and that my heart was broken in a million little pieces. He wrote me back, signing the letter Michael the Love Angel, with a drawing of the same two hearts I drew that morning on a piece of paper at my desk at The Journal. Did we have mental telepathy? This frightened me enough to never contact him again. He owed me money and took illegal drugs, and I thought he might be criminally insane. Mother called him *de classe*, which he was.

Everything in my world was wrong even though I was in the world of the upper classes including Wasps with pedigrees meeting many influential and distinguished people who attended my aunt's parties. The elites from the publishing and newspaper world were there, as well as the man who created the Golden Delicious apple, and a famous pianist, to name a few. I could have found an aristocratic wealthy and well-connected husband if I wanted to, but nothing mattered to me anymore until I found my own mother, Dorothy Lumsley.

Marrying wealth might have meant something to Mother, but it meant nothing to me. I wanted to be away from my alcoholic Republican, country club, golfer adopters and with my own tribe or clan of people to have my own authentic life or die. The charade had to end. I tried to put on a happy face, but the happy façade was hiding a very depressed adoptee.

I wrote to my married writer friend in California to see if I could come and stay with him in Three Rivers. He told me in a letter that the arrival of a beautiful blonde would not sit well with his wife and sent me a copy of an unpublished children's story he wrote called "Anatole the Mule Who Won the Grand National." Anatole was disguised as a racehorse just as I was an adoptee disguised as a Meyer. Why didn't he tell me he was Jewish and a writer/producer for Universal Studios? Or that he co-wrote *The Invisible Man Returns* and *The Invisible Woman* in 1949? I told him about my marriage to the Satanist and that it was right out of a horror movie. So was my life.

I knew from his letter that this married man had no idea about who I really was, nor did he appreciate the horror I had seen in my life. The long blonde hair made him think I was another dumb Hollywood starlet using my looks to get by. Not many knew about the secret life or death struggle that had become my life. He told me if I wanted to write the horror story and book about my marriage to Casey I should call it, "I Married a Satanist," and to write it like a woman possessed.

"Spin yourself," he wrote. "This is the door to success. Start at six in the morning or work at night. But work. See, if you want to be a writer you have to go through a valley of tears. But were there no valleys, there wouldn't be mountains. The deeper the valley the higher the mountain. So don't cry on anybody's shoulder."

The letter was encouraging, but I was in no shape to write the story. I thought if Casey found me, he would kill me. I was in the valley all right, the valley of the shadow of death.

One late Sunday afternoon, I was sitting in silence, alone in my aunt's family room and a "bear's head against a big full moon" appeared in the pattern of the fabric on their antique prayer stool cover. Why was I seeing this particular vision in the abstract patchwork? The bears had disappeared from my dreams when we left Ohio. Having the artist's eye and an abstract mind probably explained it. What did this mystical relationship with bears mean? The bears in some form were always with me. It was a mysterious and weird bond as they were always appearing and disappearing. I never understood the connection or why I was seeing them. My confusion and anxiety were so overwhelming that I got down on my hands and knees praying to God to help me make sense of it. Now I was begging Him to grant me this last wish and went so far as to promise to never ever do anything bad and that I would dedicate the rest of my life to doing good if he would lead me to my mother and the truth about myself. What I needed was a miracle!

19

The Accidental Actress

My last resort was a call to my friend Janet, the aspiring actress, writer, socialite, and secret natural grandmother living in Carmel who told me she wanted me to meet the famous ex-president of MGM and family friend of a president who was living in New York City in The River House.

I waited until my aunt and uncle left on a trip to call a driver and fly to LaGuardia Airport in New York City. There I hailed a cab to take me to the St. Regis Hotel in Manhattan. The next morning, after a relaxing massage in my room, I walked to the Museum of Modern Art and then to the Metropolitan Museum of Art to later return to get ready for my big date with Bo. My secret and deceptive plan was to be back in their house in three days before they returned as if I had been there all the time.

My date was arranged and there I was waiting in the hotel room for this King of Hollywood to come and get me for a night out on the town. I opened the door and there stood a short, fairly attractive man with pockmarks like giant craters on his face. This couldn't be the tall, handsome man named Bo Janet told me about. This man standing in front of me wore a burgundy velvet jacket with a paisley ascot and looked more like the Pillsbury Doughboy than a handsome movie star.

"I'm Bo's best friend and he asked me to escort you to his penthouse," he said in a phony British accent as he took my arm and off we went. The children's stories were tucked under my other arm as I was hoping Bo might read them and help me find a publisher. We arrived at the penthouse, and to my dismay Bo wasn't there. How rude of him I thought to myself after going out of my way to find just the right dress at Bloomingdales late that afternoon for the occasion.

"Bo had to go out and will be back later," he told me while opening a bottle of Dom Perignon and began to pour the champagne into Bo's expensive Lalique flute glass.

"I'm the owner of a tennis club where all the celebrities belong and I'm also producing the movie *The Man in the Iron Mask* in Canada," he proudly announced after our fifth glass of bubbly.

"I guess I'm the woman in the iron mask?" I said drunk out of my mind so disappointed that Bo wasn't there.

"You look like my close friend, the elegant Princess Grace Kelly except you have piercing wild animal eyes that are much more exotic and intimidating than hers. Will you be my Princess Grace?" he growled and tried to put his arm around me.

"Why would I want to be Princess Grace when I didn't even know my own name? I already was living as another person and was having to waste ten good years of my life trying to find the real me and my real name. Looking into a mirror was confusing enough. Would I really want to see Princess Grace looking back at me?" was racing through my mind like a silent movie not to mention he was reminding me of Rob.

I laughed and just kept nervously chewing my bubblegum furiously, thinking he was an idiot, and I chugged down the champagne when he held out the palm of his hand.

"Give me the gum. Grace wouldn't do that." He made me spit my gum into the palm of his hand. He reached into his pocket and pulled out a huge bundle of one hundred-dollar bills and flipped them in my face.

"If you will be my Grace, I will put you up in an apartment in Talouca Lake, have you dressed by Edith Head, and you can be one of my girls," he said with a straight face. "In fact I will change your name and make you into a movie star! How would you like that?"

I couldn't believe I was hearing this when Bo suddenly appeared in the room. If this is how the shy socialite from Philadelphia became a movie star and married a prince, I wanted nothing to do with it. This shy socialite was no dumb blonde. Bo went into his dressing room and came out in his boxer shorts and proceeded to get into his king size bed.

"Why don't you spend the night here?" he suggested and all three of us got into his bed with me fully clothed wedged in between the two of them who were in their boxer shorts. It wasn't long before I felt Bo's hand on my thigh.

"If you want a threesome you can both go straight to Hell you perverted creeps. You had better respect the power of the heart, you pieces of worthless trash. My grandfather has more class in his little finger than you could ever think of having," I said as they turned into Rob and Father in my mind triggering a panic attack. I practically flew out of the bed, making a bee-line out the door, totally forgetting to take my manuscripts.

Drunk and offended, I bolted out of the door into the elevator hitting the basement button by mistake. I ended up in the pitch black basement disoriented, drunk, and hyperventilating. The green glow of the elevator button led me back to the elevator after groping around in the dark I finally hit the M for the main floor.

It was now three in the morning as I came staggering out of the apartment building, asking the doorman to call a taxi. These powerful playboys had betrayed me and triggered my post-traumatic stress reaction from being stalked by Rob. Sexploitation was always the trigger. The reason I was in this mad, mad world in the first place was because of some untrustworthy man who was mostly likely a womanizer who probably sexually betrayed my mother Dorothy.

There went my big Hollywood career even though I could have been in my own real life movie Coming Out of the Adoptee Fog wearing a white straight jacket, breaking open the ties with a cute little outfit underneath while singing "I Will Survive," I mused and vowed to myself "I will never give up," and fell asleep in the hotel bed with my clothes on hating the world and everyone in it.

Once back at my aunt's no one knew I was gone except the maid who I swore to secrecy. I knew my time there was running out and I would be homeless again. After more than thirty unwanted moves in my life, I was very tired. Even so I took one more secret trip to New York City to go to all the art galleries and museums when they were away to a newspaper convention. The jewelry designer for Tiffany I met in a bar was my last port in the storm.

"Vhat do you vant from me?" he asked me in his Russian accent as we were standing in his tiny, dingy apartment bedroom somewhere in Manhattan.

"I don't know, but it has to do with me being adopted, having no roots, being an artist, and losing my identity, and soon I'll be homeless again," I said in a whisper.

"What? I'm sorry, but you can't live here with me. You are too high strung and mixed up to live vith me. I don't even know you. Who are you anyway? Some inbred royal bastard?"

The plane back to O'Hare had been delayed due to a snowstorm, so I took a cab from his tiny apartment to the MoMA where I felt at home.

"Where can I find people my own age? I have two hours until my flight leaves," I asked two well-dressed ladies in the museum.

"Go to Maxwell's Plum," they said in unison.

I hailed a taxi and went to Maxwell's to get some warm spinach salad and wonder what I was going to do now that Jed and I weren't getting married. My false self was so burned out I didn't want to live anymore. In walked two guys.

One was tall, the other shorter, yet mysterious, Hollywood handsome and well-built, with beautiful jet black hair and big exotic almond-shaped brown eyes. They walked by me and then sat at a little table right across from mine. The good looking stranger with the gorgeous head of black hair was so funny I couldn't help laughing as I ate my salad listening to him cracking jokes. The more I laughed the funnier he got. Pretty soon we began to talk and he invited me to his table for some wine. He was a cross between Lenny Bruce, Don Knots, Jackie Gleason, and Elvis.

Both of us had done psychedelics. Jerry had mainly smoked pot and taken forty acid trips. Timothy Leary was an acquaintance of his. Was this funny man who drove an old silver Lincoln Town car the answer to my prayers? He came from an affluent Russian Jewish family and was brilliant, handsome, a writer, and a comedian. His answer for most people was simple.

"I do think that most people need a couple of doses of acid and a lot of sleep. I dropped an LSD laced sugar cube in Manhattan and it went off like a bomb in my body in the middle of the Triboro Bridge. I thought I was dying. Totally disoriented, my instinct took over and somehow I drove to Kings Point to meet up with fellow trippers where I left my car in the middle of the street to lay down on the grass and die. An experienced head told me to go with it, and it ended up a visually stunning experience altering me forever," he told me.

"How old are you?" I asked him.

"Thirty-four," he answered.

"I'm twenty-nine."

He had me howling with laughter when he told me about the time he and some of his friends were driving around Brookville, Long Island, when they were pulled over by the police.

"We were carrying a five-gallon pickle jar full of marijuana seeds. There were enough seeds in that jar to get everyone in Manhattan high. Somehow we convinced the police we were florists and were let go," he said laughing.

"I was with a Pre-Med student once who was taking pot across the border to Canada. He was thinking the police at the border were psychic and knew where his pot was hidden. He made me think of the word 'pink' as we went through customs so they wouldn't know it was behind the car radio," I told him and laughed even harder.

"My mother started an aerospace metal business in 1955 after my father died. She's one of the first women in the country to run a successful nickel alloy metal business," he informed me.

"What happened to your father?"

"He died of a stroke when I was five. I hate my stepfather and my half-brother," he admitted.

"We have something in common; I hate one of my adoptive brothers and my adoptive father, too."

"My mother remarried and had my half-brother with her second husband," Jerry told me.

"Are you a trust fund baby like I am?" I asked him.

"Of course," he answered.

"Did you love your black maid better than your own mother?" I asked him.

"Not really, but when my mother went to work, Margaret, our black maid, took care of us. I had no one to talk to as a kid so I talked to myself. Come home with me tonight," he asked hoping I might go home with him right then and there.

"Listen, I'm too burned out to play games with you. If you want a serious relationship, call me at the newspaper," I told him and wrote my phone number on a napkin.

I began to write long letters to him explaining my predicament and how I needed to find Dorothy. He began to call me at the Journal to finally tell me about his aunt and uncle who were lawyers and that he would ask them to help me.

Oh, Lord, how long do I have to wait to find her? Being from a closed adoption had ruined my life.

I had a paying job at The Journal as a reporter and knew that couldn't last too much longer. Jerry called repeatedly to tell me that I should come and see his house in the woods. It was flattering and annoying at the same time. I wasn't going to marry Jed and I was too afraid to go to Chicago alone to become a stockbroker like his mom wanted me to. No one knew me because I didn't know me.

While in my aunt's elegant dressing room, sneaking a Seconol to calm my nerves, I saw a letter Mother had written to her. It read, "Please take care of my schizophrenic daughter." I couldn't believe my eyes. She was really crazy to think I was a schizo when it was adoption that was schizophrenic. Did she know that her son Rob was the schizo? My suspicions were right: both Jean Alice and Mother weren't to be trusted. I was so insulted, frightened and dreadfully hurt that I had to get the heck out of there to save my own soul. The only thing I wanted to be committed to was finding a safe home, the truth, and my roots. Just to see my genetic mother, father, grandparents, aunts, uncles, cousins, great or great great relatives would have helped me to become more stable and rooted in reality.

Dandelion Beer

Once again I began to trust a total stranger and off I flew to visit this fascinating man in an upscale community in the woods of Northern Westchester in New York. Sam and I had actually stopped there on our trip back from Toronto years before, and I liked the elegant and sophisticated country lifestyle and natural woodsy setting at that time. I loved to be outdoors and liked the idea of living within quiet wetlands of a deciduous forest among the foxes, raccoons, deer, hawks, cinnamon ferns, jack in the pulpits, wild geraniums and incredible natural beauty. The woods always felt like home to me and hopefully Casey would never find me there. I would also be far away from my adoptive family.

Jerry left the insanity of Long Island and purchased a cozy little ranch style house in the woods. It was now 1976.

He asked me to come and live with him and I said yes.

Spring was in full force as I lay among the returning song birds and the frogs singing in the vernal pools in the wetlands surrounding the house. The lush leaves and ferns looked as if they had been dipped in liquid light and the rocks and trees, nature's sculptures. I imagined myself a wood nymph dancing among the trees on the gorgeous moss-carpeted forest floor. It was heavenly.

Jerry was a deep thinker and extremely bright, not to mention hilariously funny. He was interesting and from a very different background. His writing was captivating as I read a screenplay he wrote about hunters and fur trappers killing wolves on his property just outside of Montreal. He and the wolves were pitted against the evil fur trappers. The protagonist's cause for animal rights was a good against evil story like mine. He and his Jewish ex-wife bought a house in the deep woods of La Macaza, Montreal where they raised and sold Christmas trees. No wonder the marriage didn't work out. He had married a Jewish American Princess, and he was an unconventional loner.

A prominent agency represented his screenplay and a very famous movie producer was going to produce it, but bought *Rosebud* instead.

I loved Jerry's writing. He was a Capricorn, and I was an Aries. Perhaps our relationship worked because I was a fire sign and had no planets in earth signs and he was an earth sign, plus we both were born on the 9th. He told me I had a man's mind and reminded him of an inbred racehorse because I was so high strung. He was Russian and had a thing for blonde WASP girls. Perhaps we had known each other in a past life. Mother said it was because I couldn't castrate him, but his mother had already done that. In reality, both of us had artistic temperaments and big loss issues and we saved each other from the looney bin.

I began to paint murals on the walls. The scenes of rolling green fields, streams, hills, and forests with big, deep, blue skies poured out of me. I didn't know why I was painting them, but felt free, happy and safe for the first time in years because Jerry let me be myself.

"My mother is cold and abusive. I know you've suffered and I understand and will take care of you," he promised.

He encouraged me to be myself and we made each other laugh. Finally, I found someone funny with a big heart who enjoyed nature and living in the woods as much as I did.

"You remind me of Vincent Van Gogh," he said.

"You remind me of funny animated cartoon character The Little King penned by Otto Soglow in 1937."

Still part California flower child, I decided to impress Jerry and make dandelion beer. The idea came from my brilliant Polish friend from San Jose State who was dying from a brain tumor. His best friends made rose petal flavored beer and invited me and his closest friends to a kind of Last Supper party for him to celebrate his life before he faced the great beyond. We had a special bond and he was convinced my IQ was 170 or higher after I wrote him a very personal goodbye letter and story about his soul. The roses weren't in bloom, so I thought I would improvise with the dandelions growing in the wetlands. I learned of his death and it seemed fitting to honor his memory with a glass of homemade dandelion beer and the Cat Stevens song *Moon Shadow*, his favorite, and *Oh, Baby, Baby, It's A Wild World*, my favorite. I put all the ingredients altogether in a glass jar and let it ferment in the kitchen cupboard and promptly forgot about it until one late afternoon when we heard a huge explosion.

"What was that?" asked Jerry in his deep booming voice after a particularly passionate love making session.

"I think I forgot to leave the top off of the jar of the beer and it might have exploded!" I told him as he fell to the floor in a panic and I ran to the kitchen to see thousands of shards of glass and bits of dandelion flowers strewn all over the floor and countertops.

"You could have killed me you idiot," Jerry yelled.

"I could have killed me and you," I cried.

I mean what more could you expect from an adopted northern European child of alcoholics? Jerry's knowledge of botany went about as far as knowing what marijuana seeds looked like and mine wasn't much better. He was so neurotic that he even tried to get me to wear a hair net while cooking so my hair wouldn't fall into his food!

Fortunately, he supported me in my search. I knew that my mother was Dorothy Lumsley and that she and my father were living within a one hundred-mile radius of Chicago. He helped me compose a search letter, taking over when it became too painful for me. I drew a circle on a map within the radius from Chicago while my tears dropped like rain. He ordered phone books and off went a letter to every Lumsley we could find in cities within that circle. I sent out over 200 letters. All the letters that came back stated they did not know a Dorothy Lumsley and if they had a little girl, they never would have given her up. Each letter was like a stab in my heart forcing me to run for the Valium for sedation.

Time passed and I once more had the courage to search. I began to correspond with a private investigator. By this time I became a force of nature and a force to be reckoned with. Jean Paton, the founder of the search group Orphan Voyage, gave me an investigator's name for search assistance. She said she hoped to get open records soon. He wrote to me and gave me some hints and ideas, but I didn't have the money to pay him for more.

"It may be years, if ever, until the records would be open to adoptees," he told me.

Slowly, I revealed my story to Jerry who seemed to get it like no one else ever had. It took a while for him to see that my anxiety and crying spells from the traumatic losses and abuses in my life had emotionally crippled me. I usually cried in the car or in the shower so he wouldn't hear me. Whenever he heard me crying and saw me shaking he made me take the little yellow pill that calmed me and stopped the pain. I couldn't regulate my own emotions during these episodes. He had a few secrets of his own.

"I couldn't fight in Vietnam because of mental troubles and was diagnosed with schizophrenia and depression from the LSD. The army sent me a letter falsely stating I had syphilis. I have been seeing a shrink and taking tranquilizers for years," he confided.

The acid trips really turned his brain into scrambled eggs. We realized diet pills compounded my problems and down the toilet they went. I still couldn't tell him about Rob and Father. Jerry sang the blues better than Billie Holiday. He sang *Good Morning Heartache* to me over and over and over, night after night, in front of the fire until I fell asleep. My spiritual self-education continued. Reading *Khrishnamurti, The Tao of Physics* and *Sai Baba and the Psychiatrist* helped me tremendously to remain loving, tolerant, positive, and strong.

I now had someone to help me with my emotions. Being a fly on the wall of my own mind took some time explaining.

20

Worlds in Collision

Before long, Mother and Father flew out to meet my new man.

"You're living in a cottage not a house. Why does it look like a Scandinavian farmhouse inside?" Mother asked with disdain as she handed me a little box with diamond stud earrings in it.

I don't care! I thought but dared not voice. *It's our cozy ranch house in the woods and I like it. It's warm and feels like home to me. What did she expect, Windsor Castle?*

"Jerry is a double-talking playboy and will most likely leave you. Why have you thrown your life away?" she asked me.

"He went to Adelphi Academy and has an MBA Degree from NYU. Did you bring the Keane painting and the Montoya?" I asked her wanting to say instead, "You are a silent enabler and unlike you, Jerry is going to help me find my mother, and I know you think I'm insane."

"Your father has them in the rental car," she answered.

I threw my entire refined and elegant WASP upbringing away in her eyes and was going to marry a spoiled New York Jewish playboy with a wealthy mother and Eastern European Russian roots. She must have died inside, thinking she wasted all that money and all those years teaching me to be the perfectly-mannered English lady. She was horrified that I didn't even have a dishwasher, let alone was in love with a Jewish prince and not a legitimate blue-blooded one.

Her dreams for me of being a proper wife were dashed, although I had been a really good adopted child. Hard as she tried, she couldn't change my basic personality, my easygoing and fun loving nature, or the past. She felt the same way about Jack when he married a middle-class German fundamentalist missionary. I knew she thought we were both lost causes and not the blank slates the social workers told her we were. We were being forced to think of ourselves as Meyer's with a sterling reputation to uphold, and yet we carried within us our natural relatives' energy patterns, personalities, talents, and genes. Mother acknowledged Jack and my unknown relatives as damaged goods or inferiors. It didn't occur to any of us that Jack and I were an invisible minority, as adoptees from closed adoptions, born into a cycle of abuse with no rights.

"The Meyer's are not who we are. I'm Baby Girl Lumsley and I plan on finding out the truth about Jack," kept running through my mind over and over again. It was becoming apparent to me that holding all these thoughts inside without being able to talk about them was creating two people inside of me and that was unhealthy and the probable source of my illness.

"Your father and I will never come back until you have a proper mother-in-law's room for us to stay in. I don't like staying in an inn," she informed me when we were at Neiman Marcus buying Jerry a sterling silver key chain. "I don't understand why you don't want a man to lean on, not one that leans on you," she uttered after a couple of drinks.

Mother was so angry that I wasn't serving them breakfast at our almost empty and poorly-furnished little cottage. Jerry, the preppie hipster and I were very unconventional and had been damaged from our traumas and losses. Jerry was giving me courage to stand up to Mother as my artificial self was making way for my authentic genetic self to emerge like a beautiful butterfly. I watched Father's hands shake as he poured bourbon into his morning coffee. He was not really welcome in my house so I played the best game of Let's Pretend You and Your Son Aren't Abusive, Alcoholic Perverts and You Aren't My Natural Father not to mention it's your fault I'm sitting here in this cottage in the woods thousands of miles away from you. As always I looked "apple pie normal" and no one would guess there was anything wrong between us.

I was beyond dysfunctional and Mother had no idea what I had been through. She didn't know me at all, but saw me through narcissistic eyes and had the nerve to blame me for ruining her relationships with Jean Alice. Later I found out she was to blame.

I couldn't stand up to either of them and made one of the toughest decisions of my life and that was to let them go.

"Do you at least know the names of any of these trees?" she asked me in the car on the way to an elegant Sunday brunch at a beautiful country estate built in 1907 by JP Morgan overlooking the Hudson Valley called Le Chateau.

"We have a tulip tree that drops beautiful green and orange flowers that land right on the dirt driveway in June," I answered hoping this and the French restaurant would impress her.

She seemed to enjoy using her famous botanist father as a weapon to make me look stupid forever talking about her father's very valuable 3-volume collection of rare prints from the Pinetum Britannicum that Rob was to inherit.

"What's a Pinetum?" Jerry asked her trying not to laugh.

"A collection of hardy coniferous pines cultivated in Great Britain. The prints were printed in 1884 in London by her Majesty, Queen Victoria, in memory, of H.R.H. Prince Consort who was the German Prince Albert."

She went on and on talking about how many of the pines were transplanted by the Queen to her Osborne Estate. She told us the Victorian masterpiece of hand colored lithography was so important that the queen became its first subscriber and then Napoleon the III.

"Did you know The Pinetum is considered to be the most important study of the English naturalized conifers ever produced and only 10 copies were ever printed? The original plates are housed at the British Museum of Natural History in London. Did you take Latin?" she asked Jerry.

"No, I took Hebrew for my Bar Mitzvah," he answered.

"How lovely," she replied with that fake and condescending tone she used when she was being snobby.

"My father's family came from Vinnitsa, Russia. I love the woods like your daughter does. These woods remind me of the ancient Baltic forests where my ancestors lived. I hear the coyotes howling at night and it's all so cosmic," he told them.

"Sometimes the dead tree trunks look like huge wolves. There are so many natural sculptures in nature. I love it here and feel at home here," I exclaimed.

"Melinda is so talented. Of course you know what a gifted artist she is," he rambled on as they sat there in silence.

The names of my own family trees were the only trees I was interested in knowing and if that made me schizophrenic then so be it.

I knew how disappointed she was that I wasn't going to marry into a family with old money from Bedford, New York, Greenwich, or New Canaan, Connecticut. There was no way she could relate to my life as a poor artist with no atelier, in a cottage in the woods, living with an irresponsible, spoiled, rich, eccentric, handsome, Russian Jewish playboy who was born in Brooklyn.

"Truth is the energy which keeps us alive. This life energy is within us as is the way to self-awareness and happiness. Did you know there is something called heart-consciousness?" Jerry asked them forgetting that they were conservative Christians and had never taken LSD.

"Really. Linda do you remember playing Prokofiev's musical composition from Peter and The Wolf on your flute, oboe and bassoon in high school?" Mother asked as if she didn't hear a word of what Jerry was saying.

"Sure, especially the part where the wolf swallows the

duck alive," I said to shock her with the insinuation that I was the dead duck.

"My favorite composition that you play is The Girl with the Flaxen Hair by Debussy. By the way do you still have that beautiful warm sweater that Nannie brought you from Norway?" she asked.

"No, but I have my flute and the rings Nannie gave to me," I replied.

Mother and I were light years apart. My Meyer self was still masochistically holding on to my love for her and did not want to hurt her. It wouldn't have been appropriate to lash back at her saying, "Let me hear you play the Bach Sonata No. 4 on my flute or actually sell a drawing and painting like I have and by the way do you know your son and husband are alcoholic perverts?"

"You know Linda, I think Jerry is the only man you couldn't castrate," she whispered in my ear as they left in the car.

A Most Wonderful Arrival

It was dumb luck that I found my way to Al-Anon, the support group for those who lived with alcoholics, after finding a little book that was sitting out of place on the grocery store shelf. The book was about coping with living with someone in denial about being addicted to alcohol. I carried it around in my hand like the Bible for days and days to help me cope with my anger triggered by my parents visit. The words helped me to feel grounded. Slowly, my understanding grew. It took me years to understand co-dependence and the effect being an adult child of an alcoholic had on a person. I wondered if my natural parents were alcoholics and I felt buried alive under a mountain of deep dark secrets, lies, and unresolved issues. My issues even had issues! It was rough making new friends as I was buried deeper than everyone else. I knew lots of alcoholics, but not one adoptee or incest survivor. How could I when these were topics no one in my adoptive family ever talked about?

The big-eyed blonde Keane and Montoya pictures went on my bedroom wall to keep me company. I loved having my own room again. Once again I took refuge in art and other artists. A local artist who owned a gallery taught me how to oil paint. Another noted female local artist taught me to draw objects and make them appear and disappear. She thought I could be an illustrator or graphic designer if I wanted to. Her drawing of a deer in the woods was magical because it would appear and disappear among the trees just as they did in our woods. This new way of perceiving and seeing would later emerge in my art.

Now that I had a home and was away from Mother and Father, my art and my cause celebre for open records for all adoptees grew from an acorn into a mighty oak. I painted an oil portrait of the daughter of the 39th president in 1977 and sent it to her at The White House. Along with the painting I wrote to the President why I thought records should not be sealed and about how adoptees should have the right to know who they are. I received a post card of a black and white photo of his daughter and a hand-printed note on the back from her thanking me for the painting. Years later, I found she was restoring old master paintings. Perhaps I had something to do with that. She would never understand what it was like being in my shoes having an adoptive mother who didn't know her daughter was an artist. I actually lugged an oil seascape all the way to California for Mother to see how good I was. She couldn't relate and barely acknowledged my beautiful painting seeming disappointed that I was a talented artist.

Upon my return from the trip home to California, Jerry and I were out having dinner one night at Nino's, an Italian restaurant in historic Bedford now The Bedford Post owned by a famous Hollywood actor.

"You're Joni Mitchell, aren't you?" a woman said to me as I sat at a table with Jerry. I told her I wasn't but she insisted and said, "Bye Joni" as she left.

"Jerry, if you don't marry me I'll leave. I'm two months

pregnant and we have to get married. You have to ask my father's permission," I said slurring my words from the vodka in my Bloody Mary.

"To hell I do," he answered defiantly as I got up from the table and ran across the street into the woods crying hysterically knowing then that I would never have a father to walk me down the isle of a church or be able to wear a beautiful white wedding dress at my own wedding. Jerry bolted from the table running to catch me, but I was already across the road hiding in the darkness of the woods when I heard him fall and moan,

"I'm hurt, help me Melinda."

I then realized he must have tripped and fallen over a low handmade stone wall and into a creek. I ran to him.

"I think I broke my arm and I chipped my tooth," he muttered in the darkness.

We arrived at the emergency room where Jerry found he had broken his wrist and needed a cast. Three days later he went to the dentist who put a cap on his broken front tooth.

The Justice of the Peace married us a week later, wounds and all. My Aunt Dorothy, Father's oldest sister, stopped sending me a birthday check because I married a Jew. Well that's what Mother told me.

My life became much more complicated because my mother-in-law despised Germans and spoke about it openly in front of me. I knew nothing about Jewish people and it didn't occur to me she had a Hebrew name before it was changed in Europe or that she might be a German Jew or have family members that were killed by Hitler. Crosses were forbidden in her household as she made it very clear to me she didn't believe in angels or Christ either. She was furious that Jerry's younger brother changed his name and he and his Jewish wife lived in Utah, became Mormons, and later had their kids convert to Catholicism. My mother-in-law made her grandchildren take off their crosses when they entered her house.

"This is a Jewish household and Jewish money. Either

you wear the Star of David or nothing around your necks in my house," she demanded of her now Christian offspring.

Now that I was a part of this alcoholic upper middle class Jewish family, every time Jerry's fat stepfather who dabbled in the business of industrial chemicals with Jerry's mother who sold aerospace metal greeted me he always tried to stick his tongue in my mouth for a French kiss just like Father did.

Seven months later, a son, my first flesh and blood relative was miraculously born to me on June 5, 1978. John was mine, all mine. I felt joy, love, and elation and showered him with a thousand kisses, love and affection. He had dark brown hair, brown eyes and looked like Jerry. Who did he look like in my family was the question?

Driving home from the hospital with our precious newborn was thrilling. We almost ran over a blonde long-haired afghan hound that ran in front of the car right across from the famous 100 year old Bedford Oak tree. She pounced on my lap when I opened the car door to escape a very angry man chasing and yelling in anger at her. He told us she had been abandoned and he rescued her from certain death as he found her loose and confused on the Long Island Expressway.

"She doesn't get along with my other dogs because she was traumatized from some sort of abuse and has some disturbing behaviors as a result," he informed us.

Now this was something I could identify with realizing I just rescued this regal creature from this man who was also verbally abusing her right in front of me. When God closes one door, he opens another.

"I'll take her," I told him and put her in the back seat of the car next to my newborn son to later adopt her for a quarter.

Jerry named her Peanuts. Her kibble would mysteriously end up in our shoes in the closet. The vet told me she was suffering from Post-Traumatic Stress Syndrome so I nursed her back to health. When she was happy, she ran around and around the house like a streak of lightning. We really formed a special bond of love, trust, and understanding.

I continued drawing lessons with Amy Jones who helped

me perfect my drawing skills until the sketches of Peanuts were good enough to frame.

"You're a female Picasso," the framer commented. "But you didn't sign them."

"I don't know what name to use: my maiden name, my married name, or my first name. I'd really like to sign it using my real name, but because I was adopted, I'm not allowed to know my name."

"Why?" he asked.

"It's illegal but I really don't know why."

"Why don't you use your first name," he suggested.

Being adopted had created a painful hidden and chaotic inner world, my artificial (fictional) self vs. my authentic (factual) self which had really messed up my head. Picasso's famous painting Guernica, depicting the bombing of Spain, looked exactly how fractured my psyche felt. Even so, the two perfectly drawn pencil portraits of my darling dog hung in my front hall with a signature M that looked like a long snake. I also painted watercolors of the beautiful loose-petal pink roses that grew next to the house. It was wonderful to create such delicate beauty.

Moth Monsters

Christmas in our little ranch house in the woods with Jerry and John wasn't complicated because I went out and bought a Christmas tree and put it in the living room and decorated it by myself. Every night I turned the lights on Jerry unplugged them. He didn't care for holidays of any kind yet he liked WASPY blonde girls while being clueless about our Christian customs. When Mother sent me gold hoop earrings for Christmas, I celebrated by myself because Jerry could have cared less.

"Why do Christians hate the Jews and they worship one?" Jerry asked me annoyed that I couldn't even pronounce Hanukkah correctly.

"It's complicated. I can't even believe that my parents never told me that Jesus and Mary were Jewish," I replied.

Jerry told me about his Jewish first wife who was an aspiring opera singer and thespian; she was both an aspiring actress and a lesbian or maybe just bisexual. Their relationship, like my first marriage, lasted less than a year.

I was deliriously happy to be married with a family of my own and to have given birth to a son, my only blood relative.

"Don't you see the French in him?" Jerry asked me over and over.

"I don't recognize him at all. I have no male biological relative to compare him to. He has your dark hair and brown eyes and looks nothing like me," I thought to myself.

"God, you lost your family and I lost my father as a child. I don't know which is worse," commented Jerry.

Jerry and I eventually slept in separate rooms because his snoring and constant body movements kept me awake.

"I can't live up to any of your expectations. In all honestly, I never travel except to the track or to Mommy's house," he confessed one morning.

"Mommy's house? You call your mother Mommy?" I asked realizing he was a real Mama's boy.

What was one more disappointment? Jerry was no woodsman. He loved nature but was afraid of moths. Worse, he had ridiculous aversion to killing insects that pestered us. His obsession with the bloodlines of race horses and addiction to Off Track Betting became apparent when I found a huge box full of his betting slips. He was gambling away all our money. What could I do but continue my search for Dorothy? I had to make the best of my situation, even though I desperately wanted to go home because Jerry was an angry, verbally abusive alcoholic who cared only for himself.

"You made your bed, you lie in it," Mother said after I called her crying wanting to come home.

"Why did you name your son John?" she inquired as if she didn't hear me.

"I don't know," I told her over the phone and hung up.

She always asked me such impossible questions which I could have answered, "Because I'm adopted, you idiot."

Time passed and it was now 1979 when Jerry's brother called to tell us about Rosalie. Bob, Jerry's brother, revealed that he had a son out-of-wedlock and located Rosalie, a search angel, through an ad in the Penny Saver they owned in a city on Long Island.

"Rosalie helped me find my lost son," he told me over the phone.

"Really, where is he? Is he alright?" I asked.

"He's depressed and angry, but I think Rose can help you find your birth mother. You must have some tall athletes in your family that's for sure because you're so tall and can run really fast and on the dance floor you dance like a pro," he said and gave me her phone number triggering a memory of the clairvoyant woman named Rose I met while sitting with my friend at Clint Eastwood's bar in Carmel.

This was my miracle! All my efforts were finally paying off and I was convinced God had heard me! It was no accident that I met this man whose brother was a birth father! It was very freaky that I was drawing and painting the pink roses growing outside our front door just before Rosalie appeared to help me find Mama. I couldn't ignore that just maybe there was some sort of synchronicity, precognition, and or higher power connecting me to my birth mother through a person named Rose, my art and God at work. Was there some big spiritual connection to my art and the truth? Was it God's plan? Was I finally channeling? God worked in very mysterious ways indeed.

My excitement grew even more as I also found out I was pregnant again. My hopes soared knowing that Rosalie might be able to help me find Dorothy at last, but I was too terrified to call her.

21

"Blood" Ties

Tim was born on December 28, 1980 after our second year together as a legitimate family. I had another baby of my own to hug and kiss. He was almost born in the backseat of our car when he arrived during a huge nor'easter. The nurse gently put him on my chest after a grueling labor and delivery.

"Look at his big eyes and his bald head," she said.

"Why is he covered in cottage cheese? His skin is so white. Are you sure he isn't an albino or an alien?" I asked the nurse.

"No, he looks like you," she affirmed.

Once again there was joy, love, and elation although I did buy a beautiful white dress hoping he would be a she. I loved being a mother, teacher, and nurturer. He was so cute and reflected my lost male and female birth relatives just as John did.

Jerry's very Jewish mother told us that when it came to his name we had to go by Jewish custom and name him after my husband's dead father Abraham.

"I'm sorry but there will be no juniors in our family," she said to me.

"I'm sorry too, but there will be no Abrahams in my family," I told Jerry.

We compromised and gave him Jerry's stepfather's first name David as his official middle name.

I finally mustered enough courage to call Rosalie to ask her if she knew how to get my birth records for me!

"Once you find your mother you will finally be able to heal the terrible grief you have lived with since you were separated at birth. Reuniting is the only answer to that pain," she informed me.

"I hope so. The search has almost killed me. Even if I hadn't been abused in my adoptive family I love my biological mother and still need to find her," I admitted.

"You were abused? I'm so sorry but so glad you called me and I can help you find Dorothy. Leave it all up to me. It may take me awhile but just know I'm working on it for you," she said.

A big fat envelope from the hospital where I was born in Chicago, Illinois arrived a few weeks later. The writing on the birth record stated that Dorothy Lumsley lived in Wisconsin Dells, Wisconsin! The document stated that Baby Girl Lumsley was born in Chicago and delivered by Dr. David Turow. Wasn't he the father of Scott, the famous novelist? Even though I had been searching for Dorothy all my life, I didn't have the courage to call her.

"Did you realize the scenes you painted on the walls look like scenes from Wisconsin and Minnesota? You even painted the sky the same color blue. The sky there is bluer than in New York," Jerry told me.

"Really? Are you sure? How bizarre. I think I have been channeling the truth through my art without realizing it. It's like some mystic chords of cellular memory are tying us all together. It must be an unbreakable bond," I said in amazement.

"Maybe you have an unseen and inescapable blood and psychic bond to Dorothy. Perhaps you are a part of the same genetic blueprint and eternally bound. That is just so far out!" he exclaimed.

Another letter to The Cradle was my last attempt to get them to tell me more. I wanted to know who might have looked like my blue-eyed son in my natural family. Jerry thought Tim was another man's baby because he didn't recognize his own sons Aryan features. I had been brainwashed to think I was English without ever thinking about what I looked like as a newborn. The only picture I ever saw of myself was when I was sitting on Gaga's lap after being adopted.

A letter from the adoption agency arrived October 8, 1981.

> My Dear, First of all, let me make this comment that we have been writing to you since 1970. Believe me; we enjoy hearing from our "Cradle Children." You are the one who told us that "Lumsley" is the name of your birth mother. You must have your adoption decree to get the name or maybe your parents told you. If Lumsley was on the decree, she did not use an alias. Attached is the letter we sent you with the descriptions of your natural parents. You could have a blonde-haired child with blue eyes. What about your father's family?
>
> If I failed to tell you of your birth mother's education, you can know now that she had one year of schooling after she finished high school. Truthfully, I have given you all that I can, practically all that we have. If you read your letters carefully, you will know that we cannot give you names and locations. Should you want more, you will have to go through court under our present state legislation. We understand your curiosities.
>
> Why don't you enjoy your family and make life for all of you not only happy but also meaningful? You are so gifted.
>
> Sincerely, Mrs. Jean McGill, Social Worker.

I didn't want to believe that my parents knew who my parents were all along and didn't tell me or that this woman from The Cradle was lying to and deceiving me.

"Let's check to see if Dorothy is listed in the Wisconsin Dells phone directory," Jerry said and picked up the phone for information.

"Thank you operator," Jerry said and wrote down a phone number.

"We did it! You finally found her," I screamed and was so filled with anxiety that Jerry had to give me two valiums to calm me down.

Jerry dialed the number for me put the phone in my shaky hands as I was barely able to breathe when a woman's voice answered.

"Is this Dorothy Lumsley?" I inquired.

"Yes, it is," she replied in a soft voice.

"Is this the Dorothy who gave up a little girl for adoption in 1947?"

"Who is this?" she asked and began to scream hysterically until I had to hang up and immediately called Rosalie for help.

"This is a normal reaction. What you need to do is to send her a letter along with baby pictures and just wait. Give her some time and I know she will write to you," she said.

Three months later, the first letter arrived.

"Yes, I am your mother," it said.

She never put her return address on the envelopes of our secret letters from the first letter in 1981 through her last letter in 1994. My mother remained just a voice on the phone.

"I kept you a secret all my life. If anyone should ever find out about you, they would outcast me for deceiving them," she said to me over the phone.

How ironic that she did to me what she feared the most. I was the real outcast. In her mind, I was to understand that I had to remain a secret and accept the very conditional relationship which made me furious at her.

Her advice to me in a letter was to say The Serenity

Prayer. The fact that she wouldn't meet me sent me into the fetal position crying uncontrollably all over again and I was inconsolable. Prince Valium and Jerry came to my rescue. This sort of raw pain surfaced often, setting me back emotionally for months. She was in control and continued to withhold valuable life and death information from me. Why? Once again I was forced to have a secret identity and now a secret relationship with my own mother as well. She made it clear that I would never receive a picture of her. I hated being a victim of manipulation again and was stuck living a double life enduring endless grief that hurt like Hell with no one to turn to.

A letter from Dorothy.

> Dear Melinda,
>
> After receiving your phone call on the 10th and the package that arrived the 22nd, I'm trying to compose myself so I can communicate intelligently. I do hope you understand the dilemma I'm in. Please bear with me.
>
> I realize you have many questions to ask but first I must be assured that I can trust you to be discreet and keep it personal between you and me, especially at this end. There is much at stake here and hopefully I can live what's left of my life at peace with myself. If you will comply with this, I shall answer as best I can the questions you have.
>
> Yes, I have kept my name all these years, but Mrs. should be put before. I've also been alone, worked for many years to eke out a living. I retired early, as it became necessary to be of assistance to my elderly parents—ages 90 and 93. I live in a small apartment, nothing pretentious, but I call it home.
>
> It's a simple life I live, good friends, unknowing of anything, have made it more pleasant. These past years haven't been easy for

> me, living with so much remorse. Trying to lead a Christian life has helped.
>
> It's a handsome family you have. I am having a bit of a problem figuring relationships. I hope you will accept this note as a beginning. I pray for strength to handle it.
>
> Sincerely, D"

"Earl Lumsley was my husband and my married name. I was divorced and used it on The Adoption Decree to keep you legitimate," she told me during our next phone conversation.

"What is your maiden name and my father's name?" I asked.

If she was having a problem with relationships, I was totally confused.

"My best friend in the apartment complex is an ex-prostitute," she informed me, but would tell me nothing about my grandparents or my names.

I still thought of myself as English like Mother, and Baby Girl Lumsley was also English. I had no sense of history or myself at all. It was she who held all the cards and continued to keep me in the dark about my identity.

The result of being a graft on someone else's family tree left me feeling cut off, like an impersonator, with no real history of my own. I had been brainwashed to be an imposter for the rest of my life and was at everyone's mercy. They stole my name, my power and hijacked my brain and I was to live my life made up of other peoples' identities. The system was evil and had failed me. Everyone but Jerry had failed me. My life made no sense until now.

Dorothy and I wrote and talked on the phone. It was very difficult for me because she was afraid someone might be listening to us on her party line. It was an emotional strain having another mother who was withholding the truth from me. I managed to juggle the two rather well and to hold my family together in between my terrible bouts with depression. Another Christmas arrived and I wondered what Dorothy's

Christmas was like. She never told me much about her life. Mother sent the usual check.

"What did you buy with the money?" Mother asked me over the phone.

"I bought ice skates for the boys and a nice pair for myself," I boldly stated finally standing up to her.

"Why in the world did you buy ice skates?" Mother asked disapprovingly.

"I want to ice skate on the local pond with the boys," letting her know that I participated in the sports my sons loved.

"Did you know I have a soprano coloratura voice?" I informed her.

"No, I didn't."

"Yes, I have been taking voice lessons with an opera teacher and she says I sound like Barbara Cook and if I keep it up I will be singing at the Metropolitan Opera one day. I'm performing the coloratura aria Glitter and Be Gay from the operetta Candide next Saturday at the recital. She also told me I looked like I had the breeding of an aristocrat," poured out of my mouth.

She obviously didn't know how well coordinated I was or nothing about ice hockey and how much fun it was ice skating on frozen ponds in the winter with my boys. The only thing she did with me was to take me shopping for clothes, out for luncheon or to see a play. The last thing she knew about me was that I was so athletic, could sing or that I might be an aristocrat as well as she. The eighties went by and I became more and more impatient with Dorothy for keeping my identity and our relationship a secret.

I called to finally confront Dorothy. "Why did you give me up?" I asked her.

"My husband cheated on me, and I kicked him out. I had a revenge affair with your father to prove to my ex that I was still attractive to other men and got pregnant the first time. I didn't want my husband to know about you because he would have tried to take custody of your sibling."

"Who is my half-sibling? Is it a boy or girl?" I asked her.

"I can't tell you."

"The truth is I'm the product of a one night stand or would you call it an affair," I said to her.

"Your life is like the ones I read in books," she said and referred to my adoptive mother as the nice lady.

"I have to go now," she said and hung up. If that didn't make one schizoid, I didn't know what would. In my mind my life was more like something out of a Grimm's Fairy Tale and not a story you read in books.

I sent her a Valentine present and she wrote back. This time her handwriting began to look very shaky.

> Hi, Melinda
>
> Just a note to thank you for the pretty valentine. I love it. However, it arrived while a good friend was visiting me and I opened it in her presence. It did cause me some anxiety for few moments and I tried to handle it. My thinking is you didn't realize this might happen. I hope so anyway.
>
> It's been a cold week here, typical January weather. The sun is out today which does make things more cheerful. Sorry about this hand-writing. It's the best I can do.
>
> Love, D

The next note I sent to her was written on one of the note cards I hand painted of an etched basket filled with tiny hand painted flowers in watercolors and sold locally.

> May 1, 1989
>
> Dear Melinda,
>
> This will be just a note to tell you I received your letter today, and was afraid to open it after reading the previous one, but not to worry. I've read and reread many times. Thank you for explaining your feelings and problems. I understand how difficult it's been for both of us to

communicate rationally.

Yes, I was getting very upset, never knowing what would happen in the future. Oh, I do hope we both are back on the right track. Be nice to each other and above all else, hope God forgives and helps us from now on. Yes, we can be friends. I want that very much.

I intend writing you about what kind of a person I really am but you'll need a bit of patience. It's difficult for me to write, until I can get my nerves under control. I had better work hard on this. My friends are noticing changes in me and wonder what's happening to me. The hard part is to bear it alone. I cannot tell them.

I cry, too. Discretion—I detest this word, but have a need for it. The last card you sent is lovely. You are truly an artist. My thought-a May basket!

Until later on.

Love, D

How did she know it was a May basket? She knew me better than I knew myself. She even knew I was a fine artist! My roots ran deep. This was my first real connection and genetic mirror. As far as the part about God forgiving us, she should speak only for herself on that one.

"What is my father's name? Who has my intense big green crazy eyes?" I asked her during our next phone conversation.

"I can't tell you," she replied, which didn't cut it for Jerry and he grabbed the phone from me.

"You will tell us who her father is or we will put an ad in your local newspaper and tell everyone what you did," Jerry threatened. "Don't you know what you have done to her by not wanting to reunite with her? You are the reason she is so depressed and she needs to see you in person to heal what you have done to her by abandoning her. What's wrong with you people anyway?" he yelled.

"His name is John Franck," she blurted out and hung up.

"So you were illegitimate. Haven't you heard of the old Indian legend that when someone steals your name they take away your power? She's such a liar! I wonder what she told everyone in Wisconsin Dells when she disappeared for months while she was at The Cradle waiting to have you?" Jerry asked me.

"We'll never know," I replied holding back the tears.

22

Righting the Wrong

We always went to visit Jerry's mother and step-father in Long Island for all the Jewish holidays. She adored my first-born because he looked like Jerry, but she didn't like my second son, Tim.

"Sig heil, Auctung!" she shouted out, giving Tim the Hitler salute after too many Johnnie Walker Blacks at the dinner table one night.

I told her to never to do that again and left the table with my precious newborn. Jerry just went along with it as he was too afraid to stand up to his mother.

Tim was too Aryan-looking to fit into a Jewish household and his mother was a German-hating alcoholic. My black haired mother-in-law, who looked Hispanic to me, even hated flowers because they reminded her of funerals. Worse yet, she didn't believe in angels.

Jerry's paternal Aunt Minnie, his decreased father's sister, was like a second mother to Jerry. She was a black-haired, very short, childless, borsht-loving, Russian Jewish Orientalist attorney who visited often with her very fair tall and not-so-handsome attorney husband.

"Who do you think you are, Lady Di? Oy vey, isn't Melinda a black person's name? I'm faklempt," Minnie said to me with disdain because I wasn't Jewish.

Her Yiddish insults failed to offend me since I had an idea what she meant. She handled a silk scarf that she was considering and looked at me with disdain.

"You wouldn't have any idea about silk, would you? Or that the Jewish presence in Oriental Studies is surprisingly overlooked," she barked and then decided not to give me the scarf.

Oy vey, did it ever end? I thought to myself. "Did your ancestors live Beyond the Pale in Russia or were they from the Hebrew Jaktan clan wandering the Silk Road?" I could have replied to her cutting remarks, but hurting people was not in me. She was such a compulsive talker that you could put the phone down, take a vacation and she would still be talking upon your return!

Of course, my brown-haired John was their little darling. Jerry's maternal grandmother, who spoke Yiddish and loved Klezmer music, lived in Brighton Beach with all the other Russian Jews. She was always nice to me when we visited my mother-in-law for Passover.

"Kaynahorah, kaynahorah," she exclaimed every time we crossed paths in the house.

"What does Kaynahorah mean?" I asked Jerry.

"It's some incantation in Yiddish to ward off the evil eye."

"I hope she doesn't think I'm evil," I cringed.

"No. There's some sort of cultural memory born into all Jews. It's so tied deeply inside us and connected to something inside your soul. Don't pay any attention to her," Jerry told me.

Now my Aryan-looking son and I were experiencing reverse discrimination and abuse. Jerry's mother disliked me because she thought I was not only the dreaded Christian goy, shiksa, but a dreaded German, too. She never said a thing to me except to tell me that I acted like a child.

Would I ever regain my identity? I was now in a family

of Russian Jews and one Irish Jew, Jerry's stepfather, with whom I couldn't relate. Would I ever get the real truth and legitimize myself so I could fit in somewhere? I felt more at home across the street with the Albanian family, even if they ate lambs' eyeballs and testicles, and had an Uzi 9mm machine gun in their front closet that their son used to shoot deer out his bedroom window.

I was mad now at everyone for keeping the truth from me and after some liquid courage, i.e. beer, called my natural father hoping he would tell me more about who I was. The information operator gave me his phone number.

"Is this John Franck?" I asked.

"Affirmative," he answered.

"This is your daughter," I said and heard a click as he hung up on me.

This went on for a few years. I had to be drunk to call him as the outright rejection always sent me spiraling out of control into a deep and frighteningly dark anxiety-ridden depression. Once I regained my emotional equilibrium, my desire to connect with him forced me to call him again and again until I finally got him to talk to me.

He finally did talk to me in 1993, and I told him my story. He seemed sympathetic and told me I had two half-brothers and a sister and that I was German, French, and Polish. He told me my mother was wild and promiscuous, something she denied, then took my phone number saying he would call me. I was filled with hope.

Shortly after the phone conversation, a letter from his lawyer arrived. The lawyer said that due to the fact that I was so rage-filled they thought it unhealthy for me to pursue a relationship. I was told not to write or call John and threatened not to show up on his doorstep because all Wisconsin residents have privacy rights.

What about my rights? They were treating me as if I was invisible, and more like a criminal than a sensitive human being in need of healing and truth. His lawyer received a letter from me telling him that the laws were unfair and that he would answer to God for keeping valuable life and death information from me. I wondered how he could sleep at night. Just who was the criminal here? I was fighting outright abuse, ignorance, evil, and corruption. If there was a painting that captured my feelings it would have been The Scream by Edvard Munch.

Another letter from Dorothy arrived.

> Dear Melinda,
>
> I told you how difficult it is for me to write, but I'll try once more. Your letter came a couple days ago, took five days in transit. Nice to hear things are fine with you after your bout with the flu and a root canal. So far I'm relatively healthy. Oh, I do get spells of vertigo still. When I feel them coming, I sit on the floor to prevent my falling. A bit scary but I put up with it and stay in a lot.
>
> Now about the second part of your letter. You said you called a certain person New Year's day. You had told me he wouldn't talk to you at one time. Anyway, he did know and is the one responsible. To use the word promiscuous was a cruel, malicious thing to say. Not true, libelous, yes. I have never made even one derogatory remark about him as you well know. I saw no point in doing so.
>
> In regard to others you mentioned in your letter. I do not have a first cousin Howard. I had no brothers and I know not of a Richard Lumsley or Paul. I have no idea who they are and you couldn't have known my father. Wish you could have, you would have liked him. I hope what I've written will be accepted as the truth because it is. I'm tired of all the insinuations, so would you have heart and write a nice letter for a change? Regardless of what you might imagine I do think of you.
>
> Love, D

These people were making me so crazy I went to see a psychiatrist in a neighboring town to see if he could help me get through this depressing nightmare.

"My adoptive mother thinks I'm schizophrenic," I told the shrink and began to tell him all about my search.

"Perhaps your mother is schizophrenic! You put a country between your parents, and your adopted brother, Jack, put a continent. You have a savage beauty," he commented as if he understood adoptees.

He confused me because after a while, I didn't know which mother he was talking about. His demeanor was so disconcerting. He had a reptilian look and darted his tongue in and out like a horny lizard from limbic Hell. He made me so nervous that I parked my car on the ice-covered hill by his office in Chappaqua and watched it slide down into the street almost crashing into oncoming traffic. Adoption was schizophrenic, but no one seemed to acknowledge that fact. My beauty always got in the way with men.

The stress of finding Dorothy and John caused my left hand to shake so badly I changed over to my right hand after realizing both of my natural parents were afraid of me. They demonized me and were determined to keep me a deeply hidden secret. My dream of reunion was shattered. I was hated and feared by my own parents, an outcast, and felt psychologically crucified. A physical death would have been easier because my grief kept being triggered over and over and I was unable to stop or control the sobbing.

Neither one of my mothers could or would help me to gain independence by telling me who I was so I could proceed with my life without being totally dependent on complete strangers for my survival and to pay all my bills. The gap was way too large to bridge. I kept treading and treading in the dangerous deep dark waters of crippling grief, anxiety, confusion, loneliness, misplaced trust, trauma, fear, insecurity and insanity with only a fire burning deep down in my soul to keep me fighting for my life.

My unconditional love for Dorothy, a proud Lutheran, remained. John and Tim kept teasing me by calling me Baby

Girl Lumsley. They had no concept about my plight as they had their original birth certificate naming their biological mother and father, whereas I had two birth certificates. One was sealed and a secret and the other was a lie.

"Mom, so my real grandfather and I have the same first name and your real last name is Franck, is that right?" asked John.

"I know and I didn't even know what his name was when I named you."

"It's almost too complicated to even understand all of it. So, John Franck is my real grandfather on your, I mean our father's side," John said holding his head.

"So, who is my grandfather on your mother's or my grandmother's side?" he asked.

"I have no idea. Heck I'm not allowed to know my own mother's last name or what nationality I am!"

"Maybe someone in your family is light sensitive like you are," John mentioned thinking that must be the reason why I wore sunglasses inside the house even after dark. The secret letters D sent and our paranoid phone conversations because she was on a party line wondering if anyone was listening in were upsetting and comforting at the same time because she never answered my questions.

"Are you having a big ham?" Dorothy asked me sarcastically that Christmas over the phone.

She was playing some cruel psychological S & M game because she was an anti-Semite. I just couldn't catch a break from anyone.

Another letter from Dorothy….

> Melinda,
>
> Yes, this is the same card you sent to me. I thought the message appropriate for you as well. After reading your enclosed note, I realized we just haven't been good for each other – you with your depressions and my anxieties. However do not accuse me of not being there for you. Think! From the start when you began all this, I've kept in

touch. I thought I did the right thing, too many times I was wrong. You didn't mean to harass me? Well some of the nasty things you wrote certainly isn't proof of good intentions on your part. I chose to overlook and forget. I too have reasons to be depressed, but must deal with it the best I can. You can, too. I just know you can. Could menopause possibly is part of the cause? It does strange things. You said God will give you solace. Also keep in mind He doesn't give you more than you can handle. This has kept me going all these years. Not too many left for me, but many more for you and yours. You have a family—be glad happy, and above all, love each other. Peace be with you. I pray for this and hopefully I can find it, too.

"To be wronged is nothing… Unless you continue to remember it"

So be it.

D

Three Brown Mice

I don't know why, but I bought a little brown rubber mouse in a local store, tied a red ribbon around its tail and put it in the window sill facing West to Wisconsin Dells, Wisconsin where 'D' lived. This mouse was me longing to love and stay connected to her spiritually even at a distance.

"I'm calling that bitch. She doesn't want to see you? Listen to this," Jerry told me as he picked up the phone.

"Dorothy, this is Melinda's husband. Melinda needs you and is dying," and hung up on her. I just couldn't be that cruel and called her back to tell her I wasn't dead.

That Christmas a card came from Dorothy. I opened the envelope and there were three little brown mice with a red bow tied to each tail holding a Christmas ornament just like the mouse I had sitting on my windowsill. One mouse was playing the guitar, and the other two singing carols, with little wings and halos over their heads. The word Joy! was written above each singing church mouse. Inside it said, "To you, you, you! Merry Christmas!" She wrote in very jittery handwriting like she was extremely nervous and stressed out.

"Why?"

"Reason deceives us often – conscience never."

So be it with me for now.

D

I couldn't believe my little brown mouse had the same red bow tied to its tail as the mice on the card she sent me. We were both on the same wavelength and had a telepathic bond that transcended time and space. I wanted more than ever to touch and see her hoping we would one day meet face to face.

The more I studied the photo of the pastel I had done of my sleeping cat back in California, the outlines turned into a map drawn within the sphere. Upon further study the lines formed a map outlining Minnesota, Lake Michigan, and Wisconsin. If you looked at it like a map, you could see Wisconsin Dells. *I channeled my birthplace from my unconscious.* This blew my mind. I actually remote viewed the location of Dorothy through my art without knowing it! My art and psyche had mysteriously contained the truth hidden in it. It was unbelievable. Could I have inherited my ancestors' memories, or was it quantum communication?

Just like the illusion of Sam's mountain that changed into a nude woman and the vegetable arrangements that changed into portraits of people, my art, too, had a double meaning. The truth was all in my mind and unconscious. We had a genetic psycho-spiritual bond and I was making works of art with the duality of my two selves in them. It was just a matter of seeing the two realities in the artworks and connecting them to the truth. The more truth I found, the more my art showed itself to have both my identities in one image.

The fact that Dorothy validated that I was a real artist gave me a true direction, the courage, and a reason to return to college in 1983 to get my degree. I took a monoprint class and drew and painted a picture of a terra cotta hen piece of pottery that I ordered from the Gumps (San Francisco) catalog. Then I filled the hen with daisies. I took my monoprint to the framer and hung it on the wall in our living room. A local store sold my prettiest orchid monoprint to a girl for her Laura Ashley room in Florida.

"People love your work. A man from the New York Philharmonic Orchestra just bought your Jack in the Pulpit watercolor," said the owner of the store and handed me a check for $1500.

Dorothy gave me more validation as an artist from seeing what she thought was a May basket drawn on the note card I sent to her. She knew I was an artist, but she didn't tell me how she knew it. I made many cards with etchings of baskets, wreaths, and bows printed on white stationery, carefully hand-painting miniature water colored blue bells, daisies, bleeding hearts, and columbine on each card. Everything I did was a one-of-a-kind work of art. My new hometown in Westchester was originally known for making baskets and the local market sold all of the boxes of my cards.

"You will be the next Grandma Moses," Mother said when I told her over the phone about my success as an artist.

Mother had no idea how good I was or that I didn't want to be an untrained folk artist or the next anybody! I already was a selling and recognized artist in my own right. Grandma Moses couldn't even draw. Not one person in my adoptive family knew how good I was and that hurt, but Dorothy knew I was a real artist.

My art really began to make sense to me after seeing Doug Henderson on Unsolved Mysteries. He was a professor, adoptee, psychologist, and expert on synchronicity from Wisconsin. He talked about a birth mother who had written the book *Synchronicity and Reunion, The Genetic Connection of Adoptees and Birth Parents*. The book was about the process of building or limiting their post-reunion relationships for adoptees, birth families, and adoptive families as they begin to "piece together" the years of separation. They often discover that uncanny coincidental behavior and meaningful information transfer occurred between them when normal sensory contact was absent. They may be astonished to learn they had annually vacationed in the same place, named children by unknown names of ancestors, or had accurate dreams and premonitions.

There was a story about one adoptee who had never seen her natural mother. The week before they were to meet she had drawn and water colored a specific room with an elaborate English tablecloth and tea set. When she went to meet her first mother, she saw the exact room, tea set, and tablecloth. This was proof of the telepathy between them, and they were connected by design.

One adoptee was stunned to find out she had fallen in love with a priest, who she learned after locating her lost family, was a very close resemblance to her natural father. Now I understood how deeply I was connected to my first relatives because it was happening to me. My art and subconscious had hidden in it real clues and connections to them. It was all about DNA, molecular biology, cellular consciousness, quantum physics and communication.

Doug belonged to The American Adoption Congress (AAC) and I called him. We talked as one adult adoptee to another and he promised he would drive out from Wisconsin and visit so we could talk.

It was no surprise to Doug when I told him about my son John's drawing. His art teacher told me he was a good artist and was using both sides of his brain. I couldn't wait to show him the framed pastel of a fish with red, yellow, and black stripes and a potato print of a school of fish hanging on my wall. John made a very sophisticated clay sculpture of a human figure when he was only ten years old. We had a long, yet hidden, genetic artistic legacy. Our blood tied us together.

Doug came to visit me and counseled me about my adoption and abuse issues, something I could have never done alone. His own life had such similarities to mine. Finally, I met an adoptee from Wisconsin who was a psychology professor from the University of Wisconsin and an expert on adoption.

"I work with adoptees and abused children. When I met my natural siblings, they also worked with abused children and told me I looked like my father. My mother would not see me and my father died of alcoholism right before I found him. I'm a recovered alcoholic," he told me.

Doug was one of the most important connections of my lifetime. I began to see we had the same adoptee experience.

He slowly helped me to see that I had been living with two people inside of me and that depression in adoptees was not unusual. In fact he told me there was a 21% higher rate of suicide among adoptees. We talked and talked until I slowly realized I was in reality a Franck. I asked questions and he answered them.

"You don't have schizophrenia in the clinical sense, but have an imposed schizophrenia by the nature of the closed adoption," he affirmed.

He explained to me why I had always felt so filled with anxiety, depression, isolation, and chronic loneliness, as well as why I was living such a strange life in the middle of nowhere. He said often that if it wasn't for adoptees, psychiatrists would be out of business. This was a revelation to me and a well-kept secret. I had no idea there were so many others adoptees and first mothers suffering in silence just as I had been.

"Adoptees usually don't know what causes their anxiety and depression until they are about thirty. Natural mothers and fathers suffer from grief and depression from the loss of a child to adoption. too. Your husband also is suffering from grief and depression over the loss of his father when he was five years old and has issues about the fact that his mother had to leave him at such a young age to go to work," he told me.

We both realized I was connected to my blood relatives on a mysterious psychic and telepathic level. He explained why my adoptive parents thought I was schizophrenic, with a dual personality, when in reality it was simply my unrecognized genetic self at work. He knew I had a false self and an authentic self—a dual identity as an adoptee from a closed adoption.

Things were finally making sense and slowly it was clear what had happened to me. He talked about it on *Unsolved Mysteries* with a famous psychic from England. Scientists have not yet totally figured it out, but they have proved the existence of a non-local (timeless space) quantum factor at work and we marveled that consciousness interfaces with creation somehow from an information base rooted in nonlocal consciousness. This was the ultimate mystery and seemed to happen faster than the speed of light. I read an article that said the cell membrane is a liquid crystal semi-conductor with gates and channels. The membrane is an information transistor, an organic computer chip. We were on to something big.

"I'll send you some articles I wrote," he said when he left.

Doug's story "There Are More like Me: Search, Reunion, and Synchronicity in Adoption" came in the mail along with scholarly articles he had written about adoption for The Journal of Social Distress and the Homeless. I read his Adoption Therapy presentations that he made to the AAC and copies of the magazine, The Decree, a publication by the AAC. His article on "Sexuality and the Adoptee" was very enlightening, explaining that adoptees have a great deal of trouble achieving intimacy in relationships due to our inability to trust. Then we talked about genetic sexual attraction and that adoptees are also attracted genetically to their unseen natural relatives.

"Adoptees are connected by design and energy to their natural relatives," he said. Wow, this was just what the doctor ordered and gave me validation and authentic power to continue on my dark primal journey into the light. No wonder I never fit in anywhere.

I still hadn't told Mother anything about Dorothy. We all had secrets I guess.

Still Juggling

Juggling both identities was complicated. I needed to resolve the cognitive dissonance due to the false information I had been forced to live with concerning my ethnicity and heritage. Mother sent me an interesting stationery card made of rice paper and pressed flowers in 1981 that she received as a party favor at a friend's birthday party. She said in her letter perhaps I could do something like it and sell it and get a wide distribution. She helped Grandfather press his botanical specimens as a little girl and related to me through pressed flowers. While in Mexico, on a mining job, she helped him pick and press flowers in his two giant flower presses. He later lost that entire collection in a freak fire. I had to give her an A for effort here.

I had a reputation to uphold in my adoptive family. There would be no Kmart in my family history. Upholding the Meyer family name was complicated and I had to be the best at everything. Each Cranes card was elegantly decorated with a design made of pressed flowers. There were hundreds of wildflowers in the woods and my explorations yielded many specimens that went into the phonebooks, left over from my search, to be pressed and glued on to the card. I pressed everything from wild woodruff to wild geraniums to decorate the cards. I found a pink Lady's Slipper orchid on one of my expeditions growing under a group of hemlocks. Gaga would have loved to have seen these. The perennial Lady ferns turned into miniature Christmas trees with red bows at the bottom for my Christmas card line. Anything that grew in the enchanting woods was fair game for my cards, but one had to know what was able to be pressed. The Maidenhair, Royal, Interrupted and Cinnamon ferns were beautiful, but not delicate enough for the fine art of pressing.

"Don't pick the wild columbine. It is a protected and endangered species," yelled a lady from her car. "I won't," I answered and waved back with my hands full of the contraband.

My cards sold locally. I was a success again! I showed them to my husband and he just laughed them off like they were ridiculous. My next step to success was to read the book about Neiman Marcus. My cards were one-of-a-kind and just right for their stores so I put in a call to the president of Neiman Marcus. The secretary told me he wasn't there. I was persistent.

"Please send me a sample," she said after the third call.

Months went by and my next call got me my first order.

In 1984 I sent the 41st president's wife a note on my pressed flower stationery. I told her about my views on open records for adoptees. I knew she had an adopted son. She sent me back a thank you note on the standard White House stationery, as did the next president in 1994 who had interviewed a cadet named Lumsley, and I thanked him for letting me see what I thought was a natural relative. It could have been my maternal half-brother I thought. I also told him about my wish for open records, open adoption, and above all, truth in adoption. Hopefully he understood being adopted himself.

By this time, I felt like a broken record, realizing opening records for adoptees was not a big legislative priority in Washington D.C., but a State issue. I had no political power and why should they care about me? I was the powerless and anonymous one thinking the lawmakers thought they knew what was right for adoptees more than we did, but I never gave up.

Having two mothers and fathers took a bit of getting used to, especially when one set was invisible and under deep secret cover. Thinking about my four grandparents, great grandparents and great-great grandparents totally boggled my mind. When anyone asked me a question about my mother or father I began to ask, "Which one?" I was slowly getting my identity and my authentic voice back!

To add to our problems, my mother-in-law, who was a chain smoker all her life, was diagnosed with cancer and died within a year. I tried to comfort help her by putting earphones on her ears to hear her favorite singer Barbra Streisand sing as she lay in the ICU tied down and unable to move.

"Why are you crying? I'm not dead yet!" she said to me in a defiant tone and died the next day alone.

I had never been to a funeral, but now was on my way to the Jewish funeral home where she lay like someone from the house of wax in a simple pine box. Jerry's brother made the Rabbi mad because he wouldn't wear the yarmulke and put it in his pocket like a handkerchief. After the funeral, Jerry's brother opened the casket and we kissed her stone cold forehead goodbye. She was the first dead person I had ever seen that I knew personally. We drank vodka out of Bob's flask in the limo heading the funeral procession to the cemetery. Bob told me his family dropped the "sky' from their last name when they emigrated from Russia. He decided to drop the first three letters of his last name as well, making it sound less Jewish. It was interesting to me that I was trying to find my own name and identity and reclaim it while he was trying to lose his.

The next day I walked out of the door of my house and hyperventilated so badly I fell to the ground and couldn't breathe remembering the dead body of my mother-in-law.

My husband and his half-brother inherited the business and we continued to raise the boys. Bob was given a lump sum and went back to Arizona.

23

The Journey Continues

The matriarch of the family was dead and Jerry was now co-owner of her aerospace metal company along with his half-brother who managed to get to her safety deposit box and take all her jewelry behind our back. We drove down to her house in Long Island. All I wanted was a watercolor of a pheasant in the woods in winter that her friend painted, her gold plated flat wear, and formal bone China set of plates, dishes, coffee cups etc.

I was trying my hardest to raise the boys while Jerry began to commute to work and always arrived drunk upon his return. Tim luckily found a friend whose stepfather began to take them fly-fishing for trout. Fly-fishing was as alien to me as my talents were to my adoptive parents. He was only ten when he began to tie his own flies while fishing in his waders and vest with other professional fly fishermen. His natural talent won him a handmade fly-fishing rod from the Trout Unlimited organization.

"Your son is a fly-fishing prodigy and will probably write articles for the fishing magazines. He's the youngest one I've ever seen," assessed the oldest and most respected local fly fisherman.

"My son is a very gifted fly fisherman and sports writer? Where did that come from, I wonder," I said as we were all mystified.

Mom, would you buy me the magazine Field and Steam?" Tim asked.

Both the boys drew well as I did and were gifted with abstract minds, large vocabularies, and could sing. However, they were not about to be sensitive artist types. They were macho and all business like their father. They were reflecting me genetically, but it was difficult to recognize because they were boys. I never before had a biological female or male to see the genetic mirrors. We were all looking through the identity glass darkly. They had a much better self-concept than I did.

While in the local book store looking for fly fishing magazines, a charming salesman behind the counter began to talk to me. I learned he was an artist; I wanted to see his watercolors and he wanted to see mine. I was so lost, lonely, and unhappy that I befriended the very married Bill who told me he was in an open marriage and that his wife didn't mind if he was close friends with other women. He was Irish, 6"3", in AA, an artist, a drummer, an intellectual, a poet, a Berkeley graduate, a romantic, and a serious writer who kept a secret journal. We had so much in common and I was able to talk to him about all the active alcoholics in my life. Jerry was so self-involved and wasn't at all interested in talking about anything related to me. At last, I found someone who conquered and wasn't in denial about his drinking problem.

Bill wasn't a hunter, but was more like a long lost brother and possibly like John, my father, a real outdoorsman. He was a distant relative of Daniel Boone and loved the woods. The watercolors and drawings in his sketch book were sensitive and beautiful like mine. His first wife was a relative of Mr. Randolph Hass of the Hass avocado family which I could really relate to because these were growing in Gaga's backyard in South Pasadena. We seemed to have so much in common. I let my guard down and read him letters I received from Dorothy and told him about Rob and Father.

"So you're a Kraut. Your mother mentioned her husband's name was Earl Lumsley and he lives in Phoenix. Have you tried finding him?" he asked. He was rather insensitive for being so romantic.

"Yes I have written a letter to him and am waiting for his reply," I confided. "My maternal adoptive grandfather was a geologist and mining engineer who went down to Mexico to live until about 1912. He and my grandmother lived in The Woods Hotel in Guanajuato where there were many gold and silver mines and my mother's sister was even born there."

To answer his question, I continued, "I guess I'm a Kraut, but my friend Wendy thinks I'm a Shaman," I confided in him.

"Really, why?" he asked.

"I did a color workshop with a New Age psychologist friend of her brothers. She took us into a deep trance and asked us questions and we were not allowed to look at anyone's drawing until we were finished. I drew everything in a book Wendy was reading by Carlos Casteneda right down to the colors, the tonal and the nagual, and there was no way I could have known she was reading the book. My clairvoyance totally freaked both of us out. She told me that was why I didn't fit into my adoptive family because I was a Shaman. She began to write my adoption story but gave up after the third chapter."

"I'm very into this, too. In fact, I go into New York all the time and eat at a Mexican Restaurant where I talk to a Mexican man who is a Nagual and knows all about this. Would you like to meet him? I speak Spanish and Melinda means 'beautiful' in Spanish," he said.

"No, thanks. It's so crazy to me and gives me the creeps, so let's drop the subject. It's hard enough trying to find out my biological identity," I told him emphatically not wanting to get involved with the occult ever again after my year with the psycho, Casey. Still, was I perhaps possessed by the spirit of a Mexican Nagual?

Jerry the compulsive gambler alcoholic who had very strange tics and made crazy sounds, was busy going to work in Long Island and I began a secret friendship with this fascinating man. We took the train to the city to see the Whitney, The Strand bookstore and sip cups of cappuccino at a café like intellectuals in Paris. I was in seventh heaven being with a writer who graduated from Berkeley where Gaga's herbarium was housed, an accomplished and sensitive artist, writer, poet, musician who played the drums and intellectual who took a personal interest in me as well as being so like me with whom I could really communicate. He was nothing like Jerry who could have cared less about me except to have his kids, cook, clean, verbally abuse, and make fun of my small breasts and big butt.

"Look at this picture," he said and beckoned me toward him as he opened a book about slavery.

"It's very sad really, the African slave being auctioned off on the wooden block makes me feel like I, too, was auctioned off to the highest bidder," I said sadly.

"That's what I was thinking too and how abusive being adopted and separated from your own mother and father really is. The endless grief from the total separation, loss of family and identity is almost too painful to contemplate. You don't even know who you get your beautiful long silky straight hair from do you or your sexy tall, lean, and lanky body?" he asked.

"I wonder if there are any famous people in my biological families," I mused.

"You never know. Maybe your father married into wealth like I did in my first marriage and that's something he doesn't want you to know about," he answered.

"I hope that isn't the reason he would not want to meet me," I thought to myself.

Bill taught me about Gnosticism, the Nag-Hammadi codices, finding the true self and Oswald Spengler. Spengler, a German historian and philosopher, exalted the spirit of the Prussian and wrote some papers on metaphysics in 1965. I had no idea what a Prussian was.

I was beginning to realize after a while he was trying to seduce me and that he and his wife liked kinky sex. He was replacing his alcohol addiction with multiple couple sport sex.

"My mother sexually abused me as a child. I'm like the character and drug addict out of the movie The Drugstore Cowboy, and I like to hurt women because of it," he revealed after calling me a bitch and a whore triggering a flashback to Rob abusing me in the woods in Kettering sending me into a total panic and a deep depression.

I ran to the closest shrink for help. This relationship was my last attempt to bond with someone who had things in common with me and now he tells me he was being sexually abused by his mother?

"You might as well put Rob's head on all your boyfriends. Do you see the connection between the verbal and sexual abuse from your husband and his gambling and alcohol addiction and Rob's verbally and sexually abusing you and his poker and alcohol addiction? I want you to see a psychiatrist who will put you on anti-depressants," the psychologist told me.

It was obvious that I had been living on the dark side as an abused adoptee for quite a while. Everyone always thought they knew me but how could anyone really know me because I didn't know myself. The doctor failed to tell me I should also put the heads of my unknown lost genetic relatives on their bodies as I subconsciously sought out those who were genetically like me without realizing it, trying to bond with them as if they were my own flesh and blood. Prozac made me nervous and affected my short term memory. Valium stopped the anxiety reaction from the flashbacks and the intrusive thoughts that were creating such deep emotional pain for me. I had to face the fact that I was hopelessly psycho-sexually attracted to angry abusers and alcoholics like Rob and Father and others who had been abused in some fashion. My dysfunction was even more complicated by the fact that my lovers most likely had been sexually abused as well and reflected traits from my lost and unknown natural relatives.

There also was a deep dark hidden genetic sexual

attraction at work creating dysfunction in all my relationships. If this genetic confusion and an unresolved oedipal complex didn't make me crazy, I didn't know what could.

"Bill's a schizophrenic, an addict and doesn't care about you. Don't you realize that if you leave him he will find someone else to replace you? Is there mental illness in your family?" the doctor asked me.

"I don't know. I was adopted, remember?" realizing even this doctor was confused about my intertwined complicated dual identity as an adoptee from a closed adoption and all my traumatic abuse and loss issues. He really would want to put me away if I told him I was a Nagual from Mexico.

It was the same with any doctor who asked me if anyone in my family had certain illnesses. How could I know when it was against the law for me to find out? He did rule out Multiple Personality Disorder although I could have had this due to the sexual abuse. What I didn't know about my biology and genetic background was hurting me terribly.

"You must end it with Bill. He's hurting and trying to use you to fulfill his own selfish perverted sexual fantasies. In fact, he is just like your brother, Rob. Does your husband know about your friendship?" the doctor asked me.

"No," I admitted.

"I wouldn't tell him," the doctor advised as I sat in front of him in tears.

"It's time I write a letter to Rob, but I don't want his wife to read it. What happened to me is his fault," I told him.

"Why don't you send him a registered letter," he suggested.

"I also want to tell Mother about Rob and her husband. Do you think I should?"

"Yes, I think it's time you told her the truth," the doctor affirmed.

I wrote Rob a registered letter stating what he did to me was wrong and that he needed to get out of denial, come clean and admit to the sexual abuse and apologize so I could heal. He didn't reply. I called and told Mother what had happened.

"Your brother is the devil himself and your father must have been drunk," she said coldly. That was the extent to which she helped me. In other words, she went back into denial and the subject was dropped. She avoided facing the entire situation all the while remaining close to Father, Rob, Darin, Jack, and their families. It became obvious to me that I was supposed to remain in denial as the secret keeper of the family or get out.

"Your adoptive family 'stinks on dry ice.' If anyone is satanic, they are and the snake nightmares come from Rob and the abuse. I would like to hypnotize you because I think your father may have abused you as a child and you have repressed it or don't remember," the doctor said.

"I don't know if I could handle that. Let me think about it."

I was too afraid to find out or to let any man have that kind of control over my mind or emotions and decided to stop therapy. He gave me a sheet with the diagnosis of Borderline Personality Disorder on it. I never knew if he thought I was a borderline or Jerry was. Something told me the shrink didn't understand my issues as an adoptee. He must not have known the symptoms of adoptees and borderline personalities are almost identical. A treatment plan was out of the question. I wondered how many adoptees had been misdiagnosed. Did anyone know that we suffer from emotional trauma and we all have something more like Post Traumatic Stress Disorder which is very different from having a mental illness or being a borderline personality? There was no way I could trust anyone at this point in my life.

I walked in the door one late afternoon after therapy.

"Your mother died in her sleep last night," Jerry informed me.

"You mean Ellie? How did she die?"

"She had a heart attack."

"Oh, no, she was supposed to get a pacemaker and didn't. Maybe she wanted to die," I informed him thinking she died to avoid confronting the truth about the abuse.

I called Father, and he told me they had seen the movie *Home Alone* starring Macauley Culkin the night before she died and the famous flautist James Galway the week before she passed away. What a terrible way to leave me. I felt so powerless, far away and alone in my anger and my grief.

The next morning I stepped outside to take Heidi, my Pomeranian puppy, for a walk when she brought me a little leafless rhododendron branch that was shaped like a ballerina on point. Was this a sign that Mother was finally free, in Heaven, performing her ballet dances on stage as she always wanted to? It was autumn and a few days later I found a miniature blood red autumn leaf with two holes in it for eyes in the shape of a perfect mask. Out came the glue and I glued it on to make a masked face for my magical Bolshoi dancer. Nature was such perfection, and it reassured me that she was happy and free to dance for eternity on the other side.

Mother belonged to the Neptune Society and her ashes were spread out to sea under the Golden Gate Bridge instead of going back to her father's family mausoleum in Illinois. I went to the beach to walk and cry and feel close to her. It was sad that I didn't get to say goodbye and I grieved alone. She never knew that I signed with the top agent and seller of art cards in New York City. Mom might have been impressed knowing that my agent represented eighty world class artists and sold their cards all over the world. My bio was even printed on a piece of paper slipped in the back of each envelope. Each copyrighted card was labeled "A Little Piece of Art" by Melinda where I signed my name. I was finally a recognized artist in New York. Just like the song says, "If I can make it there, I can make it anywhere."

Did she figure out while she was 'watching' the movie *Home Alone* that when we were home alone with Rob back in Kettering he was verbally and sexually abusing me? Was she thinking of me when she was 'watching' Galway play his flute and figuring out that I didn't want to perform in an orchestra because it triggered bad memories of abuse by her voyeuristic son Rob who was always stalking and trying to 'watch' me strip and dance for him among other things? My dream of riding my very own three gaited black stallion and competing in horse shows all over the world and perhaps singing jazz or the blues didn't count because everything I did usually was something she wanted me to do which was an extension of her and what her own biological daughter would want to do. Did she forget I wasn't her biological child and was genetically programmed in a total different way than she was?

While walking on the beach and wondering about all the lies, deception, and bad things that happened to me that went unsaid between us, I received the inspiration for one of my best selling handmade cards; little glitter squares with waves and in the waves were real shells, miniature seahorses, sand dollars and starfish. While I appreciated the guidance from perhaps a heavenly angel in the form of Mother's spirit or soul, the down side of her ashes being spread under the Golden Gate was every time that I ate tuna I thought I might be eating Mother.

"Your crown is waiting for you in Heaven," Mother said to me before she died. After her death, Reverend Jack told me she admitted to him that they had failed me. Jack's son was getting married so I flew to San Diego for the wedding and our Mother's Remembrance Day gathering at Darin's house after the wedding.

Rob's wife Becky and I were sitting together alone by the swimming pool when I finally opened up.

"Rob abused me when I was a little girl," I told her. She was speechless and stared into the air and I got up and left for my room upstairs. The conversation was dropped until much later that evening.

"Come, let's sit down and talk," Darin said when we were alone after midnight. I began the conversation and gradually brought up the abuse.

"Rob abused me, too," Darin admitted.

"He did?" I exclaimed in shock and disbelief.

"Yes, he threatened to break my arm if I ever told."

"I told Becky about Rob today after the wedding and she

didn't believe me," I said thinking he would approve.

"You what? How dare you ruin his relationship with her," he angrily yelled at me as I began to shake.

"I want you to leave the house right now," he ordered. My sobs began and I said trembling, "I don't have anywhere to go and it's one in the morning." We ended the conversation because his wife walked in and I went to bed shaken and in tears.

Darin later admitted to me that he never knew I was so talented and so good. It wasn't until two years later that Becky called to tell me she realized Rob was sick and had a perverted side.

"When I confronted him about it, he said you were a very sick person. You won't believe this, but when I discovered he had been cheating on me for years and filed for a divorce guess what the real estate agent found in the house?"

"What?" I asked.

"She found that he had installed a two-way mirror between his office closet back wall and the guest bedroom."

"How did the agent find it? I asked her.

"She noticed a black piece of cloth pinned to the back of the closet wall. When she pulled it up there was the mirror and he even made a shelf and a hole through the wall above the mirror for a video recorder. I didn't find any videos. I'm sorry I doubted you. I'm experiencing night terrors and have to go on anti-depressants," and hung up on me too upset to talk any further.

Finally he was caught and now my sister-in-law knew Rob was a pervert! Thank God I never stayed in that guestroom! She called again after calming down to tell me more.

"He came on to my sister and my sister's friend. My sister was staying at our house because she was going to pick up a poodle at the breeder close by. When she was going to brush her teeth, she found a note on her pillow saying, "Brush your teeth before you come to bed." The note was crazy she thought. When she got into bed, Rob was in it!

"Can you believe he told her he had never loved me and

loved her and you know what else? Rob always told me he wished I was sexy like you when we were first married," she said sobbing.

I was so glad to know that the truth about Father, who we called Pop, and Rob was finally out.

"Pop came on to Jack's daughter, too. Perhaps Rob was the real schizophrenic? What a bunch of womanizers and sick perverts," I told her.

Rob lost his boys who call him 'dick head' and no one dares to tell Darin's kids about their Uncle Rob's perversion. Darin and his wife cut me off thinking I might tell their children. Not until the year 2003, a year after Father died, did we communicate again. There was still much neither one of us knew of my adoptive family secrets.

My recurrent nightmare of walking on thousands of snakes began to make sense to me because she was having night terrors and woke up screaming. The more I learned and revealed, the more the snakes began to bite me in my dreams. The dreams ceased when I realized they were really my fear of Rob. The monster dreams finally ended after a dream I had while running from a monster bear. In my dream I ran into a house and hid from the bear in one of the rooms upstairs. The bear began to come after me and I took a shotgun and hid around a corner waiting to shoot. As it came toward me, it turned into Father and I shot him dead which put an end to my stalker dreams.

My hopes were way up as I wrote to John, my biological father, explaining what happened to me by Rob and Father hoping he would care and respond favorably to the pictures of the boys and me that I sent to him in one of my cards. A letter arrived from a lawyer of my father's in 1992 telling me to stay away. I kept trying to break through so we could reunite and I could get answers to heal some of my endless sorrow. Another letter from his lawyer arrived in 1993 threatening me and reminding me that Wisconsin had extensive laws concerning the protection of its citizens' privacy.

I still didn't know Dorothy's maiden name which was my biological maiden surname. What about honesty, my rights, and all my unmet needs? I called my father John, "You people stole my heritage. You should be locked up in jail for that, not me. God will punish you for what you did to me," I blurted out and hung up on him like he always hung up on me.

My letter to Earl Lumsley, Dorothy's ex-husband, was never answered, so with the help of a search angel, I wrote to his summerhouse in Phoenix, Arizona to tell him who I was. He sent me pictures of his oil paintings of the spectacular red rock formations in Phoenix and Sedona with their 'mirror images' reflected in a still pool of water and told me I had a half-brother named Leigh who was ten years older. He wouldn't tell me where he lived, but said they stopped talking years ago.

It made me wonder about how surreal it was that I painted the pink roses before I met Rosalee, who was the psychic bridge to Dorothy and then to think my half-brother's name was Leigh. Rose.a.lee, did it get any stranger? Was Leigh an artist, I wondered and I totally forgot to ask his father, Earl. Then I remembered that creep from the commune in California named Lee, too, and was thankful someone was finally being honest with me, suddenly realizing that I for the longest time was bonding and loving unconditionally total strangers similar to the ones I was really related to. By this time, it was as if my story was something out of fractured fairy tale. LSD was nothing compared to this twisted and cruel mind game. Everyone I was physically intimate with ended up betraying or hurting me and never did I receive unconditional love, something I needed and craved because that was really only possible with a blood relative. The only way I got physical affection was through sex. I never let anyone hug me, put their arm around me, or hold my hand, and if they did I just froze and didn't feel it. My husband never received any physical affection from his mother or stepfather either which was another reason why we were together.

Another letter from Earl arrived and the truth slowly helped to restore my sanity. He told me that as a youngster he used to ride his bike to his aunt's house. The boy next door and he got to pal around together and played cards by the hour with his sisters in the back yard. Directly across the alley from his aunt's place lived the Franck family. Rich, my natural grandfather was an engineer for the CB&Q Railroad and considered a wealthy man. He drove the Zephyr, the first train with a diesel engine. There were three children: John, my father, Marge, my aunt and Bill, my uncle. He used to converse with my Uncle Bill who was in high school and worked each evening handling phone calls for the local paper for people who had not received delivery.

> Dear Melinda,
>
> "I can only recall meeting John a couple times after he was out of high school and college, as he was teaching at the junior high school on the south side of Wisconsin Dells. He was quite a hunter, fisherman, and fur trapper, and on one of the occasions I met him he had his big blonde lab hunting dog with him.
>
> John passed away and his sister died from lymphoma when she was only 37. Bill followed in his father's footsteps and became an engineer on the CB&Q also. He was a registered stockbroker as well. I ran into him quite often when I was running to Wisconsin Dells on the railroad and staying at a south side hotel.
>
> He was an avid walker and would walk from the home up on Hayward St. down the south side with his dog and back again. He married later in life and his wife then would pick him up for the return home. He now owns every house in an entire block except two people who would not sell. He fixes them up and rents them at very reasonable rates."

This information helped me to begin to make some sense of myself and my boys. The more I learned, the more I understood some of the genetic parts that had been hidden and kept secret, creating my need to connect with total strangers who were like me and my blood relatives. This information and the fact that there was a shared genetic consciousness between me and my natural relatives helped me understood my love of nature, woodsmen, the woods, train conductors, the railroad, Germans, teaching, lakes, writing, writers, intellectuals, artists, funny people and some of the types of songs and people I was drawn to.

The unidentifying information in the letter from the adoption agency told me my father was funny, and so was I. It was no joke that I wasn't like a Meyer, but was very much like a Franck. You can't change who you are just as you can't change the sun into the moon. I was finally becoming real, but I still felt like 'Franckenbaby,' the baby girl monster who was made up of other people's identities without one of her own. Everyone was firmly rooted and connected to their family name and identity but me.

"Dorothy's sister, Mrs. Lois Small, lives in Cincinnati. Woops I wasn't supposed to tell you," Leigh said during a phone conversation quickly pretending to be passing a painful kidney stone and hung up on me.

Who was the professional musician in my family tree I wondered? It became apparent there had to be at least one singer and instrumentalist. How I wanted to go incognito and meet Dorothy and John to resolve my omnipresent grief. How could they have the right to keep me away or to put me in jail when I needed to reunite so I could see them with my own eyes to heal from all the painful emotions that consumed me on a daily basis because of losing them?

During my many drives past the gorgeous Park and Reservation I began to notice a giant rotting old oak tree trunk in the shape of a bear standing straight up on its hind legs like a giant sculpture. What did it mean? Why were the bears always appearing to me in some form or another?

I located my biological Aunt Lois and wrote her a long

letter to tell her that the times had changed and Dorothy should come out of denial and meet me.

Dorothy must have found out that I had written to her. She moved into a nursing home and said she could no longer write to me. I was so hurt by all her mind games. I promised her I would keep it all a secret but just couldn't.

The letter from D…

> Well, well, well, so you are at it again. That card you sent me took 16 days to get here. You knew I was no longer at my address and it would have to be forwarded. You ignored my telling you no more correspondence—period!
>
> I also told you I would accept a phone call only. I am not amused. If you are checking to find out if I really am where I say I am, it's a crude tactic and easy for me to suspect that you are. Believe it! I am here and trying to adjust to my new way of life. I have met many good people here who are helpful and understanding. We are all in the same boat—next to the last stages of our lives. Think about it, it might happen to you some day.
>
> Happy Holidays.

The next little note came and was written on two smaller pieces of paper after I had written to her sister Lois Small in Ohio.

> M-
>
> So you are still snooping and invading the privacy of people's lives. You call it doing heritage? Let it go, M. I have been fair in giving you info. But no more.
>
> You latest message didn't arrive until 11-13. Postman couldn't read my name on envelope due to your poor handwriting. I also have a new address which was not the problem. Thanks to

> you and your harassment which affected my health, I now reside in a home for the aging, elderly and disabled. I hope hearing of this development in my life will make you happy.
>
> Still trying to be fair with you and if you want to keep in touch for just "chitchat" try calling in the early evening.
>
> Signed by
> "The Gullible One"
> After thought-quote
> "What fools these mortals be!!!"

"I don't do 'chitchat' you wretched witch," I screamed out loud where no one could hear me and just wished she would stop withholding information and being so cruel to me. If only she was a nice person and would just talk and share the truth with me. Instead she was treating me like a stalker. I didn't dare tell her about Rob or Father after realizing it may drive her away from me forever.

My last hope was an adult adoptee, a black market baby, who ran a support group in New York City. I sent away for all his tapes and learned about the trauma I had endured and the answers to my depression and anxiety from being abandoned at birth. I called him and he put me in touch with a professional searcher and advocate for truth in adoption living in Wisconsin who was happy to help me. No matter what, I had to be strong to continue my search and managed to find time juggling being a secret, an adoptee, a mother, a wife, a Meyer and now a Franck. She was a search angel in the open record adoption movement and actually went to the public library and sent me yearbook pictures of my father, John, and his three children—my two half-brothers and half-sister. At last, the masks were coming off.

In the interim, I lived in the Hollywood of the East and kept getting mistaken for an actress. Different women came up to me in the grocery store to ask me if I was that actress they just saw in a movie or on television and strangely they couldn't quite figure out the name of the actress.

"No, I'm not, but I certainly could use the income," I always replied. Since living in New York, I had been mistaken for the folk singers Joni Mitchell, Emmylou Harris, the actresses: Catherine Deneuve, the dead Sharon Tate, Lindsay Wagner, Jill Claiborne, Peggy Lipton, Sandy Dennis, Elizabeth Montgomery, Michelle Phillips, Rene Russo, Shelley Long and Michelle Pfeiffer.

The more I looked at the pictures of my birth relatives, the more I began to see the family resemblances. Tim was twelve and looked like the picture in the high school yearbook of my paternal uncle, Bill Franck. The picture in the newspaper article about my father John when he retired from being the principal at a high school looked like me when I was one and again at sixteen. I had his beak-like Roman nose and long face. God, we were Germans from Minnesota and Wisconsin.

"It's a good thing you were adopted or you would have been a Nazi," a friend said.

"I know. What really blows my mind is this. I lived in Kettering, and Charles Kettering invented the first diesel locomotive engine that was used in the Zephyr that my natural grandfather Rich Franck drove! Kettering designed the engine for Ralph Budd who was the president of the CB&Q railroad. Budd was friends with my grandfather who drove the Zephyr and was also a griever who met with Budd often to tell him what the passengers or staff weren't happy about. I too was a griever having lost my families to adoption. Then to add to that Kroehler, who my adoptive father and grandfather worked for, used the CB&Q freight cars to take his upholstered furniture all over the country. My natural father's brother, my Uncle Bill was also a railroad engineer for the CB&Q as was my natural mother's ex-husband, Earl Lumsley. So they are all connected by the CB&Q and I wasn't ever supposed to find that out. It was a well-kept secret until now."

The truth slowly emerged. I was blind and now was beginning to see the genetic fit. The Franckenstein monster was becoming a real Franck. I was bridging the chasm of two separated worlds, rejoining what was divided and bonding previously separated parts of my lost self with my original family. The two people inside of me were beginning to understand each other and become one. There were real people with whom to identify. I didn't feel crazy anymore or like I had two heads, but I did cry about it often.

Two articles from a local Wisconsin Dells newspaper arrived in the mail about my father. A photo of my father John was enclosed.

> The article began "WE SALUTE… John Franck
>
> "The Pied Piper of Harding School is retiring.
>
> "John Franck was honored by the little ones this morning in the school gymnasium. Special poems, pictures and songs were presented to their special friend along with a trout basket, which he can use on his frequent fishing trips.
>
> 'He reminds us of the Pied Piper when he has the children trailing behind him every day,' said Lorna Peebles, instructional media director at the school. She said that every day Franck would walk for a half-hour before school started and at each recess break with the children following close behind.
>
> 'They would all fight to take his hand so they could talk with him,' she said.
>
> 'The kids just love him,' said Nina Mullins, a teacher at the school. She said Franck walks the sidewalk around the school each day and learns more about the students' families or just talks about hunting and fishing, two things he loves.
>
> 'He sort of grandpas' them,' said Mrs. Mullins, 'especially the boys. He "protects" them, and takes them to the sick room when they need a bandage.'
>
> "Mullins said, 'He's quite a gentleman. I

> don't know if there is a person in the state of Wisconsin that can fill his shoes. He leaves quite a void.'
>
> Mullins also mentioned his love for the outdoors, saying that he was quite a good writer and had several articles published in a fish and game magazine.
>
> The other article was titled, "Kids Will Miss His Walks and Talks."
>
> "When a student misbehaves in the classroom, he or she may be punished and sent on a trip to the principal's office. But winding up in John's office might not be such a bad experience. There is a certain feeling of warmth in those quarters in the old elementary school. The office is decorated with a smattering of wildlife art, coffee and donuts for most visitors.
>
> "Every morning before school and during recesses, he may be seen meandering alone around the school grounds. In a short time, two or three students will gather beside him and walk along."

The curse was broken! The veil had been lifted.

"Jerry, come here, I have something to tell you. So this was why I have such an attraction and am vulnerable to the woods and woodsmen. Read this about my father," I told him.

"Wow, Tim inherited his talent and love of fly-fishing, and you are so much like him, too," he exclaimed.

"Look at these pastels of our son John's. The fish he drew are red, yellow and black, the colors of the German flag. This is mind blowing. The pieces to this incredibly complex genetic puzzle are finally coming together."

While sitting quietly one day on the living room couch trying to understand the truth about my birth family including myself, I was looking at my original monoprint of the terra cotta hen filled with daisies that hung behind me on the wall in the reflection of the mirror across the room. Suddenly, after the mirror gazing, the hen shape morphed into a 'trout basket' with the wild daisies coming out of it! What? Had I done it again? What was going on? John was a trout fisherman and the little children gave him a 'trout basket' when he retired! This was as bizarre as my cat pastel. I was drawing and channeling 'the truth' from two realities! Were our brains and memory banks entangled or melded in some cellular way? It wasn't an optical illusion or tromp l'oeil either. Was there such a thing as multiple intelligences? How could my art be so complex to contain both of my identities? Could it be a right and left brain function or encoded in my brain?

"I think the writing and producing of that children's magazine *The Pet Elephant* was the natural part of you that was also part of John who was in reality writing articles for fishing magazines like Field and Stream and teaching children as a profession. No wonder your Mother didn't understand why you were writing it. It didn't fit her genetic model. How could it? Your dual identities were tangled together. It's so complicated and confusing. I guess it's no mystery now why Tim is a fly fisherman because your father, their grandfather was one too," Jerry said.

"Mother used to tell me that her father told her genetics were everything, and yet she seemed to ignore mine," I replied.

"Mom, I think we came from a long line of great German artists, musicians, teachers, writers, engineers and fly fisherman," John proclaimed proudly.

24

True Identity

Crossing over is the term used for adoptees when they have become aware of their natural identity. They have become conscious of the fact that they have an entire lost history, and they cross over consciously to the reality of their original relatives and authentic self. Adult adoptees call the process coming out of the fog.

My psych professor friend Doug Henderson from The University of Wisconsin and I talked more about our many issues as adoptees.

"I'm a board member of the American Adoption Congress (AAC) and working for open records. Working with adoptees is like working with coma patients. Recovery and healing the split off part of the adoptee from a closed adoption takes a long time," he told me.

"I've had this insatiable craving to be with my blood relatives all my life," I admitted to Doug.

"Why don't you send some of your art to the AAC conference?" he suggested.

"I'll send the three shadow box paper collages of the three-dimensional opened doors," I told him enthusiastically.

Each door was open representing and advocating for open records and open adoptions. The curator of the show told me they looked like French Chauniieres, German Hauschens or Russian spirit houses. That was news to me. Did they know something about me that I didn't know? Didn't everyone?

I learned from the AAC that Edward Albee, the famous playwright, was an adoptee and had a similar story to mine. He came to speak at an AAC conference and said he never fit into his wealthy adoptive family, bonded with the black maid, and definitely felt schizophrenic. All his plays were about his adoption without ever saying it. Sadly, his fear of rejection kept him from finding his natural mother.

I joined the Concerned United Birthparents (CUB), the Council for Equal Rights in Adoption (CERA), the American Adoption Congress (AAC), Orphan Voyage and the Adoptees' Liberty Movement Association (ALMA) to learn as much as possible about the adoption community.

It was now 1995, and right in the middle of trying to make sense of my insanely complicated personal mess, Tim asked me to take him on a fly-fishing trip to Missoula, Montana. He wanted to hire a guide and go on a fly fishing trip after reading an article about it in one of his friend's fishing magazines. We went by train, and to my surprise, the train stopped right at a little train depot in Wisconsin Dells, Wisconsin where I managed to wave at an old man dressed in overalls and railroad cap sitting on a bench next to the station. He waved back at me and I was hurled back to my abandoned baby self, homesick, sick at heart, and consumed by raw emotion.

I wanted to get off the train right then and there to find and embrace my parents to put an end to my constant mourning their loss, but knew that they would call the police and charge me with stalking and harassment if I showed up on their doorsteps. Tim could have gone fly-fishing with his grandpa, and I could have run into Mama's arms. My child led me right to them and once more we were so close and yet so far. The train continued on and while traveling through Winona, Minnesota at 4am in the morning I sat in the top of the train car looking out the window at the wooded landscape with tears streaming down my face wishing I could see them face to face so my tortured soul could reunite with my mother and father and find a place to rest.

When we arrived in White Fish, Montana I rented a car and we began our drive to a motel right on The Clarks Fork River in Missoula. The next day Tim and a guide went out to fish and when he arrived back at the motel around midnight the guide was calling him “the boy wonder” after catching the biggest trout under a full moon that they had ever seen!

A woman in the motel lobby began talking to me the next morning. I told her I was a musician and an artist.

“You look like Emmylou Harris the singer. Have you ever heard of the town of Silesia? It’s an entertainment and artist community south of Billings. Silesia was named after the mineral springs in the area located along the Clarks Fork River by one of the early inhabitants, Julius Lehrkind of eastern Germany, who named the springs after his homeland province of Silesia,” this woman told me.

“I wish I could, but I have to go home to New York. How I wish I knew my homeland. I was adopted and am trying to find out my heritage. All I know is that my parents live in Wisconsin Dells and that I am a Franck. What is so painful is that they live right on the train route, and I can’t get off the train to meet them or I will be put in jail.”

“Oh, I’m so sorry dear, aren’t your adoptive parents your real parents?” she asked.

“I have two sets of parents. One set are my biological parents and the other my adoptive parents and I love them both,” I informed her as she turned and left me standing there.

There were awe inspiring ten feet tall hand-carvings of giant bears made out of huge tree trunks standing outside the driveways of many of the Montana houses and in all the stores the caved bears were for sale. These bears reminded me of the dead tree trunk I photographed to show the boys standing by the Ward Pound Indian Reservation back in Westchester that was shaped like a thirty foot standing grizzly bear. This old, dead oak tree sculpture kept drawing me into its bear-ness as did my bear dreams as a child.

The following day while Tim was away I sat watching in fascination from the motel room balcony a fly fisherman and his black lab on the riverbank out of the motel window. They kept turning into my father John and his blonde lab until Tim finally walked into the room at dusk all smiles from his fishing excursion.

"Mom, help. My arms are covered with mosquito bites," he said itching hundreds of bites.

Off we went to the emergency room for a shot of cortisone. Once we were back in the motel room I began to think about that man and his dog.

"I feel like a ghost. If only we could stop and meet our relatives on the way home," I told Tim.

"Mom, I love you. Try not to think about them, ok," and gave me a big hug.

The night before we were to leave for home I sat quietly on the motel bed gazing at the evening sky when I saw silhouetted against the huge white moon a dark cloud in the shape of a large black bird that looked like a hawk or eagle with a leviathan wing span. What did it mean? I had seen the same black eagle cloud before my mother-in-law died. Why was I having this vision?

Tim and I packed up, hit the road back to White Fish and began the long train ride home. He drew wonderful sketches as the days went by and it was evident that he also had inherited my artistic talent. I watched two guys making drawings and watercolors in the smoking car of the train and wanted to ask if they knew anyone with the last name Franck from Wisconsin Dells, but was too afraid.

I kept picturing getting on a ghost train with my father and grandfather and great grandfather reunited and riding our way to Heaven one day.

We finally returned home after three long days on the train.

"There's a message from a Leigh Lumsley on Tim's answering machine," Jerry told me.

"My half-brother called?" I said with a huge smile on my face and ran to listen to the message.

I called him and we began to talk like two old long lost friends. Leigh was an artist and a genius, too. We even loved the same lobster bisque soup with a shot of sherry. At last I had a person who really was related to me and was also like me down to our artistic talent, laugh, and our thoughts. He was a great sense of comfort to me.

"I hope you don't need my kidney," he jokingly said.

It was so exciting for all of us. His wife Sheila was listening to us on the phone and thought we sounded like twins. He was a successful insurance broker living in San Diego. Perhaps he was that guy at the bar who seemed so familiar to me when I was out there with my family after Mother died.

"I'll send you a copy of the family genealogy."

"Leigh, what's my maiden name?" I finally asked.

"It's Bartz! Our German great grandparents came from Kolberg, in East Prussia which is close to the Baltic Sea. Magdalena, your great grandma spoke German," he said as if it was no big deal.

"I'm from East Prussia, oh, my God!"

"Don't feel bad, but our mother didn't mention you in the family tree."

It hurt to know that none of my relatives even knew I existed and I would have to resurrect myself alone to get back on the family tree. Leigh sent me pictures of my mother, Mrs. Dorothy Bartz Lumsley. There she was at four years old with the same toothy grin, dimples and big blue eyes with her right eye appearing smaller than her left one like mine. Then another picture at thirty dressed in a Bavarian dirndl; another of her at her wedding with her sister Lois, and another of my grandparents. It was Grandmother Martha who had the moonstone blue cat eyes. She was so beautiful and exotic looking and my grandfather Ernest was very blonde, tall, thin and handsome. The photos were in black and white and they all appeared to have blue eyes. I began to see and feel a real connection to them. It was slow. My eyes looked and studied their pictures endlessly. Tim looked exactly like Leigh's high school yearbook picture. It was amazing to see this. I never knew that children go through such genetic changes.

"Our German-speaking great grandmother Magdalena, grandmother Martha and mother were abusive hissers and spitters. Mother was wild and loved to ride on motorcycles when she was younger. Would you believe when I was a kid she punished me by hiding from me when I came home from school to make me think she was gone. She was abusive. I belong to Mensa do you?" he asked.

"No, because no one in my adoptive family knows I'm an artist or a genius. Remember I don't know my genealogy, family background or true identity," I replied with such excitement I could burst.

Looking at Dorothy's wedding picture made me feel queasy. There she was with huge eyes standing next to her husband on one side and her sister and her husband posing for the wedding photographer.

"I received your letter back in 1977, but decided to remain silent until Mother's or rather Dorothy's death. The letter you wrote to her sister forced her out of denial. Mother called me and cried over the phone, 'I had a baby!' I told her it was okay and she then proceeded to go back into denial after calling you 'that woman' and 'her big sin!' My psychiatrist told me Dorothy was in partial denial," Leigh informed me.

Leigh's wife took the phone.

"Dorothy's a manic-depressive and should be on medication. Leigh and I have been seeing psychiatrists for years. You should read the book *Touched with Fire* about manic-depression and the artistic temperament. We understand the way you think and express yourself," they revealed. Was I a manic-depressive too? This was a stunning revelation.

Another photo Leigh sent revealed a framed master pencil sketch on the wall behind him of the back of a peasant woman's legs that he had drawn. He had the same style as the pencil sketch I had done of my dog Peanuts. We were not only fine artists who drew like, Albrecht Durer, the German painter, printmaker and theorist from Nuremberg but he drew in pencil, too. I finally fit in and had a real connection and a genetic mirror to my artist half-brother! My artistic talent was genetic and yes there was real genius in my family. This took my breath away. We even named a stuffed dog my son John carried on his shoulders everywhere Herbie after an unknown maternal great uncle, Herbert Bartz who lived in Missoula, Montana. That was telepathic.

The hidden blood connections went so far back in time. How did I know the unknowable? How far back into our genetic history did this connecting thread go?

"I am sending you something of our mothers'," Leigh informed me over the phone.

"What?" I asked in anticipation.

"Dorothy's hand-crafted sterling silver baby spoon from a set belonging to our great grandparents, Rudolph Bartz and Magdalena Klatt Ewald, who were both born in 1849. They brought the silverware with them to America from Kolburg, Germany in East Prussia in 1868," he said.

A week went by and a box arrived for me. Inside it was a small sterling silver spoon with a beautiful B for Bartz engraved in fancy Old German script on the handle. I finally had an authentic piece of sterling silverware with my surname initialed on it. My own silver spoon arrived in an envelope hand written by Dorothy that began, "To Whom It May Concern." I was deliriously happy. Leigh told me that many of the "Old Lutherans" from East Germany were persecuted and moved to the United States.

The black and white baby picture of Dorothy, my mother, who must have been no more than six months old, looked more like someone's perfect German doll sitting on my grandmother's lap than a real baby. She was perfect! I still didn't realize Tim and I looked exactly like her as babies because I had never seen a picture of myself as a baby.

He also sent her fragile and delicate Nippon-porcelain

baby cup that her parents brought from East Prussia. Inside was a piece of paper with something written on it from Leigh's wife.

> "I always intended to give these things to you one day, but if she found out about our relationship, she would demand everything back that she entrusted to us. I have a doll for you too, made in Germany that was hers. Dorothy gave this baby cup to us. She said that she didn't like milk and so she had just a little in her cup herein. Her doll is in Chester for now.
>
> P.S. She'd punish us by forcing the return of the German doll too. Love, Sheila"

The tiny cup had tiny Bleeding Hearts hand painted in gold moriage upside down on it that were exactly like the ones I had hand painted on my baskets! Did our blood and DNA connections go back to German artists in Europe? The family ancestral artifacts had finally arrived and so had I. We were all genetically connected and I had part of the family treasure back. I shed my false self like a snakeskin and dropped my abusive brother Rob like a bad habit.

Suddenly I had a reason to care about history and found that the Austrian Empire once included Silesia and Prussia. Now it became clear to me that Silesia and Prussia were real places and my genetic homelands. Now I understood why people told me I looked German, French, Swedish, Russian and Polish. According to the newspaper article I received from the genealogical society, my great grandfather August Franck came from Silesia, Germany to live in Wisconsin. My European roots came from Silesia, Prussia on my father's side and then East Prussian from Kolberg (Kolobreg) on my mother's side. No wonder I was drawn to the talented Germans. Kolberg was a city in middle Pomerania and was part of Sweden in 1637-1721, Prussia (Germany) in 1761 and then captured by the Russians during the Seven Years War and in 1871 part of the German Empire and a seaside resort along The Baltic Sea complete with beer gardens. When I read about the Prussian Order of the Black Eagle, my memory of the black eagle vision in Missoula came to mind as part of my secret history and identity. The truth was so unbelievable. Now I understood why Mother thought I was a witch. Can you imagine a Prussian trying to be a British aristocrat? Impossible.

Dorothy's sister, Lois Bartz Small, looked like my Northern German ex-sister-in-law who was married to Rob. My ex-sis-in-law was a German from northern Europe and so was I. This must have been a genetic connection. I slowly began to realize I was not English, but German, and that my mother married an Englishman and my aunt was married to a Scotsman like my first husband. What a fraudulent deception and dirty trick. The secrecy in the system was insane, not me. No more would I have to pretend to be someone I was not and the pretense of being a Meyer was over.

I bought two Pomeranians way before I even found out that Pomerania was just a bit West of Kolburg, East Prussia, back in the 1700 and 1800's. Pomeranians, before the royals bred them to be lap dogs, drew the barges on the waterways in Pomerania. Wow! Talk about cellular memories, genetics and family ties. Even Queen Victoria had a beloved Pomeranian. I began to jokingly refer to myself as Baroness von Frankfurter.

"Where did I get my witch's nose?" I asked Leigh.

"Haven't you ever seen the witch dolls from Germany? They have that nose that looks like a beak. Are your eyes big and do they look sort of Chinese?" he asked.

"Yes," I answered in amazement.

"Some think the slanty eyes come from way back in the 11th century when the Mongols invaded. Our grandmother had those eyes too. Germans are very tribal," he informed me.

"Is your right eye smaller than your left one like mother's and mine?" he asked.

"Yes," I answered in amazement realizing I had inherited it as well as her dislike of milk. "Does Dorothy have a rough time swallowing pills like I do? I have to chew them or I gag."

"This is crazy. You have to chew your pills, too? Oh my God!" he exclaimed. "She also has something called Raynaud's Syndrome and—"

"So do I," I interrupted him in mid-sentence.

"You really are my sister," he exclaimed.

It was now 1996. The next day some more information arrived from one of the searchers in Wisconsin Dells. I had three half siblings and their names and dates of birth. Somehow I found one that was from Wyoming and asked information and found his address. It was 1996 and once again a letter was sent to him in hopes he might reply. His reply never came so I tried the phone leaving messages on his answering machine and yet again total silence.

25

Past Life

To complicate matters, I knew I was clairvoyant and a seer into another dimension called having the sixth sense. If reincarnation was real what could I have possibly done in a past life to be so badly abandoned and punished in this one?

Was there a connection to a past life as an Indian princess like Tarquin who read my Tarot cards in Carmel said? I knew Dorothy was a believer in American Indian spirituality, and we had an uncle who lived in Montana with the Indians. I began to research Winona, the town in Minnesota where Dorothy's parents, my grandparents, lived and died and where she would eventually be buried next to them. It was wonderful knowing I came from Minnesota and Wisconsin after feeling like a Martian all my life.

Could I have done something in a past life that would carry over into this life where I was doomed to wander like a refugee, abandoned and alone far from home?

Then I read the Legend of Princess Winona from a newspaper article that another search angel sent to me.

The legend—

The most romantic legend associated with the Mississippi Horicon (Lake Pepin) is the story of Princess Winona. She was the daughter of a Dakootah chief. An old medicine woman related the legend.

About 150 years ago, the band of Dakootah to which Winona belonged, lived near Fort Snelling. Their village was on the site now occupied by Good Road's band. She was extremely beautiful and universally beloved.

Her father had promised her hand to a favorite warrior, but her heart had been pledged to another, not less brave, but more noble and youthful. For many months, she would not listen to the wishes of her father but his sterner nature was roused, and he vowed that she must marry the object of his choice. Weeks passed on, and she knew that she must yield. Nightly did she meet her accepted lover, but always talked to him of the Spirit Land, as if she had been a queen of that fantastic realm.

The marriage night had been appointed, and the chief had proclaimed a feast. To all outward appearances, a change suddenly came over the daughter's mind, and she smiled and talked, like one about to be a happy bride. Among the delicacies that were to be eaten on the occasion was a certain berry that was found in perfection upon a certain hill or bluff. It was a pleasant summer afternoon, and all the female friends of Winona accompanied by herself, were picking the desired berries.

Carelessly did they wander up the hillside, while an occasional laugh would ring upon the air; but Winona was only seen to smile, for (though those loving friends knew it not) her heart was darkened by many a strange shadow.

> Carelessly did the berry-pickers wander; when all at once a low melancholy song fell upon their ears, and lo! Upon the very edge of a beetling precipice stood the form of the much beloved Winona.
>
> Her song was death-like and when her companions were intuitively convinced of the contemplated deed, they were stupefied with horror. Winona motioned to keep back, while her song increased until it became a perfect wail.
>
> "Farewell, sister--- I am going to the Spirit Land; My warrior will come after me, And we shall be blessed."
>
> Having finished her song, the maiden answered her parents. "You have forced me to leave you. I was always a good daughter and never disobeyed you; and could I have married the man I love, I should have been happy, and would never have left you. But you have been cruel to me; you have turned my beloved from the wigwam; you would have forced me to marry a man I hated; I go to the house of spirits."
>
> One moment more, and Winona, the pride of all the Indian villages of Lake Pepin, was deeply buried in its clear cold bosom. And this is the story that hallows Maidens Rock the loftiest peak of this lake. As to Winona's warrior, it is said that he lived for many years a hermit, and finally died a madman. So runneth many a song of life.

A big, mysterious, wooden box arrived for me from an art gallery in Wisconin Dells. Who sent it was a mystery until I lifted 'Spirit Horse,' an authentic Lakota Indian artifact, from the box with a note on it from Leigh. His gift of a beautiful painted horse sculpted out of clay was showcased in a glass-covered red-velvet-lined wooden shadowbox hand made by an Indian artist from the Pine Ridge Reservation. This made me wonder even more about my spiritual connections to Dorothy and Leigh. He also sent me an authentic dream catcher.

"Our uncle lived in Montana with the Indians. He gave me some authentic Indian moccasins and other artifacts," he said to me during our next phone conversation.

Was that why Tim and I had such a strong mystical connection to Missoula when we were there? Is this why I bought that top in the Indian store with my friend Dotty when I first moved to New York? What about the bear dreams and visions?

Inside the box printed in red on a silver square gave the history of the horse.

> Spirit Horse
>
> The name of this horse is ThunderCloud; therefore, its Spirit name is painted on the horse. This horse wasn't only created for the pleasure of the owner but to let the spirit of a horse rest. Many years ago, the horses were brought to my people by the creator, when we were in great need.
>
> This is how my people thank the creator and honor the horses. The horse's mouth was made open to allow his spirit to enter and leave at any time. This horse had a pouch to carry its own medicine.
>
> (Reverse side)
>
> The medicine it carries are sage and sweet grass. Sage is used by my people to chase bad spirits from mind, body, and surroundings. Sweet grass is used to welcome good spirits. The Shield and War Club are used to protect the spirit your spirit horse houses. The red circle around the eye allows the spirit of this horse to see the red road. The red on the

> bottom of the hooves indicates this horse is on the red road. The red road represents everything good, kind, and honest in life. The white circle around the eye shows that the spirit housed can see other spirits while resting.
>
> Artist Michael Roberts—Winnebago

How did Leigh know I could see spirits and loved to ride horses? My friend Janet thought she had been a horse in a past life and my master flutist friend thought I was a Shaman. Did anything get any stranger?

I also was shocked to see that the little miniature vine wreaths I was making for my hand made cards was also used by the Indian artist as the shield on Spirit Horse. We were all connected?

The art gallery where Leigh bought Spirit Horse tried contacting the artist who was a real Lakota Indian for me. They called to tell me he couldn't be reached and to call the fellow who made the boxes for the artifacts. We talked and I told him the amazing story about my connection to my half-brother, my dreams and visions.

"My best friend is an Indian woman named White Feather, and we like to go to a special lake to help find peace of mind and go on vision quests. I have an anxiety disorder and lost my big city job. She just carved and gave me a bear fetish made out of granite, and I want you to have it," he said.

"Why?" I asked him.

"I don't know really but the great spirit told me to."

This was a sacred moment! I had my jeweler friend bend wire around the 2" stone bear so I could wear it on a piece of leather around my neck for protection and as a connection to my lost Indian tribe from a past life. At last, a real connection to my soul and other souls. This was a full circle moment and very healing.

Soon after Spirit Horse arrived, another type-written letter with no return address also appeared in the mail. I opened it and there typed on a one-inch strip of white paper like a fortune in a fortune cookie was, "May God Help You."

Did Dorothy write this? If so, she finally dealt the fatal blow as those were her last words to me.

The darker side of this reunion began to show itself. Leigh was very proud to be a German and collected Nazi memorabilia from WW II.

"Leigh is bi-polar and an alcoholic. His IQ is 160 and he's a Mensa member. He actually got up and danced on the table tops in Mexico yelling, 'Sieg heil' once when he was drunk," Shirley told me.

John was learning he was German and wanted his uncle to send him some memorabilia from the The Third Reich. Jerry was listening to our phone conversation.

"Tell Jerry not to worry, I won't send any lamp shades," Leigh said and laughed.

That comment sent him into a rage.

"These are the people who murdered us! Don't you dare have him send John anything from the Nazis," he yelled and headed for the Valium and the vodka.

It became apparent that I could have been brought up on Mein Kampf instead of Emily Post had the adoption not taken place. More truth began to unfold when my sons told me about something they had seen at the local mall. There was a vendor who had information about family surname history and family crests. We went to look up our surname Bartz.

"What does the name Bartz mean, Mom?" John asked. "Oh, my God. You won't believe this, but it means BEAR in High German."

Bartz, bear, Bartz, bear ran through my mind like a tornado. Bear was a sacred symbol and a true connection to my lost tribe. I was clairvoyant and really did have an unbreakable telepathic bond with Dorothy and my natural ancestors. This was huge. It was unbelievable. Was this some sort of cosmic joke? The boys and I were in total shock and awe. In an instant, we had our identity back. The three of us bear hugged and jumped up and down smiling and cheering at the mall.

This explained all my childhood bear dreams and visions

of bears in clouds and in wood. It also explained the Franckenstein dreams because I was a Franck. I had broken the dream code. We were all genetically and psychically connected! Who would ever believe it? Was this the Jungian archetype or the universal mind at work? Thus began my history lesson.

The Genealogical Society in Wisconsin sent me another newspaper article about my great grandfather August Franck who was born in 1836 in Guensthersdorf in the Province Silesia, a former Hapsburg province, and his wife who was born in Gleiwitz, Prussia. He had studied to be a tailor in London. Now I realized where my sewing and designing talent originated. It was finally sinking into my brain that my ancestors came from Prussia and I was Prussian! My love of serene forests went as far back as the forests in the ancient Baltic regions including Lower Silesia. The article was pictureless, but at least it was more genetic information finally bringing me down to earth giving me my identity back. August was a Knight of Columbus and his son, my great Uncle Paul, was a Priest. These Knights could only be Catholic men in union with the Holy See and had to have knightly qualities of spirituality and serve the Catholic Church by doing the work of God on earth. This was amazing information!

"The worst sinners are liars. I'll send you what I have found about your Franck ancestors," said the genealogist over the phone.

"You can take the girl out of Prussia, but you can't take the Prussian out of the girl," I said with a laugh thanking her for finding this information for me.

I thanked her and joyfully received pictures of my grandfather, the railroad engineer and school board member, who I resembled in first grade. The paperback book about the railroad had an article about my grandfather written by my railroad engineer Uncle Bill. "Rich actually ran the first diesel engine the Zephyr in 1935 on the Burlington. He was also a well-respected griever. He could leave Wisconsin Dells in the morning, get to Georgia and have lunch, and be back home on the return trip by 7:30 in the evening. Firing the Zephyr was the best job you could have. Rich was the conductor for The Great Northern Railroad in St. Paul, Minnesota."

To my astonishment, I saw an engineer in the book with the same last name as my sorority sister at college in Arizona. It gave me the shivers to think that my friendship with her as well as my traumatic depressions and anxiety reactions at college to the song Locomotive Man, A Rainy Night in Georgia, my railroad lantern project at the séance, my love for the train conductors at Gaga's in South Pasadena, riding on trains and driving were real connections to my lost relatives and secret identity. The steamrollers chasing me in my childhood dreams were really symbolic trains!

Uncle Bill's high school picture arrived and he looked like Tim. He also looked like my son John's best friend. The power of genetics was so obvious now. I wished Mother was still alive so I could tell her who I was and that I named my son John after my father without realizing it.

Dorothy told me my paternal grandmother, Mary Barth Franck, was tall and stately. I read that she was a devout Roman Catholic and very active in St. Michael's Home for Children and yet she was the only one I couldn't get a picture of. Finally I was connecting all the dots.

My family tree on both sides was finally complete and recorded at the County Genealogical Society for eternity, even though my letters to my youngest biological brother, Nick, in 1994, my uncle in 1995, and the one to my oldest brother, Mike, in 1996 were never answered.

A letter arrived in 1998 from my father John's lawyer. I was shocked to find a copy of a page from his last Will and Testament. Section 10 that read.

"I have made no provision in this Will for Melinda as, regardless of her claims, she is not a part of my family circle or otherwise recognized by me as a natural object of my bounty."

"Bounty? What bounty," I wondered.

He died and left money to all sorts of people. It was all about money to him and where did a teacher get so much money? Was this another big secret he was hiding from me? What was wrong with these people, I wondered? Whatever happened to love? All I ever wanted was to be Daddy's Little Nature Girl and feel his love so I could finally fit in somewhere and feel normal. I had so much love to give yet no one cared and they all, including the system, continued to abuse, lie and punish me for just being born. I hoped there was Divine Justice and that God would punish them.

This made me so mad that I wrote a very nasty letter to his lawyer. They left me paralyzed, speechless, powerless with no identity of my own and now I knew I was unloved! Would I be an outcast for eternity? The pain these people kept putting me through was inhumane and should be against the law. The psychiatrist did try to tell me to repress all this desire to find my roots, but I couldn't.

In my fantasies, I went to the cemetery, under the cover of darkness; dug up John's grave and opened the casket just to get a good look at him. I would have crawled in with him if I could have.

There were days I imagined all my dead blood related ancestors' skeletons sitting around my table having dinner with me. I lost aunts, uncles, great aunts and uncles, first, second, third cousins, nieces, nephews, parents, grandparents, great grandparents and it was just too painful to think about for too long.

Then out of the blue, another surprise letter arrived from a girl named Mary Ann from New Jersey who said she was the great granddaughter of my great grandfather August's best friend, a shoemaker, who came over to the U.S. from Gunthersdorf, a village of Silesia, with their wives in 1868. She informed me that both were in the Civil War and stationed in an artillery battalion in Missouri before they brought their wives over from East Prussia. My great grandmother came from Gleiwitz (Gliwice), a city in Upper Silesia. Mary Ann was a genealogist and told me we were fourth cousins as her great, great grandparents from Pomerania and Prussia had a daughter who married one of my great grandfather's sons. She sent me a picture of August

Franck and two of his nine children. He was tall, dark, and handsome like my son John. I was astounded to see that there was a page with about nine pictures of priests on it, too. One of the priests was my great uncle Phil who also looked like my son, John. My eyes almost popped out of their sockets when I saw all the genetic similarities. What a revelation! I really did have a heritage of my own and I was German to the bone.

Another priest looked like Andy, my son's friend, another like my boyfriend, Mark Moore, and one looked like my adoptive father! They were all German priests and friendly ghosts. My adoptive mother, father, and the closed adoption system did their best to invent my heritage, but alas it didn't work. I was Prussian German on both sides and resembled my Great Aunt Hannah Franck when she was about ten in a picture of her with the nuns and her Catholic schoolmates in Potosi, Wisconsin.

If my great grandpa studied to be a tailor in London in the late 1850's it was no longer a big mystery why I was so good at designing and sewing in high school. It all made sense. We were all cut from the same cloth. Mary Ann asked me if I was light sensitive and prone to migraines because she was, too. Finally someone was alive in New Jersey who wasn't in denial and cared and knew the truth about me. My authentic self possessed real substance and was growing stronger and stronger. As I read down the cemetery list the genealogist sent to me, I saw a Frances R. Franck, Cash, born in 1899 who died in 2000. Cash's song Locomotive Man and my breakdown at SJS flashed in my mind as another deeply imbedded yet hidden DNA and psychic connection to my identity.

My grandfather Rich was conducting a train to Georgia, Wisconsin and back to Wisconsin Dells! No wonder I broke down in San Jose when Brook Benton sang *A Rainy Night in Georgia*. The hidden subconscious connections or inherited intrusive memories to my lost birth relatives went so deep and were now healing memories instead of hurtful ones. The more I learned about my lost ancestors, the stronger my spirit and self-esteem became. The truth about my lost families finally emerged and was setting me free from some of the trauma, confusion, depression, and anxiety at last.

A wonderful man and genealogist in Wisconsin sent newspaper articles and pictures of my paternal grandmother's parents. The Weikers were one of the oldest families to live in Wisconsin Dells. They had a lovely and amazing story. Sitting in the front row of a family picture in the newspaper was my ancestor wearing almost the same long patchwork granny dress I wore and loved in California at Mark Moore's. In fact Michael Weiker looked like Mark! Could we really be related after all? My real ancestors gave me a sense of family pride and normalcy after all I had come from and been through with the closed adoption and my crazy adoptive family. I felt like I was finally coming home and fitting in. My spirit was beginning to stop spinning and relax. These were my people who were hopefully were good, wholesome and normal families. They were the real deal and so was I. Finally I was figuring out the fact from fiction about myself.

These ancestors, the Weikers, came all the way from Holzen, Luxembourg in April 1855, built their own log cabins and created their own farms. In June 1905, the eight children celebrated the 50th anniversary of their settlement. They were children again as in procession by two's they walked from place to place, recalling the days gone by.

Surviving members of this family tell interesting anecdotes of early life in Wisconsin Dells. While their first 'log house' was being built the family lived for three months in a tent. Mr. Weiker cut by hand all the shingles which roofed over the log house. One of their most valued possessions that first year was a cow, brought from Galena on the boat. My ancestor gave to the parish the logs, which built the first Catholic Church.

Game was plentiful in the county in the 50's and it was no uncommon sight to see deer drinking out of the creek close to their farm home. The old homestead, boasting one of the finest springs, is now a favorite rendezvous for festive automobile picnic parties, and the trout fishermen wander along the creek where the Weiker family had had a home for 67 years. Nannie Haas (from Luxembourg) married Michael Weiker and their daughter Anna married Fred Barth whose daughter Anna married my grandfather Rich. Knowing I was related to this family gave me some real family history, clarity, comfort, and joy.

It was no secret why I loved to sleep alone in the tent in Kettering, ended up at Casey's log cabin or living happily in New York in the woods in Northern Westchester. So many of my ancestors lived in and loved nature and the woods in Germany, Wisconsin and Minnesota. I was feeling less lost and like I finally fit in realizing I was following in their footsteps all along. My sanity was slowly returning, and my soul began to stop spinning round and round as I became more grounded in reality learning there were others like me.

"Well, Mom, who would believe it would take you thirty years to find out the truth. I guess we can add a tailor and locomotive engineers to our family tree," John said.

A package arrived for me in the mail from Doug in Wisconsin. Wasn't it pretty amazing that I even met Doug and he was from Wisconsin? He sent me a videotape of my second cousin once removed, Barb Franck, who was a basketball player for The University of Wisconsin. She was NCAA like my friend the runner and ST who played pro basketball for the Chicago Condors. It was magical. Could the black-winged bird vision I had in Missoula be a psychic connection to her, too? I began to watch the videotape and was amazed to see the number 44 on her jersey, the same mystical number that ended up in my hand up in Canada! She was pretty, 6'2" with long, brown, curly hair, brown eyes and resembled John, my son! I realized there were both blonde-haired, blue-eyed Germans and Germans with brown hair and brown eyes in my ancestry. Yes, yes, my children also became real. Doug's appearance in my life was no accident. He, along with the truth, was sent from God. In fact, everyone in my life had been sent from God to help me find the truth of my being. Doug bridged the gap between the two worlds of reality and fantasy I was living in by connecting me to a living Franck girl. She was the second blood-related female I had ever seen! Now I understood the significance of that basketball and my love of tall athletes, black or white! My inability for true closeness and intimacy with anyone except with my boys became clearer.

Doug called me on the phone. "I have intimacy problems, too," he told me. "If you can't trust your own mother, who can you trust? The adoptees I work with have big trust issues and a very difficult time with intimacy. They can attach, but can't bond. I bet you that you have shut everyone out and are still waiting to get physically affectionate with your natural mother and father. Do you freeze when someone hugs you? You can't hug or kiss anyone and really feel it? Am I right?" he asked.

"Yes," I admitted and cried like a baby after we hung up realizing that my real love and affection was waiting to be loosed only on my own mother and father.

This was a genetic amazing grace unfolding. "I once was blind but now I see," had real meaning and how sad and happy it made me freeing up a bit more buried and unresolved grief which was only making me stronger.

"Tim, come here," I said. "Look, there is a blonde, curly-haired boy standing by a train wreck from the railroad book of Wisconsin Dells in the 1800's who looks exactly like you."

That train wreck was symbolic of my life. I finally knew where many of the Franck skeletons were buried and they were in the Roman Catholic cemetery in Wisconsin Dells. Another wonderful man who knew my father took photos of the beautiful marble gravestones and the lovely French iron urn planters filled with beautiful flowers for me. My descendants were there together for eternity. I was so happy knowing that I was related to them and now knew where they were all buried together in a real cemetery, as a real family should be. How I wanted to see, know and love them but it was too late.

I was determined to educate my kids about their true blood ancestors and restore our family pride.

"Kids, our paternal surname goes all the way back to the

German tribe the Franks and ancient France. The family surname derived from the ethnic or regional name for someone from Francken, a region of Southwest Germany, so called from its early settlement by the Franks. The Franks were a member of the Germanic people who inhabited the lands around the river Rhine in Roman times," I told John and Tim.

"I guess we're German. Maybe that's why you drink so much beer," Tim said and laughed aloud.

Additional Meaningful History Unfolds

Arcane mysteries began to unfold as I delved deeper into the past. In the sixth century, Ancient France and the Franks, under their leader Clovis I, established a substantial empire in central Europe, which later developed into the so-called Holy Roman Empire. Their most famous leader was the Emperor Charlemagne (742-814) of the Merovingian Dynasty, who may have used The Spear of Destiny which lanced the side of Jesus, to win his 53 battles in the 7th century and now resides in the Habsburg Museum in Austria. The tribal name can be traced back to the Old High German word Frank that means courageous or free in spirit, and would have reflected the character of these people, my ancestors and me. Fantastic!

The Bartz surname came from St. Bartholomew back in the medieval days when they named children after Saints for protection. This information was so empowering. I learned about my German surname Bartz and its variants Barz and Bartsch. The name Bartz indicates son of Bartz; a pet form of either Bartholumaus or names derived from the Old High German word hero, meaning bear. This became the root of personal names such as Berolf (bear-wolf), Berowin (bear-friend), Gerhelm (bear-helmet), and Nerfrid (bear-peace).

"Jerry, you know what is so amazing? My best friend in Ohio, Annie Bertschy, had the same surname as mine and my best friend from California was also German. I have been genetically attracted to Germans like the ones I lost even though the government tried to keep this a secret from me."

"It is unbelievable. You are such a genius. I wouldn't have believed you if I hadn't gone through it with you," Jerry said mystified that I had figured it all out.

"Just think, my name means Bear in High German. The bear dreams and the bears that appear to me in cloud formations are a part of my stolen identity. Did you know that Oak trees were the holy trees of the Germans and worshipped by Aryans? There were oak tree cults connected to ancestor worship," I told Jerry.

"I guess they are sacred blood bonds and connections to your ancestors and spirit guides. Do you think your father has stayed in denial because his wife doesn't know about you and she might divorce him if she did?" he asked me.

"Anything is possible and it probably is all about selfishness, holding onto power and money like everything else in this world is," I surmised.

"Isn't it amazing how I tuned into that forty foot dead tree trunk that looked like a huge grizzly rearing up on its hind legs on the road by the Ridge Reservation shortly before I found out my real name meant bear? Who would believe it!

"The Franck's also have an incredible history," I said.

"Slow down! I am exhausted just listening to you. Tell me more later. I have some serious business problems and I have to make money," he said.

"Their history went all the way back to the Merovingians and the Simcambrians. Paris and Orleans were land holdings within the Emperor Charlemagne's empire in ancient France. I was a Franck, but was I ancient French going back to the 5th century, maybe? My research led me to find out that the Germans originated from Scandinavia. The German men were hunters and the women were soothsayers! Was seeing in my blood?" I wondered.

The extent to which they had covered up the truth of my true identity was incredible. No one would have cared if I ended up in jail, dead, or in a mental hospital for the rest of my life with a misdiagnosis like schizophrenia or borderline personality disorder like so many other adoptees do. When I asked Dorothy, my own mother, who I looked like she said, "You look like you," which was just cruel.

26

The Artist

It seemed like my adoptive family history was repeating itself except it was now the year 2000 when Jerry came home one day to tell me we were bankrupt! I knew how my adoptive mother must have felt back in Kettering, but it was worse for me as I was all of a sudden being forced to hock my diamond heirloom rings to pay the mortgage and had to find a job in order for us to survive until Jerry could figure out what to do.

A local art center hired me to teach drawing and painting. It wasn't long until I convinced the owner to open a gallery so I could work on the weekends to sell art and teach private flute lessons. Now that I knew Leigh and I were gifted artists I finally felt empowered and at home there. After a lifetime of abnormality and spinning like a top I was finally beginning to become grounded in reality.

The Saturday before the opening of the gallery after everyone was gone I took a box of student pastels and began to draw a picture of the old French quarter in New Orleans from an ad I found in a travel magazine. The primal energy poured out of me onto the paper like it was drawing itself. I was channeling again.

The Old French stone building I was drawing began to resemble a vintage abandoned broken-down dark and haunted gray stone French chateau or castle. The shutters on the windows were old and broken. The rotting slats of the shutters took on the look of a face and lips whispering secrets outside the blackened rooms within. The piece began to look dark and haunted. My hands magically began working in grays, blues, reds, browns, gold, copper and straw colors throughout the pastel. The stone path began at an old gray stone pillar continuing under a stone archway through a tunnel leading to a tiny soft amber colored sunlit stone room with a tiny darkened window surrounded by stones representing yet another deep dark secret that was yet to be revealed to me. While I was feverishly working on the pastel for the exhibit, Leigh called the gallery.

"Mother has died. She starved herself to death. I'll send you some of her personal things from her room at the nursing home. I never told her but I have a house on Lake Alminor in Chester," he revealed.

"You're kidding me. I went there with my first husband and you were there all the time? Oh, my God. What are you sending me?"

"Just some pictures and a few prayers I found in her room," he said.

"Would you send me some of her ashes?"

"Sure."

My heart sank like a stone after the phone call. I brought my pastel home to work on it and have it close to me while putting the finishing touches on it for the gallery opening. Signing it M. Franck, my biological surname, gave me legitimacy and the title I gave to my channeled masterpiece was *Silent Witness.* Back it went to the gallery and up it went unframed on the push pin wall for the world to see.

"Who is M. Franck?" asked one of the art teachers at the gallery opening.

"I am. I'm adopted and I signed it using my natural paternal surname, Franck," I replied.

"This looks like the Via Delorosa," the teacher said to me.

"What is that?" I inquired.

"It's the street in the Old City of Jerusalem which Jesus

is said to have walked on the way to his crucifixion. It means 'the way of grief.' The wall looks like the Wailing Wall. Your journey is also 'the way of grief' isn't it?" she commented as if she was a docent in a museum.

"Yes, it is. I wanted so much to meet my own parents and now they are both dead and it will never happen," I told her holding back the tears knowing it was because of their absence that I couldn't trust and kept everyone but my sons at an emotional distance.

Later that week a box arrived from Leigh. Inside it was a small tin filled with Dorothy's ashes, and a newspaper article about my grandmother, Martha, with a picture of her on her ninetieth birthday. The article revealed how she met my grandfather at a dance. He played the trumpet in a dance band and she introduced herself to him during a band break.

I called Leigh to find out more.

"Our grandfather had perfect pitch, great ears and could play and improvise with anyone. He loved to play jazz especially and was quite the swing dancer," Leigh revealed.

"I have perfect pitch and wanted to be a jazz flutist," I told him.

"You would have really loved him. His best friend played his favorite song by Segovia on the guitar while he was dying," he said.

"What song was that?" I asked.

"*The Girl with the Flaxen Hair* by Debussy, have you heard of it?"

"I play the song on my flute along with Segovia from a tape. Segovia is my favorite classical musician. Isn't that crazy that my grandfather and I loved the same artist and song? Leigh, I have always loved my grandfather, Ernest. So, he was the musician! I am a musician, too, and have been playing my flute with professional musicians! Oh, my God! There is another genetic mirror. Tell me about Grandmother," I said excitedly.

"She was tall, blonde, beautiful, and so psychic. People back then thought she was a witch and weird so she hid her ability to know and see things," he said.

"I think I inherited it," I replied.

"Did you inherit her big, green, sexy cat eyes? You must be one tall, blonde, hot babe then," he assured.

"Yes. People have told me that looking into my eyes is like looking at a mood ring because they change color all the time. Some guys even growl when they look into my eyes," I laughed.

"I also have a Pickelhauben which is one of those Prussian spiked helmets worn by the German military. It was one of our ancestors who rode in the Prussian cavalry," he said proudly.

The shadow world and the shattered mirror were now being pieced together bit by bit. No more would I be at the mercy of total strangers for validation.

Leigh also sent me another picture of Dorothy as a baby sitting on beautiful Marta's lap alongside my gorgeous tall and slender grandfather. She looked like Tim when he was a baby and I suddenly began to realize that I must have looked like my own mother when I was a baby! I finally made the connection to my lost baby self and was now able to say aloud that I looked like my mother. Martha, my grandmother, the East Prussian, looked a lot like Madame Blavatsky, the Nobel Russian, but Martha was much prettier! Grandfather Ernest Bartz looked like me after my nose was done. He had the cutest pug nose, straight fine blonde hair and was so handsome in a gentle and sensitive way.

The little orphan misfit was finally born of real flesh and blood. A real fit at last. I had Martha's big, almond eyes and Ernest's beautiful long fingers plus his musical and artistic talent.

I pulled from the envelope Dorothy's birth and death certificate, plus some prayers she had written on parchment paper she kept in her room.

"If I knew certainly the world would end tomorrow, I would plant an apple tree today."

By Martin Luther

A Prayer

"The table I approach Dear Savior, Hear my prayer. Oh, let no unrepented sin prove hurtful to me there."

Matthew 26 v. 41

An Evening Prayer

"We beseech Thee Lord, to behold us with favor, fold of many families and nations, gathered together in the peace of this roof. Be patient still; suffer us awhile longer to endure, and (if it may be) help us to do better. Bless to us our extraordinary mercies.

Be with our friends. Be with ourselves. Go with each of us to Rest. If any awake, temper to them the dark hours of watching; and when the day returns to us call us up with morning faces and with morning hearts-eager to labor-eager to be happy. If happiness shall be our portion-and if the day be marked for sorrow-strong to endure it."

Robert Lewis Stevenson (ironically the author of Dr. Jekyll and Mr. Hyde)

I looked at the colored photos of Mama with a very red-headed Leigh on their trip to Germany in 1983.

"She was very proud of being one hundred percent German," he told me.

I saw from looking at her in the photo that I had her small bones, tiny long waist, and fair complexion. We were tall, thin, and small-boned. I had to keep looking at the pictures over and over again to believe what I was seeing. We looked alike and I was finally seeing parts of my own tall, slender body and tiny waist on her. It was very strange at first. She even wore sneakers like I do and a red scarf tied around her neck just like the red scarves on the mini polar bears on my Christmas cards I designed for my agent. Dorothy was an Aryan, and so was I. She was my mother, for God's sake! I certainly wasn't English and didn't have to pretend to be like my adoptive mother anymore. It all began to make perfect sense. This closed adoption practice of hiding the truth from me and the permanent separation from Dorothy was an abomination of nature and a terrible abuse of power by the closed adoption laws. There was indeed a natural genetic pull within me to Germans as well as to those similar to the ones I lost. We were all connected by a deeply embedded grand genetic design.

There she was in another photo with a huge toothy grin on her face just like mine in a Munich beer garden on Oktoberfest right next to Leigh holding a beer stein in one hand and a cigarette in the other wearing a Tyrolean hat! They both wore glasses and were smiling.

"The only time she was really happy was when she was back in Germany," Leigh told me over the phone.

I really saw myself reflected in her especially in the picture of her next to a huge monument on the Palace Grounds in Wurzburg, Germany.

"When I went to empty out Dorothy's safety deposit box, I saw my birth certificate and realized I was a 'had to get married' baby. She was a manic-depressive and should have been on medication you know."

He began to refer to our dead mother as the vulture on his shoulder. My realization that I was exactly like her was a sobering thought. Leigh began to threaten suicide, unlisted his phone number and never wrote to me again.

This was a lot of information to absorb all at once. I certainly was German all right and continued my research on the Franck surname.

The Francken Kings and the Simcambrians, ancestors of the Franks, were a Moon-worshipping cult. They were known as the "People of the Bear" for their worship of the bear-goddess, Arduina, connected to the constellation Ursa Major, the Great Bear. Could I possibly include these ancient people in my heritage? I certainly had a strong yet mystical connection to bears and I was a Franck. My vision at my aunts of the bear and the moon seemed no coincidence but another mystical connection to my lost tribe and secret identity.

The Merovingian Frankish sacred longhaired kings from the Dark Ages gave me more German history. Their robes were fringed with tassels, which were said to have great magical healing powers. They were known as occult adepts! They have even been proclaimed by some as the Fabulous Race descending from extraterrestrials from Sirius. Like the Nazarenes of old, the Merovingian monarchs never cut their hair, and bore a distinctive birthmark-said to be a red cross over the shoulder blades. In one Merovingian tomb was found such items as a golden bull's head, a crystal ball, and several golden miniature bees. Many skulls of these monarchs appear to have been ritually incised – i.e. trepanned.

I was getting ancient history on both sides of my natural families. Could I be related to these incredible people, too? Is this where all my psychic powers came from? Was this the connection I was searching for? I checked my sons out for the birthmark. Needless to say, it wasn't there, but I finally had a real connection to my genetic history.

My attempt to explain my pastel *Silent Witness* to a psychologist who came into the art gallery while I was adding some of Dorothy's dove gray ashes above the archway to the pastel paper wasn't easy.

"This pastel is fascinating. Who did it and how much is the artist asking for it?" she asked me.

"It's mine and it's not for sale," I told her as I rubbed Dorothy's gray silken ashes between my fingers after secretly using them on the archway in my pastel.

"Is this in New Orleans?" she inquired.

"I think it's in France somewhere and has something to do with my lost identity," I told her thinking I was quite the DNA and psychic detective.

"It looks like it could be in the labyrinth of the 13th century walled town of Chartes where The Chartres Cathedral was or the Palace of the Popes in Avignon, which was the first Seat of the Catholic Church. It could be in Beaujolais where the stones glow with the same golden yellow light from the sun like you have here on this pastel," she enlightened me.

"The colors seem to look like various colors of soft gold and amber light I think? How strange. My life has been such a mystery to me because I'm adopted and my real name is Franck which is German. I thought I was an English aristocrat like my adoptive mother until now. I'm an activist for giving adoptees their original birth certificates and medical information when they are 18 so they can at least know the truth about who they are and their medical history. That's the least they can do for us."

"I totally understand and agree with you," she said.

"*Silent Witness* is the title because there's an almost invisible outline of a man's face right there wearing glasses if you look at the upper left corner which I think is symbolic of my natural father. He's hidden there in the picture if you know where to look and a silent witness to my conception and existence. I know as an adoptee from a closed adoption that there was a conspiracy of silence, secrets, lies and many silent witnesses to my birth who were then purposely put under a gag order by the state government as the records were sealed as was my fate," I explained to her.

The psychologist looked and looked at it. "At least there's light at the end of the tunnel!" she commented.

"I'll drink to that," I said jokingly feeling somewhat queasy and disoriented.

One of the other art teachers who came from a long line of prominent Scottish painters told me *Silent Witness* was a holy painting as I needed him to put some finishing touches on the pastel. Did he see something more than I did?

To me, my channeled piece symbolizes a mysterious eternal room where something miraculous or secretive had taken place that transcends time and space. The planter outside one of the windows took on the appearance of a stone cradle with a headboard that changed to a headstone symbolizing the death of my original identity at birth. The smaller French street lamp next to the planter on the outside of the building also turned into an urn with ashes in it or a womb carrying an egg within it depending on how one looked at it. This work of art was mysterious because I was drawing it without knowing that Mama was slowly passing away leaving me and this earth forever.

I never got to see or touch Mama because she wouldn't let me. I wanted and fantasized about loving and meeting her face to face until the day she died. It seemed I truly had captured the blending of our spirits and souls in this transcendental work of art. When I showed the pastel to my adoptee friend Doug he interpreted something new for me.

"The walls and pillar are obstacles you had to get around as an adoptee from a closed adoption, and the brick wall stopped you from ever having a true reunion with either natural parent or blood relative," he said.

"Do you think adoptees can ever be normal?" I asked him.

"Funny you should ask this. Just about a week ago I had the realization that I don't know a single adoptee who does NOT have problems, ranging from mild to serious, many of them in the sexual area. Everything an adoptee must know on some level about their 'self' having to do with their adoptive identity is a disconnect," he answered.

Time went by and I had *Silent Witness* framed and hung it above my couch in the living room. My old friend Susie from the condo called and I told her everything.

"You have to read Dan Brown's book *The DaVinci Code* and about The Priory of Sion and the hidden symbolism in Leonardo's paintings," she said.

I began to research the Priory of Sion. It was hitting a chord with me. Pope Paul II's ancestry went back to ancient France and the land holdings of Charlemagne and the Carolingian Empire in the 8th century.

I explained my pastel to friends as a channeled piece done during the time Dorothy was dying. Each object had a double or triple meaning representing my original natural family, my psyche, soul and my true identity. The work of art was deep and seemed to go back into time containing mysterious symbols and dark secrets.

No one knew that it contained Dorothy's ashes over the

archway.

There was one thing I didn't quite understand about Silent Witness and that was just why, was I having such trouble shading in the center of the arch to the point of having to ask my Scottish artist friend to help me with the shading.

"You have for some reason drawn what looks like a bird shape almost like an eagle right above the arch," I remembered him saying as he took a blue gray pastel stick and smudged it out.

I didn't even notice the bird there and let him fix it for me.

When I began to look through the pictures of Dorothy again there was one I missed of her standing under the archway entrance to a castle in Nurnburg, Germany. There above her on the archway to the entrance was a black German eagle just like the bird appearing over the archway in my pastel. On either side of Dorothy at the castle entrance hung a red, yellow and black German flag leaving no doubt that Dorothy and I certainly had a spiritual psychic connection through telepathy even though The Cradle Adoption Agency had squashed the truth of my German roots at birth. I couldn't physically see her but some part of my spirit saw and was connected to her through our unbreakable blood bond. Could two minds think the same thing? Apparently so. Did we have the same spirit and mind?

Perhaps true love never dies and neither time nor space could keep our souls apart. Just maybe she was a part or me and with me all the time.

The yellow flowers drawn on my pastel also symbolized the wedding bouquet that Dorothy and John never had. I didn't have a wedding either. There was no wedding and no bouquet for us yet there was the golden yellow light glowing throughout the piece for some reason. The light was trying to tell me something but I just didn't know what.

I was finally able to come out of the sealed record adoption closet as my authentic self into society with a signed work of art no longer feeling spiritually or physically misplaced or so disconnected from reality. So what if I was born out-of-wedlock? I was able to authenticate myself, drop the shame everyone inflicted upon me and tell the truth about my lost identity to everyone and anyone that was interested.

I was still Meyer to all my friends from Kettering and California and Mrs. to those in New York, but those in the adoption community understood the importance of finding my real identity at last.

"I'm East Prussian on both sides. My mother and her family are Lutheran and my father and his family are Roman Catholic and I finally have a legitimate life!" I began to proclaim to the world trying to become normal.

After Dorothy died, my big psychic connection to bears seemed to disappear. I was disturbed about it because the bear theme was always in my awareness as if it were an unseen spiritual bond of eternal love and protection between us.

There was also the bear head rock I always saw on the side of the road next to the Reservation making me feel a connection to her and a sort of primal and spiritual connection transcending space and time. The bear tree trunk at the reservation had been removed and I felt the loss and wondered what it meant until one day in 2003, I saw something new within the yellow-white light of my pastel. There was the head of a pure white bear reading what looked like an ancient copper colored scroll or some old parchment-like document within the radiance of the yellow flowers surrounded by a circle of white light. I saw with my own eyes the white bear head was encircled in white light like the moon. The ancients called the moon The Lady of the Night ruling over fertility and magic. Was this a portal into another world or a Divine Vision or was it trying to reveal to me some important secret I had yet to find out? How in the world did I paint that? What did it mean? The veil had been lifted and there was no boundary between us. I was a bit shocked to suddenly see it. There it was again, the double way of seeing. One way it looked like yellow flowers, and if you looked at it another way you could see the ghostly bear's head looking down reading something sacred and copper colored silhouetted against the moon.

Susie read my story and hadn't realized the depth of what I was going through back in the late 60's and early 70's.

"Remember Linda, our roommate back at the apartment in Palo Alto, California who had the long blonde hair? Her last name is Frank and her parents owned Lawry's Seasonings. Perhaps you two are related. Remember how you always thought you were like Veruschka the supermodel. She was really from East Prussia and changed her name from Countess Vera von Lehndorff- Steinort to Veruschka and told everyone she was from Russia to create a mystery about herself when she signed with Ford Modeling Agency. She had a traumatic childhood too like you, but hers was because her father was in the German resistance and tried to assassinate Hitler when the Nazi's were beating and killing Jewish children and her family was put in a labor camp. Her family became homeless. She was discovered in Italy after she left art school in Hamburg, Germany. She was really from Konigsberg in East Prussia which is now Kaliningrad, Russia. It's a bit bizarre that I was once mistaken for a Russian aristocrat when I was living and going to school in Germany. But you were really East Prussian all along," she said.

"Oh, my God, how insane. Maybe your natural father was Russian. It's so freaky that my DNA knew I was East Prussian. Frank is German Jewish and I'm a Franck so I don't think I'm related to Linda, but I am German. Who really knows? Some historians think we are all related to King David and I read somewhere that one in every 200 people on this earth is related to Genghis Khan," I replied.

"Does your adoptive brother Jack know his natural parents?" she asked me.

"No, but I'm going to get his birth records from The Cradle for him. They want $500 for his records and are still treating him like a child. He won't pay them a dime and thinks it's extortion. He wrote a nasty letter to them."

"It's sick," she said.

"It's worse than that, it's torture being forced to live a life in secrecy swirling in a deep dark hole of fantasy, blackness and despair always wondering who you are and to whom you are really biologically related, not to mention who you are like or look like in your lost families. And we are supposed to live in denial about our biological families and pretend to be normal? I doubt it. This is what messes us up so much," I answered.

I sent the money to The Cradle and read his birth records. "Do not recommend for adoption due to spina bifida," was clearly stated on the paper. Did they tell my parents about his condition or were the records sealed? If they did know they never told Jack who was Baby Boy Burns and Baby Boy Burton on the hospital medical records. He thought he was Welsh, but in reality was German, French, and Polish. Once he came out of denial he tried to search for his natural mother. Unfortunately he was unsuccessful and gave up.

Susie will never know her biological father, her last name or her lost half-sister. I will probably never be able to use my surname Franck legally or meet a biological relative. My brother Jack will never know anything about his first relatives. Janet will never know her lost granddaughter and Doug will never know his lost parents, but we will forever be soul sisters and brothers adrift in the cosmic mystery of life like millions of other adoptees like us.

When I'm lonely all I have to do is look at the white bear in my pastel *Silent Witness* above me as I sit on the couch and I feel connected to Dorothy and my tribe knowing that our DNA not only holds our genetic code but also our genetic memories and our story. After all, I can't suck my thumb anymore.

My adoptive father died and left me $100,000. Jack forced Rob to send me the beautifully framed lithograph from Gaga's Pinetum Britannicum collection that he inherited of a Spanish church and courtyard in Mexico titled 'Taxodium Montezumae' that was hanging in Father's living room. Rob gave lithographs from Gaga's collection to everyone in the family, but me. Come to think of it, he never gave me anything but trouble.

My father never came out of denial, and before he died he sent me a letter blaming me for every bad thing he could think of instead of taking responsibility himself. He ended the poisonous letter with a quote he carried around in his wallet.

"Life is mostly froth and bubble, Two things stand alone, Kindness in another's trouble, Courage in your own."

I've done everything possible to heal myself, fill in the blanks of my existence, get my power back and reclaim my stolen heritage for my children, my grandchildren and myself. The best part of it all is that I have my identity back, a new sense of purpose, and a wonderful family of my own!

There is nothing that gives me more pleasure now that I have found myself than a heartfelt thank you note or gift from one of my darling art or flute students. You see I know now that I am my father John's daughter and so proud to be following in his footsteps as an educator. My studio walls are decorated with a smattering of wildlife art and lots of donuts and coffee just like his! I'm not out of the woods, but I am beginning to finally see the forest for the trees.

The Beginning

From the Author

A Legitimate Life has an active Facebook Page that is supportive of anyone in the adoption triad, as well as anyone interested in educating themselves about the many issues inside the hearts and minds of adoptees, including why our suffering is so profound. Please feel free to join us and discuss anything.

For more on Melinda's life, past, present, and future, her reunion with biological relatives, including family photos and adoption-related research, please visit:

www.melindaawarshaw.yolasite.com

Please visit and "like" *A Legitimate Life* on Facebook.

~ Melinda A. Warshaw

About the Editor

Best known for her bestselling Christian Thrillers, Ellen C. Maze is *The Author's Mentor*, offering book preparation and publishing services to aspiring and accomplished authors all over the country. Assisting in the self-publishing of more than one hundred books for forty-eight authors, covering all genres, from non-fiction, to children's coloring books, Ellen's joy is watching writers' dreams come true. Ellen is also an oft-sought speaker at writers' conferences, and has edited a nine-author anthology entitled *Feckless Tales of Supernatural, Paranormal, and Downright Presumptuous Ilk* (Little Roni Publishers, 2010).

Check out Ellen's ground-breaking 5-star vampire novels on Amazon.com under "Ellen C. Maze," as well as her darling self-illustrated children's books.

Ellen lives with her family in North Alabama. She invited all who will to "friend" her on Facebook. Search, "Ellen C. McCraney Maze."

www.ellencmaze.com
www.theauthorsmentor.com

Made in the USA
Middletown, DE
17 December 2014